A GLIMPSE OF CHINA

By Jin Bo

 China Intercontinental Press

图书在版编目（CIP）数据

中国概览：英文 / 金帛著；王国振，关威威译 . -- 北京：五洲传播出版社 ,2014.6
（当代中国系列 / 武力主编）
ISBN 978-7-5085-2796-3

Ⅰ . ①中… Ⅱ . ①金… ②王… ③关… Ⅲ . ①中国－概况 Ⅳ . ① K92

中国版本图书馆 CIP 数据核字 (2014) 第 124449 号

当代中国系列丛书

主　　编：武　力
出 版 人：荆孝敏
统　　筹：付　平

当代中国概览

著　　者：金　帛
译　　者：王国振　关威威
责 任 编 辑：王　峰
图 片 提 供：中新社　CFP　FOTOE　东方 IC
装 帧 设 计：丰饶文化传播有限责任公司
出 版 发 行：五洲传播出版社
地　　址：北京市海淀区北三环中路 31 号生产力大楼 B 座 7 层
邮　　编：100088
电　　话：010-82005927，82007837
网　　址：www.cicc.org.cn
承 印 者：中煤涿州制图印刷厂北京分厂
版　　次：2014 年 6 月第 1 版第 1 次印刷
开　　本：787×1092mm 1/16
印　　张：23.25
字　　数：280 千字
定　　价：128.00 元

Contents

Foreword

China is a country the outside world sometimes struggles to understand. It is experiencing the fastest economic growth and social change in human history. This rapid development of the most populous country in the world provides economic opportunities for other countries; and this in turn brings China increasingly closer to the outside world. China's development calls for a peaceful international environment, and global prosperity needs continuing development in China. In this environment it is necessary for those outside China to come to a better understanding of this vast country.

China has a history of over 5,000 years. Throughout China's long history, China has developed a unique culture which has greatly enriched world civilization.

Currently China is powering ahead to open its door to the outside world and to learn from others. China is dedicated to peaceful relations, and is always sincere in its dealing with others.

Throughout history, many people have come from the outside world to

explore China. Some of them gained a good understanding of the country. Of course, impressions of China varied according to the period.

Some 400 years ago, Alvaro Semedo (1585–1658), a Portuguese missionary who came to China, described China in the following way in his book on China:

It is a big country with a large population, with endless villages and towns, each in close proximity to the next. Houses fill the horizon. China has varied climates according to latitude and region. The country abounds in fruit, giving the impression of being a warehouse of fruit gathered from around the world. It is self-sufficient in food production, and in fact produces a surplus to trade with other countries. Many countries yearn for the chance to visit China. It produces mainly rice and wheat. Many countries consume mainly wheat or rice, and China grows both in large amounts.

When talking about the Chinese society Decades ago, John King Fairbank (1907–1991), said in his book *China: Tradition and Transformation:*

In viewing China, however, foreign advisors must remember the following: First, the Chinese society has families, instead of individuals, government or churches, as its basic unit. Each family provides its members with major support for their financial needs, education and recreational activities. China's ethic system also has families as its center, instead of God or country. The family system calls for its members to be faithful in social behavior. Law is the indispensable tool for management while individual morality constitutes the foundation of the society. In China, there will never be anarchy due to a lack of importance being attached to the law in mind; Chinese society is closely united under Confucianism.

Several years ago, William Overholt with the Asian-Pacific Policy Center of the US Research and Development made the following comment in *China and Globalization* on the changes in China:

China is making social adjustments which are beyond description. China does so quite willingly, with the result being that no large country in the world can match her in terms of achievement in improving the life and labor conditions of its people. China follows the rule of law, and its people have strengthened awareness of competition; English is used extensively, and foreign modes of education are widely followed. All these, plus the introduction of many foreign legal systems, help improve the Chinese system and, at the same time, make Chinese culture more sophisticated.

With the deepening of the ongoing reform and opening-up, and with more efforts made to deepen economic globalization, China has become more closely connected to the rest of the world. In this context, getting to know more about China has become a vital priority. This book has been created with the expectation of being of some help in this regard.

Geography and Civilization of China

As an old Chinese saying goes, "Man is conditioned by the natural environment he lives in". It emphasizes the significance of the environment for the development and survival of a country.

China, being a united multi-ethnic country, is blessed with a special geographical environment. In the process of its formation and evolution, China became a country featuring readily identifiable and cohesive characteristics.

Geography and Climate Features

   Situated in the east of the Asian continent, the northern part of the Eastern Hemisphere, as well as forming a shoreline along the edge of the Pacific Ocean, China is a country exhibiting both maritime and continental topography. Its

Sketch Map of China's Geography.

territorial area of approximately 9.6 million square km accounts for one-fifteenth of the terrestrial globe, or a quarter of the landmass of Asia. To put this in a global perspective, its terrestrial area is smaller than that of Russia and Canada, but larger than that of the United States and Australia, and approximately equal to that of Europe. With its land borders extending more than 22,000 km, and over 18,000 km of mainland coastline, China is adjacent to 15 countries and has six neighbors across the sea.

China has a terraced terrain, which descends, through a series of gradations, from the west to the east before meeting the shores of the sea. Thanks to various landforms, the Chinese topography consists of mountains, plateaus, basins, plains, lakes and hills. China has many mountains, with mountainous areas accounting for two-thirds of the country's total landmass. Its major mountain ranges include the Himalayas, Kunlun, Tianshan, Qilian and Altai Mountains in the west, and the Hengduan, Daba, Taihang and Yinshan Mountains in the central

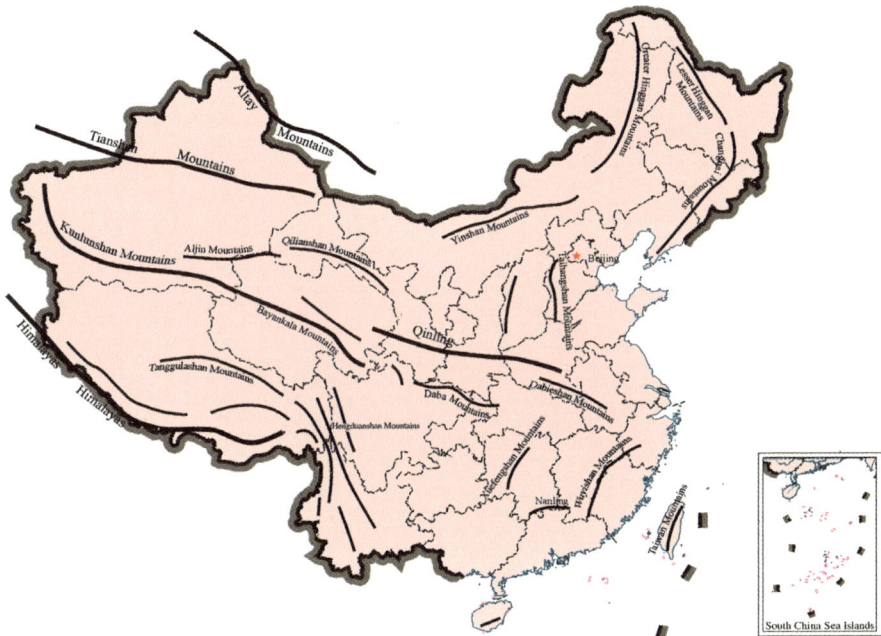

Sketch Map of Major Mountains in China.

part, as well as the Wuyi and Changbai Mountains in the east. These towering and majestic natural features comprise a network, ranging from hundred of meters to thousands in height, giving shape and perspective to the entire country. China also has many basins, mainly distributed in the west; major ones include the Junggar Basin, the Tarim Basin, the Qaidam Basin and the Sichuan Basin. There are also famous plateaus which can be found in the west and the north, and these include the Qinghai-Tibet Plateau (often called "The Third Pole" or "The Roof of the World"), the Yunnan-Guizhou Plateau, the Loess Plateau and the Inner Mongolia Plateau. In addition, China's three major plains are all situated in the low-lying area in the eastern part of the country, namely the Northeast China Plain, the North China Plain and the Middle and Lower Yangtze Valley Plains. So far as the hills are concerned, these are mostly to be found in the southeast. After comparing the topography of China with that of Europe, North America and India, Fei Zhengqing (John King Fairbank), the famous Chinese-American Sinologist, concluded: China has a disunited topography, with a subsequent lack

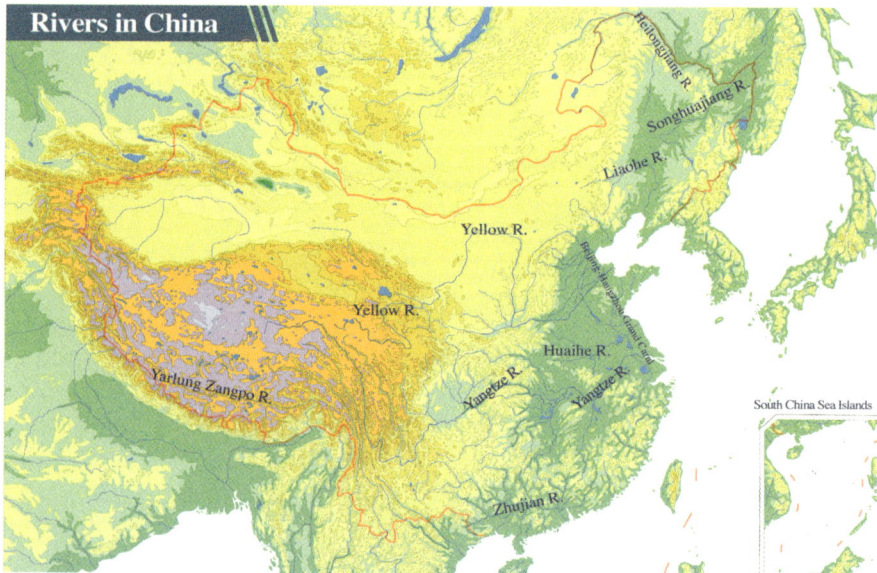

Sketch Map of Major River Systems of China.

14

of good transport access. On the other hand, its North China Plain, although certainly very large, is in fact significantly smaller than the north plains in India, let alone the large plains in Northern Europe and middle-west plains of North America.

China has numerous rivers. Principle among these are the Yangtze River, ranking first in terms of length and water volume, the Yellow River, Pearl River and Heilongjiang River. Whereas rivers in Central Asia and North America tend to flow either north to south or south to north, Chinese rivers, due to the terraced topography mentioned earlier, mainly flow from the West to the East or Southeast. There is also a significant drop in elevation during a river's course, resulting in tremendous water resources.

China's territory extends south of the Tropic of Cancer from 50 degrees of northern latitude. As a consequence of this vast size, its climate is wonderfully diverse, although the majority exhibits temperate, warm and subtropical zones with a generally mild range of temperature and four distinct seasons. The greater part of China's territory, an area approximately the size of the United States of America, lies at a degree of latitude to the south of Europe. The continental monsoon climate is the major feature of the Chinese weather system. During the summer months the southeast wind leads to higher temperatures than are experienced in other parts of the world at similar latitudes. On the other hand, owing to the severe north wind, this same area is both drier and colder in winter, with a lower mean temperature than at the same latitude elsewhere.

As the cooler continental air currents meet the moister air currents over the Chinese landmass, a great deal of rainfall is the inevitable result. In the southeast area covering the Huaihe River, the Qinling Mountain Range and the Qinghai-Tibet Plateau, the annual precipitation is over 800 mm in its east and south; the annual precipitation is less than 800 mm in its north and west. And this figure decreases the further north-west one travels: by the time we reach the Tarim Basin we discover that the annual rainfall has reached an upper limit of just 50

mm. Most precipitation occurs during the summer, although there are important regional variations due to the topographical features to which we have previously referred. In the south, there is a long rainy season from May to October, but in the north a shorter season from July to August.

Geographical Environment and Inward Movement

China faces the Bohai Sea, the Yellow Sea, the East China Sea and the South China Sea in the east and southeast. With a long curving coastline, these vast seas were taken as the end of the land by the ancient Chinese.

In the northern part of China lies the vast Mongolia Plateau which is bisected into Inner Mongolia (south of the desert) and Outer Mongolia (north of the desert) by the Gobi Desert and the Yinshan Mountains. To the north of the Mongolia Plateau are mountains stretching thousands of km from east to west. Further north of these mountains is chilly Siberia. The special geographical

Ends of the Earth (Tian Ya Hai Jiao) in Sanya of Hainan, which is regarded as the end corner of China.

17

Sky-scraping mountains in the Tibetan Plateau.

environment forced various ethnic groups on the grasslands to turn to the area south of the plateau, namely the Central Plains in the valleys of the Yellow River and the Yangtze River, to seek opportunities for development. In ancient times, the ethnic groups living on the Mongolian Plateau were mostly nomadic tribes. They, being attracted by the culture of the Central Plains, kept moving southward. Some of them established regimes in the Central Plains.

In the northeastern part of China, the Greater Hinggan Mountains screen the Mongolian Plateau off in the west; the Lesser Hinggan Mountains lay in the north; the Changbai Mountains extend in the east; further east is the vast Pacific Ocean; and the vast Northeast China Plain covers the areas between these mountains and the ocean. A long narrow corridor winds its way from the south of northeast China along the coastline of the Bohai Sea, serving as an extremely important route connecting northeast China with the Central Plains. Historically, it was the corridor used by most of the ethnic groups in northeast China to move westward or southward to the affluent Central Plains. Also, it is the same corridor used by the Han people of the Central Plains to spread into the Northeast China Plain for a new life, bringing advanced civilization there with them.

In the northwestern part of China, the border areas are covered with steep high mountains and the desolate Gobi desert, forming a natural barrier. The Tangnu and Altai Mountains sit in the north; the Pamirs Plateau at an elevation of above 4,000 meters is located in the west; the lofty Kunlun Mountain Range towers in the south; further south is the Qinghai-Tibet Plateau, a lonely area. For local ethnic groups longing for a better life, the best choice was to turn eastward. The Central Plains in the east possessed the material conditions necessary for the development of the northwest. In old times, various races here maintained very close relations with the Central Plains by way of the Hexi Corridor. Located west of the Yellow River, it is called the He (river) Xi (west) Corridor. Extending 10,004 meters east-west and 100–200 km south-north, it lies to the north of the Qilian Mountains in west Gansu Province.

In the southwestern part of China, the Himalayas with an elevation of 5,000 meters and the Hengduan Mountains with deep ravines and rapids extend along the border area; these mountains join the Qinghai-Tibet Plateau and the Yunnan-Guizhou Plateau in making the region the most inconvenient in terms of transportation in ancient times. Dozens of ethnic minority groups inhabit the region, making it the most heavily populated area by ethnic minority groups. In history, many of these ethnic minority groups moved northeastward to the Central Plains.

Such a geographical environment restrained the ancient ethnic groups from expanding outward; the terrain even formed impassable natural barriers in some places. Thus, various ethnic groups in remote border areas were forced to turn to inland areas, especially the Central Plains which boasted proper conditions suitable for human existence, such as mild climate, plenty of natural resources and flourishing culture, and enjoyed political stability and followed ethnic policies good for them. This helped promote the migratory trend.

Origin of the Word "China"

Many think that China is called China because the country was famous for its chinaware in ancient times. There are also some who believe the word China evolved from the word Chin, the name of the ancient Chin (Qin) Dynasty (221 BC–206 BC). Chin (Qin), the first feudal dynasty in the Chinese history, was formidably powerful.

No matter how people argue, it is indisputable that the word "China" appeared some 3,000 years ago and was used to refer to the area under the control of tribes in the middle reaches of the Yellow River. With the passing of time, the word expanded to refer to the area of the Central Plains. The word China even found its way into the great classic of Ancient Chinese literature, the *Spring*

In February 2013, the National Museum exhibited blue and white porcelain of the Qing Dynasty period (1644–1911) unearthed from a shipwreck at No.1 Wanjiao Reef in Pingtan, Fujian Province.

and Autumn Annals, created some 2,500 years ago. However here it was used to represent the capital of the country which exercised jurisdiction over areas other than the Central Plains, including the border areas where ethnic minorities lived. This meaning is also found in another ancient classic-*The Book of Songs.*

In ancient times, people in East Asia described their lands with terms such as "Under Heaven" , "Four Seas" and "Within the Four Seas". These terms existed alongside "China" and refer to areas including minority regions. This is why ancient Chinese people created phrases such as "those who win popular support will eventually win all" and "all under the heaven belong to the same family" as well as "all men are brothers within the four seas". At that time, the emperors were deemed superior to "all under heaven".

In Chinese history, all dynasties had dynastic titles to distinguish one rule from another, and these included "Great Han" (206 BC–220 AD), "Great Tang" (618–907), "Great Song" (960–1127), "Great Yuan" (1271–1368), "Great

The National Palace Museum of Beijing, formerly known as the Forbidden City, was the Chinese imperial imperial palace from the 15th century to the early 20th century.

Ming" (1368–1644) and "Great Qing" (1616–1911). The Western countries once referred to China as the "Ming State" or the "Qing State", and referred to the people as the "Tang people" or "Qing people."

This situation lasted until the Qing Dynasty collapsed in 1911 and the Republic of China was founded in the following year. From then on, China became the name of the country.

Today, China is short for the People's Republic of China, which was founded in 1949. Composed of 56 ethnic groups, it is administratively divided into a number of regions as follows:

The country is administratively divided into provinces, autonomous regions and municipalities directly under the Central Government;

The provinces and autonomous regions are divided into autonomous prefectures, counties, autonomous counties, and cities;

Relief sculpture of Zhongshan Academy: On January 1, 1912, Dr. Sun Yat-sen (Sun Zhongshan) (1866–1925) was inaugurated at the Presidential Palace in Nanjing when the Republic of China (1912–1949) was founded.

The counties and autonomous counties are divided into townships, ethnic townships and towns.

At present, China has 34 administrative units at the provincial level, including 23 provinces, five autonomous regions, four municipalities directly under the Central Government, and two special administrative regions.

Beijing is the capital of the People's Republic of China.

Map of the People's Republic of China.

China Provincial Administrative Divisions				
Name	Abbreviation	Administrative center	Area (10,000 sq. km)	Population (10,000)
Beijing	Jing	Beijing	1.68	1,961
Tianjin	Jing	Tianjin	1.13	1,294
Hebei Province	Jin	Shijiazhuang	19.00	7,185
Shanxi Province	Jin	Taiyuan	15.60	3,571
Inner Mongolia Autonomous Region	Meng	Hohhot	119.75	2,471
Liaoning Province	Liao	Shenyang	14.57	4,375
Jilin Province	Ji	Changchun	18.70	2,746
Heilongjiang Province	Hei	Harbin	46.90	3,831
Shanghai	Hu	Shanghai	0.62	2,302
Jiangsu Province	Su	Nanjing	10.26	7,866
Zhejiang Province	Zhe	Hangzhou	10.18	5,443
Anhui Province	Wan	Hefei	13.90	5,950
Fujian Province	Min	Fuzhou	12.00	3,689
Jiangxi Province	Gan	Nanchang	16.66	4,457
Shandong Province	Lu	Jinan	15.30	9,579
Henan Province	Yu	Zhengzhou	16.70	9,402
Hubei Province	E	Wuhan	18.74	5,724
Hunan Province	Xiang	Changsha	21.00	6,568
Guangdong Province	Yue	Guangzhou	18.60	10,430
Guangxi Zhuang Autonomous Region	Gui	Nanning	23.77	4,603

Hainan Province	Qiong	Haikou	3.40	867
Chongqing	Yu	Chongqing	8.20	2,885
Sichuan Province	Chuan	Chengdu	48.40	8,042
Guizhou Province	Gui, Qian	Guiyang	17.00	3,475
Yunnan Province	Yun, Dian	Kunming	39.40	4,597
Tibet Autonomous Region	Zang	Lhasa	127.49	300
Shaanxi Province	Shaan	Xi'an	20.50	3,733
Gansu Province	Gan, Long	Lanzhou	45.00	2,558
Qinghai Province	Qing	Xining	72.00	563
Ningxia Hui Autonomous Region	Ning	Yinchuan	6.28	630
Xinjiang Uygur Autonomous Region	Xin	Urumqi	165.58	2,181
Hong Kong Special Administrative Region	Gang	Hong Kong	0.1104	710
Macao Special Administrative Region	Ao	Macao	0.0028	55
Taiwan Province	Tai	Taipei	3.60	2,316

Note: The population of various provincial-level administrative regions on the Chinese mainland is the population verified during the 6th National Census conducted in 2010. The population of Hong Kong and Macao Administrative Regions was provided by governments of the two in 2010. The population of Taiwan Province was determined accordig to the registered population released by Taiwan authorities concerned.

Different Parts of China

China is blessed with a diverse topography and also exhibits an enormous range of climate across its various regions. These two factors not only shape the country's various modes of production, such as crop raising, livestock breeding, fish farming and hunting, but are furthermore responsible for the development of distinct life styles, customs and entertainments in different regions. They even influence the physical attributes and character of the people in various areas.

The Chinese are also usually spoken of as being either Southern, Northern, Northeastern or Northwestern people. In the past, the people's modes of production varied greatly between the south and north, between the east, west and central parts of China. Some of this diversity can still be found today. On the whole, speaking in terms of natural conditions, the south and east of China

Xitang in Jiashang County, Zhejiang Province: The ancient town is representative of the area south of the Yangtze River.

are particularly suitable for the development of agriculture, with relatively less emphasis on fishery, while the north and west of the country have tended to be more dependent on livestock breeding, with relatively less emphasis on raising crops.

The south and east of China consist of hills, plains, and lakes, as well as some big mountains, although these are relatively modest when compared with those of the more rugged north and west of the country. Taken as a whole, the area boasts a moderate climate, with many hours of sunshine and plentiful rainfall. It is particularly suitable for the cultivation of rice, which can be harvested twice a year. Furthermore, its abundant rainfall enables efficient water transportation and fishery; indeed the southeastern part of China has always been known as "The Land of Fish and Rice". Crisscrossed by many rivers, it has, throughout history, been more affluent than the north. People in this region enjoy a comfortable life, despite the threat of floods, and the consequence is a large population with densely peopled towns and cities. People here are noted

Qilian mountainous scenery in Haibei Tibetan Autonomous Prefecture in Qinghai Province.

for their mild and temperate disposition, combined with qualities of diligence and goodness, thus forming the distinguishing cultural feature of the inhabitants south of the Yangtze River.

The north and west of China, by contrast, is characterized by numerous mountain ranges and high plateaus. The climate is typically continental, being significantly colder than that of South China, the natural environment much harsher. Historically, the people here have always lived primarily on animal husbandry, combining this with growing wheat, corn and *kaoliang* (Chinese sorghum) in the places which are suitable for crop cultivation. Many rivers in north China are seasonal: in the summer, some of them become so shallow that only paddle boats can navigate them and most are never suitable for heavier shipping. In ancient times, animals were the only practical conveyance for passengers or freight throughout the entire region. Although the northwestern part of China boasts a vast area, it has a small population. Due to the tough natural conditions, famine was a constant danger in the past and, as a consequence, the people of this region are noted for their hardiness and courage in the face of adversity.

The differences inherent in the character of the people of north and south China finds full expression in the ancient literature of China. Consider, for example, this traditional folk song dating from the Southern Dynasties (420–589):

I am like the Northern Star

Whose position in the topmost hemisphere

Is constant and unchanging

For thousands of years.

You are like the sun

Which rises in the east at dawn

But in the evening

Disappears into the west.

Hulun Buir Grassland in Inner Mongolia.

The song delicately depicts a woman is firmly loyal to her lover and blames her husband for his betrayal.

Here, too, is a folk song produced in the Northern Dynasties (439–581) in approximately the same period, which acts as a counterpart to the one quoted above:

Beneath the vault of sky, under the Yinshan Mountains,

Far and wide are spread the wide Chinese plains.

Beneath the heaven blue, over the vast country below,

A passing wind discloses the herds amid the grasses low.

It gives expression to a most characteristic and attractive scene of the vast, magnificent steppe where the nomadic peoples in North China still live.

In China today, to achieve a coordinated development among different

regions, the state initiates and carries out various development programs, including pushing forward the development of the western regions, revitalizing the old industrial bases of northeast China, promoting central China's modernization, as well as encouraging the eastern region to lead the country in development. Here, it should be noted, western, northeastern, central and eastern China refer to specific geographical concepts.

West China includes Sichuan, Guizhou, Yunnan, Shaanxi, Gansu and Qinghai Provinces, Chongqing municipality directly under the Central Government, as well as the Tibet, Ningxia Hui, Xinjiang Uygur, Inner Mongolia and Guangxi Zhuang Autonomous Regions. The 12 administrative regions cover 6.85 million square km, making up 71 percent of the total area of China. Its 2010 population was 360.38 million, accounting for 27.04 percent of the national population. Their GDP hit 11,391.5 billion Yuan, or 16.9 percent of the national total.

Sketch Map of West, Northeast, Central and East China

Northeast China encompasses Liaoning, Jilin and Helongjiang Provinces. It covers an area of 790,000 square km, or 8.2 percent of the country's total. The region had a population of 109.52 million in 2010, or 8.22 percent of China's total. Its 2011 GDP was 4,506 billion Yuan, accounting for 9.3 percent of the national total.

Central China comprises Shanxi, Henan, Hubei, Hunan, Anhui and Jiangxi Provinces, covering 1.027 million square km, or 10.7 percent of the national total area. In 2010, it had a population of 356.72 million, accounting for 26.76 percent of China's total. Its GDP reached 3,208.8 billion Yuan, accounting for 19.7 percent of the national total.

With an area of 913,000 square km, or 9.5 percent of the national total, East China is composed of Hebei, Shandong, Jiangsu, Zhejiang, Fujian, Guangdong and Hainan Provinces, as well as Beijing, Tianjin and Shanghai municipalities directly under the Central Government. It had a population of 506.16 million in 2004, covering 37.98 percent of the population in China. Its GDP was 8,843.3 billion Yuan, making up 54.2 percent of China's total.

Primitive Chinese Civilization

There is no evidence to show that early Chinese ancestors migrated to China from elsewhere.

In the 1960s, the remains of Homo erectus Yuanmouensis, dating back 1.7 million years, were found in Yuanmou County in Yunnan Province in southwest China. Two incisors from the upper jaw of the Yuanmouensis were discovered. Animal bones with traces of cuts, and archaeological evidence showing the possible use of fire were also unearthed. Also in the 1960s, the remains of Homo erectus Lantianensis, which lived between 800,000 and 600,000 years ago, were found in Lantian, Shaanxi Province in central western China.

Another major archaeological study in 1927 discovered the remains of Homo erectus Pekinensis (Peking Man), which lived between 500,000 and 200,000 years ago. The remains were found on Longgu (Dragon Bone) Hill at Zhoukoudian, about 50 km southwest of Beijing. With narrow teeth and jaw bone, and a larger skull, Peking Man is quite similar to modern man in terms of skeletal morphology-bone size, shape, proportion and muscle attachment points-especially when compared to other prehistoric humans. With a height of about 156 cm, Peking man has shovel-shaped incisors characteristic of Mongoloid races. Besides Peking Man fossils, some 100,000 fragments of stone artifacts, rock fragments and large amounts of mammal fossils were also found at the site. They provide evidence that shows Peking Man could do simple work with stone tools. Signs of fire were found in the Peking Man Cave. Ten years later, in 1937, Japan launched a war of aggression against China, and unfortunately the Peking Man skulls were lost.

Early Homo sapiens existed between 200,000 and 100,000 years ago. Human fossils from this period include Maba Man found in Qujiang in

Guangdong Province in south China, Changyang Man found in Changyang in Hubei Province in central south China, and Dingcun Man found in Xiangfen in Shanxi Province in north China. From the Dingcun site, some 2,000 stone artifact fragments were found, the most representative being stone balls and triangular pyramid shaped tools, which were technologically much more advanced than those of Peking Man.

Human fossils and relics of activities of later Homo sapiens, who lived 100,000 to 10,000 years ago, were found in southwest, northwest and north China. Upper Cave Man was found in the early 1930s in the upper cave of the Longgu Hill at Zhoukoudian, where Peking Man was found. Upper Cave Man lived 18,000 years ago, and in physical terms was basically devoid of ape-like characteristics. It was basically the same as modern people. The stone artifacts discovered were quite delicate, and bone needles were used for decoration and repair. This proved that drilling, grinding, and other technologies had been mastered to meet the people's aesthetic requirements. Fish and other animal bone

Restored image of Peking Man.

Monument to Site of Yuanmou People.

Stone axes unearth from the Hemudu Site
in Yuyao, zhejiang Province.

Restored image of Cave Man.

fossils unearthed prove that Upper Cave Man's life involved fishing, hunting and gathering.

After more than 1 million years of evolution, humans left caves and moved to settle down in the plains some 5,000–8,000 years ago. They began to live in permanent farming settlements. This marks the point when Chinese civilization entered its primitive period.

Water is the origin of life, and also the source of civilization. When the major life-sustaining activities of humans evolved from fishing and gathering into farming, water played an even more important role in people's lives. The Tigris River and the Euphrates River were major sources of irrigation for the Mesopotamian civilization, the Nile River for ancient Egyptian civilization, the India River and the Ganges River for ancient Indian civilization, and the Aegean Sea for ancient Hellenic civilization. Similarly, Chinese civilization was nourished by two rivers-the Yellow River and the Yangtze River.

The Yellow River is the second longest river in China. It runs through north

China, flowing through nine provinces and covering a drainage area of 750,000 square km. Known as the birthplace of Chinese civilization, the Yellow River is regarded as the Mother River in China and it contains many cultural relics throughout its drainage area. These sites were named according to the cultures they represented, including Yangshao Culture (in Henan Province), Qijia Culture (in Gansu Province), Dawenkou Culture (in Shandong Province) and Longshan Culture (in Shandong Province).

The Yangtze River is the longest river in China, covering a drainage area of more than 1.8 million square km, nearly one-fifth of all Chinese territory. Many cultural sites are found in its middle and lower reaches, such as Hemudu Culture and Liangzhu Culture (in Zhejiang Province), and Qingliangang Culture (in Jiangsu Province). Hongshan Culture was discovered around the Liaohe River in northeast China. All these sites indicate that ancient Chinese people were making constant progress not only in terms of production and improved livelihoods, but also in terms of enlarging the area of their activities.

Hukou Waterfall of the Yellow River, the Mother River of the Chinese nation and birthplace of the Chinese culture.

The farming economy dominated primitive Chinese civilization. A primitive farming civilization is the main feature of all of the cultural sites mentioned above. At that time, people were farmers: they engaged in livestock breeding, fishing, but also retained elements of hunting and gathering. During the period of Yangshao Culture (5,000–6,000 years ago), maize was the main crop. From the ancient site of Banpo Village during this period, over 100 kg of maize were found in one pit. From one Dawenkou Culture site, tracing back to between 4300 BC and 2500 BC, one cubic meter of maize was discovered. Rice was found in one site representative of the Hemudu Culture (5000 BC–3300 BC). All these discoveries show the rapid progress that was being made in terms of farming tools, especially stone implements.

During these periods, handicrafts also witnessed enormous progress. Stone implements found at some of these sites were much more intricate and delicate than earlier discoveries and included stone axes, stone shovels, stone knives, and stone sickles.

Hemudu Cultural Site exhibited in the China Agriculture Museum.

The statues of Yandi Emperor and Huangdi Emperor in the Yellow River shore, Zhengzhou , Henan Province.

There was also pottery created to meet the needs of daily life. Some pottery items excavated from sites have decorated symbols, which represented certain meanings to their producers. As they were similar to the later ancient Chinese characters carved on tortoise shells or animal bones, these symbols are considered to be an embryonic form of Chinese characters.

The development of agricultural civilization made it possible for ancient peoples to put down roots and form communities. This created opportunities for marriage between different groups. In turn some related groups would unite to form a kinship group which would later involve into a tribe. Friendly tribes might then form a tribal union. The Yandi Emperor and Huangdi Emperor in Chinese mythology were leaders of such tribes or tribal unions. They organized armies and fought to protect their territory and ensure their survival. They established a rudimentary administrative system necessary to handle social interactions. Some of these tribes and tribal unions became stronger and formed the rudiments of early states in China.

Unification of China in History

Xia (about 2070 BC–1600 BC), Shang (1600 BC–1046 BC), Zhou (1046 BC–256 BC)… Qin (221 BC–206 BC), Han (206 BC–220 AD)… Wei (220–265), Jin (265–420)… Sui (581–618), Tang (618–907)… Song (960–1279), Liao (907–1125), Jin (1115–1234), Yuan (1206–1368), Ming (1368–1644), and Qing (1616–1911) are all ancient dynasties of China.

For nearly 4,000 years, China had been in a period of dynastic rule, and the situation lasted until the early 20th century when China founded a modern State.

Though China suffered from divisions, the end result was unification which features the flourishing of the culture of the Central Plains that. held the most prominent position. The replacing of dynasties did not change the system of passing down and inheritance but continued the tradition of inheritance and maintained the integrity of Chinese culture. In the long historical development of Chinese culture, it was inherited and carried forward continuously. In spite of foreign invasion, it was never replaced by other cultures. The ancient history of China is mainly different from the histories of other countries in its length, continuity and unification.

Continuity of Chinese History

"Since Pan Gu separated heaven and earth… Since the Three Sovereigns (usually referred to as usually referred to as Fuxi, Suiren and Shennong) and Five Emperors (usually referred to as the Yellow Emperor, Zhuanxu, Di Ku, Tang Yao and Yu Shun)" is a phrase much heard in China not only in the past but also today. It shows the continuity of Chinese history from antiquity to the present.

Pan Gu's story is a Chinese version of Genesis from China's remote antiquity. It indicates ancient people's imagination and understanding of the origin of heaven and earth. Legend has it that in ancient times, the universe remained in chaos until one day, a god named Pan Gu, cracked the darkness with a big ax. Light and clear things rose to become heaven and heavy and turbid things fell down to become the earth. Thereafter, the sky rose higher and higher and the earth became denser. To prevent them from combining again, Pan Gu held up the sky with his hands and stood on the earth. This condition lasted for 18,000 years until the sky and earth eventually came into being. Unfortunately, Pan Gu exhausted all his energy and died.

As recorded in the *Bible,* it is God who created Adam and Eve. China's legend says Nu Wa is the mother of all Chinese. After Pan Gu separated the sky and the earth, the earth was desolate and lifeless. Nu Wa, a goddess with a woman's head and serpent's body, made a clay baby beside a clear pool. Finally, the clay baby turned into a lively human being. She continued to make many men and women. In order to maintain the proliferation of the human species, Nu Wa created marriage between men and women to give birth to new generations.

The Three Sovereigns and Five Emperors were deemed as the ancestors of the Chinese people and also the creators of Chinese civilization.

The legend of the ancient times is thought to have originated in the clan tribe period. It is said that about 10,000 years ago, a tribe, which originated in the Kunlun Mountains in west China, called Suiren-shi, moved to the Hexi Corridor of the Qilian Mountians (present-day Gansu Province). There they invented a method of making fire by drilling dry wood. Their invention enabled human beings to cook foods, which contributed to disease reduction, and the enhanced ability to stand coldness. A new era, called the era of the Suiren, began, and Suiren-shi was respectfully addressed as the Heavenly Emperor by later generations.

The Suiren-shi era was replaced by the Fuxi-shi era about 10,000 to 7,000 years ago. Fuxi issued an improved calendar and began to raise the livestock, farmed crops and invented written characters. As a master of science and

Sculptures of Nuwa and Fu Xi.

humanities in the ancient times, Fuxi was widely respected by all the clans and became their leader. He was addressed as the Human Sovereign. Legend says, in this period, a hole was torn in Heaven, resulting in disasters such as floods, fires and so forth, which threatened the existence of human beings. To save the people, Nu Wa melted five colored stones to patch the sky. People lived peacefully afterwards. This is the story of Nu Wa Patching Heaven, which is so well known in China's history.

In the mythology of ancient China, after the Fuxi era, some influential tribal unions came into being 6,000 to 7,000 years ago, including the tribes of the Yan Emperor, the Yellow Emperor, and Chiyou. The Yan Emperor's tribe, surnamed Jiang, lived in the Jiangshui River drainage area (the eastern part of present Shanxi Province). According to historical record, the Yan Emperor was Shennong, the god who invented farming and created medicine. He taught the people to cultivate the land and use dead stocks. Legend has it that he tasted all kinds of herbs to identify medical herbs and taught people how to cure

Ceremony held on the ninth day of the ninth lunar month to worship Emperor Huangdi.

Sculpture of Da Yu Harnessing
the Over-flooding River in the
Yuexiu Park in Guangzhou of
Guangdong Province.

diseases. He was regarded as the Emperor of Farming for his familiarity with
the productive use of land and farming skills. As land is the base of farming, he
was also regarded as the Emperor of Land, and the creator of the agricultural
culture of China. The Yellow Emperor's tribe lived in the Jishui River drainage
area. Surnamed Ji, they were also called Xuanyuan-Shi and Youxiong-Shi. Many
talented people were in Yellow Emperor's tribe. They invented many things,
including sericulture, vessels and vehicles, character, swings, medical science,
mathematics, etc. The Chiyou Tribe, also called Jiuli tribe, lived between the
Yangtze River and the Huaishui River. In all the tribal unions, the tribes of
the Yan and the Yellow held the leading position. Because of their inventions'
significance to later generations, they were both regarded as joint ancestors of
the Han Chinese. The Han Chinese called themselves descendants of the Yan

and Yellow emperors. Even now, the Chinese people pay homage to the Yellow Emperor Mausoleum every spring.

About 4,000 years ago, floods happened frequently and endangered the existence of human beings. A story titled Yu the Great Subdued the Flood, which spread among the Chinese, occurred in this historical period. It is said that at that time, rain poured down and floods occurred everywhere. People suffered greatly from the disasters and many of them died of starvation. A leader of a tribe from the middle of the Yellow River, whose name was Gun, was appointed to control the flood. Unfortunately, he failed in this task and was killed by the Shun Emperor. His son, called Yu, was appointed to complete the task. Having learned from his father's experiences, Yu led people to dig ditches and dredge rivers before diverting the floodwater into the sea, other than blocking them up. His method not only harnessed the flood, but also created advantages for agricultural production. Yu was highly praised by later generations because during his more than ten years of struggle with the floods, he didn't visit his family even when he passed by his house.

According to historical documents, the demise of the era of Yao, Shun and Yu happened in this period. When he was old, Yao, as the leader of the tribal union, chose, Shun as his successor and transferred his power to Shun, with the permission of a meeting of all tribe leaders. Later, Shun handed over leadership to Yu. However, when Yu came to power he was actually a monarch of a dynasty, which was titled Xia.

Formation of the Ancient Country

The Xia (about 2070 BC–1600 BC), Shang (1600 BC–1046 BC) and Zhou (1046 BC–256 BC) dynasties were the early regimes of ancient China.

The Xia Dynasty is very important in Chinese history because it was the first regime to feature national characteristics. The establishment of the Xia Dynasty, a slavery society, marks the formal beginning of Chinese civilization. From then on, the ensuing dynasties followed the Xia practice of all emperors coming from the same family. The Xia was an ancient tribe that inhabited the Central Plain (middle and lower reaches of the Yellow River). They expanded their territory after Da Yu (Yu the Great) came to power. The central area of the Xia kingdom was the modern day western part of Henan Province and the southern part of Shanxi Province. The Xia conquered other clans and tribes and made them slaves. After the death of Da Yu (Yu the Great), his son came to power

Rao-Shun-Yu Tai in Yongji, Shanxi Province, which allegedly was where Yao and Shun gave their ruling power to their predecessors.

and created the system of hereditary rule which replaced the original abdication system. This would greatly influence China's history. Jie, the last emperor of Xia, led a licentious life. He once compared himself to the sun, claiming that as the sun never dies he and his kingdom would never die. Later, Tang, the leader of an eastern tribe led his troops to defeat Jie, ending the Xia Dynasty.

The Shang Dynasty was the second regime in China's history. The Shang tribe had long inhabited the lower reaches of the Yellow River. When Xia established its state, Shang created a powerful alliance with other tribes. Tang, the leader of the Shang, defeated the Xia and established the Shang Dynasty. The Shang Dynasty continued to expand its territory, and the central area stretched from the modern day areas of northeast Henan Province to southwest Shandong province and south Hebei province. Compared to the Xia Dynasty, the Shang Dynasty had more well-developed administrative organs, military

Tripod with three animal face patterns supported by three tiger feet, an exhibt of the Nanjing Museum.

forces, criminal laws and prisons, which combined to ensure a brutal system of slavery. The emperor of Shang had total power. During the Shang Dynasty, much headway was made in bronze smelting techniques, making it possible for bronze wares to be widely used in common people's daily life. They include Ding tripod cast as cooking utensils. In Chinese traditional culture, bronze Ding, round or square with three or four legs, is a symbol of the imperial throne and power; it also symbolizes peace and prosperity. The Shang capital moved several times until eventually Shang Emperor Pangeng moved it to Yin (around Anyang, Henan Province today). Thus, "Yinshang" was widely used in ancient documents to refer to the Shang Dynasty. In the latter period of the Shang Dynasty, several years of military invasion decreased the power of Shang, and the Zhou tribe which had prepared for many years took advantage and conquered Shang.

Fragment of oracle bone inscriptions unearthed from Anyang of Henan Province. Archaeologists believe they bore the earliest script of China.

The great progress made during the Shang Dynasty was the vast quantities of inscriptions on bones or tortoise shells. These inscriptions on bones or tortoise shells are among China's oldest written characters. This is of incomparable significance because it marks the beginning of written records of China's history. This was a great achievement of one of mankind's major civilizations. It is still the common fortune enjoyed by the culture circle of Han characters in Eastern Asia at large.

The Zhou tribes, who had been in existence as long as the Xia and Shang

Dayuding Tripod with inscriptions
on it of the Western Zhou Dynasty
(1040 BC−771 BC).

Jade Cong of the Zhou Dynasty
(1040 BC−771 BC).

tribes, established a new country, Zhou, after defeating the Shang, and set up a feudal lord system. In China's history, Zhou is divided into two periods: the Western Zhou Dynasty (1046 BC−771 BC) and Eastern Zhou Dynasty (770 BC−256 BC). The Western Zhou established its capital in Haojing (Xi'an, Shaanxi Province today). The emperor of Zhou was not only the leader of the central government but also the governor of dukes and princes. Zhou adopted the system of "Granting Lands to Officials". The area around the capital was divided into "Wangji", meaning land governed directly by royal family members. Besides the Wangji, vast areas of land were granted to royal family members, officials and tribal leaders. Based on these lands, various kingdoms were established. At the beginning, these kingdoms maintained a close relationship with the central government. In the Zhou Dynasty, the State possessed all the land and all land transactions were prohibited. It was called "System of the Well Land". (The land was separated into several squares by paths, channels in the fields and roads, resembling the Han character " 井 ". It can still be seen in the central plain of

China today.) Progress was made in agriculture, the handicraft industry, and business during the Western Zhou Dynasty. Its territory stretched to the eastern part of today's Gansu province in the west, seashore in the east, Huaishui River in the south and northern Hebei province and south-west Liaoning province in the north.

In 770 BC, the imperial court of the Zhou Dynasty was divided by internal conflict, and the capital was moved to Luoyi (Luoyang, Henan province today). This marked the end of the Western Zhou Dynasty and the establishment of the Eastern Zhou Dynasty. Luoyi was located to the east of Haojing, the former capital of Zhou, therefore, the dynasty was called Eastern Zhou, and the former dynasty with its capital in Haojing was called Western Zhou. The Eastern Zhou Dynasty is divided into two parts: the Spring and Autumn Period (770 BC–476 BC) and Warring States Period (475 BC–221 BC). Since the events which happened during 770 BC–476 BC were all recorded in the Spring and Autumn, an historical book, it is called the *Spring and Autumn* Period. The following years saw continuous battles between kingdoms, so people called it the Warring States Period. At that time, various kings were estranged from the royal family and the Zhou Dynasty's power began to decline. These kings ruled over their respective lands and savage conflict was commonplace. Kings rose to hegemony including "Five Hegemonies in the Spring and Autumn Period" and "Seven Powerful States in the Warring States Period". This was a period of turmoil in China's history but also a period witnessing the emergence of various thoughts and culture. Numerous ideologists, politicians, litterateurs and militarists including Confucius, Lao Tzu, Mo Zi, Mencius, Xun Zi, Zhuang Zi, Sun Tzu and Qu Yuan all emerged at that time. Various schools of thoughts such as Confucianism, Taoism and Legalists were all shaped at that time. All these theories exerted great influence on the nation.

The situation of separate states did not end until the State of Qin united the whole country and established the Qin Dynasty (221 BC–206 BC).

First Unification and Separation of China

The Qin and Han Dynasties from 221 BC to 220 AD witnessed the first unification and prosperity in China's history, exerting great and deep influence on later generations.

After the Han Dynasty (206 BC–220 AD), the formerly centralized and unified country separated. The ensuing 400 years saw the emergence of many kingdoms and coexistence of various dynasties.

The Qin Dynasty was the first dynasty to establish the emperor as the ruler of the entire country. The first emperor Ying Zheng took the throne at

Sculpture of Emperor Qin Shihuang of the Qin Dynasty (221 BC–206 BC) and the Mausoleum of Emperor Qin Shihuang in Lingtong of Shaanxi Province.

the age of 13 years old. He adopted the policy of "making the nation affluent and strengthening military forces" and implemented the strategy of preventing alliances between different kingdoms in order to defeat them one by one. In 221 BC or the 26th year of his reign, he unified China and established Xianyang (in Shaanxi Province today) as the capital and the nation of China was born. From this point forward various forces always desired to be the emperor and establish a new dynasty.

The Qin Dynasty established a relatively complete central government. It replaced the system of "granting titles to kingdoms" with the "prefecture-county system". The country was divided into 41 prefectures governed by prefects. During this period, the currency, weights and measurements, the vehicle axle length and written characters were all standardized. The Qin's reign lasted only 15 years, but exerted great influence on China's history. It laid a solid foundation for the unification of China's politics, economy and culture. The Qin's tyranny destined it to a short reign. The Qin's rule came to the end shortly after the first emperor's death. His son ascended the throne but was quickly overthrown by a peasants' uprising. The country plunged into conflict and chaos until the Han Dynasty came to power.

Qin emperor Ying Zheng is regarded as the greatest emperor in China's history. He made great contribution to China's history. He lifted China out of the "Warring States Period" and unified all the ethnic groups to form the nation of China. Regardless of these achievements he was an arrogant and violent emperor. He granted himself "Huangdi (meaning emperor)" implying his virtue and merit had surpassed "the three sovereigns and five emperors in ancient China's history". He hoped his offspring would govern China forever. During his 12-year reign, he levied heavy taxes, imposed serious punishment, and built many extremely luxurious palaces. He also engaged in wars for several years. He placed a heavy burden on people and life was harsh. He burnt books which were opposed to the Qin and buried scholars who spoke against the Qin. This was the

famous event known as "burning books and burying Confucian scholars alive" in China's history. He organized many large-scale projects and recruited tens of thousands of people to build the 5,000-km-long Great Wall and the marvelous Mausoleum of Emperor Qinshihuang (The famous Terracotta Warriors and Horses are part of it).

The Han Dynasty was the next monarchy after the Qin Dynasty. It was controlled by one family (Liu Family) throughout its history. The Han Dynasty was divided into the Western Han Dynasty (206 BC–25 AD) and Eastern Han Dynasty (25–220). because the emperor reestablished the regime and moved the capital in 25 AD. The first emperor of the Han Dynasty, Liu Bang, was born to a common family. He was a low official of the Qin Dynasty. He had great talent and bold vision and employed all kinds of talents despite their family or educational backgrounds. The Han Dynasty was totally different from the previous dynasties in that the emperor came from the ordinary people and his

Qin Shihuang Terracotta Army Museumin Xi'an, Shaanxi Province.

generals and ministers also rose up from the grass-roots level. The ensuing dynasties followed suit.

The Western Han Dynasty had its capital set up in Chang'an, present-day Xi'an of Shaanxi Province. It followed the Qin policy of strengthening centralized power. It also learnt from the failure of the Qin Dynasty and introduced the policy of "developing economy and increasing population". At the beginning of the Han Dynasty, many soldiers were allowed to return home, and their taxes were reduced or abolished. Efforts were also made to support agriculture and discourage businesses. This period saw a stable society and fast economic development. Peace and prosperity appeared for the first time in China's history. In the later period of the Western Han Dynasty, social conflicts intensified, and the peasants revolted repeatedly. Other families coveted the imperial power and tried to usurp the throne, which resulted in a war. Finally Liu Xiu, a member of the royal family, reestablished the regime of the Family Liu as

Emperor Wudi Liu Xiu (6 BC–57 BC) of the Eastern Han Dynasty (206 BC–220 AD).

the Eastern Han Dynasty with its capital in Luoyang (Luoyang, Henan Province today). At the end of the Eastern Han Dynasty, the famous Huangjin (Yellow Turbans) Uprising broke out. Taking advantage of this, various warlords set up separatist regimes and the Eastern Han Dynasty only existed in name. Much headway was made in foreign relations during the Eastern Han Dynasty. In 57 AD, Japan sent an envoy to China, marking the beginning of the Sino-Japanese relationship. Ban Chao, a famous general of the Han Dynasty, visited the western regions of Asia. During the Han, the western regions refer to Xinjiang and Central Asia, located to the west of today's Yumen Pass of Gansu Province.

In the latter period of the Eastern Han Dynasty, various warlords fought to take the throne. Peasants revolted. The most famous peasant uprising was the Yellow Turbans Uprising. After a long-period of fighting, there were three kingdoms left: Wei, Shu and Wu. Cao Cao, a famous politician who had built a solid foundation for the Kingdom of Wei, unified north China. In 220 AD, Cao Pi, son of Cao Cao, forced the last emperor of the Eastern Han Dynasty (Emperor

Relief sculpture of Cao Cao (155–220).

Xiandi) to abdicate. He came to power, named the Kingdom Wei and established a capital in Luoyang (Luoyang, Henan Province today). Liu Bei, espousing the slogan of "Restoration of Han Dynasty" established the Han Kingdom in 221AD in Chengdu. It was also known as "Shu" or "Shuhan". Zhuge Liang, the famous militarist, was the Primer Minister of the Kingdom of Shu. In 229 AD, Sun Quan, the representative of southeast China, established the Kingdom of Wu with its capital in Jianye (Nanjing, Jiangsu province today).

After the Three Kingdoms, there were the Western Jin Dynasty (265–316) and Eastern Jin Dynasty (317–420). Both dynasties are ruled by the Sima family. The difference is their choice of capital: the Western Jin's capital was in Luoyang (Luoyang, Henan Province today), and the Eastern Jin's capital was in Jiankang (Nanjing, Jiangsu Province today). The Jin was derived from the reign of the Wei. The Sima family had high official ranks in the Kingdom of Wei. Later, after years of struggle, the Sima family managed to take over the reign. The Western Jin won a war against the Wu in 280, ending 90 years of turbulence since the end of the Eastern Han Dynasty and China was temporarily unified. Before long, China was plunged into separation once again during the Eastern Jin Dynasty, and the chaotic situation lasted for about 300 years.

Chinese Empire Reunified and Split Again

During the Sui and Tang Dynasties (581–907), the second reunification period in ancient Chinese history, the Chinese Empire experienced prosperity again and unprecedented power.

The Sui Dynasty (581–618) ended centuries of division, and achieved the reunification and the establishment of the centralized state. The first Emperor of the Sui, Yang Jian, had been a court minister holding a key post in the last regime of the Northern Dynasties (386–581), the Northern Zhou Dynasty (557–581), who monopolized the political and military power. In 581, Yang Jian replaced the Northern Zhou with the Sui. Thus the Sui Dynasty was founded, with Chang'an

Modern buildings flanking the Beijing-Hanzhou Grand Canal.

(currently Xi'an in Shaanxi Province) as the capital. After the north was well consolidated, the Sui Court defeated the last of the Southern Dynasties, Chen, and unified the whole nation.

The Sui Dynasty lasted a very short time, less than 30 years, only some 10 years longer than the Qin Dynasty (221 BC–206 BC). The Sui Dynasty was often compared to the Qin Dynasty, which had a far reaching influence to the Han Dynasty (206 BC–220 AD). There would be no the Tang Dynasty (618–907) without the Sui. The Sui ended a long period of division, laying an important foundation for the future development of the Tang Dynasty. The Sui period saw great pioneering undertakings unparalleled in history: the one imperial civil examination system, which connected studying, the taking of examinations and attaining an official position, profoundly influencing the selection of talent in Chinese history; another the grand canal, which has always been the main artery in the nation's transportation between southern and northern areas, playing an important role in economic and cultural exchange between southern and northern

Illustration
- - - Sketch Map of the People's Republic of China
▬▬▬ Sketch Map of the Tang Dynasty
▬▬▬ Sketch Map of Political Regimes and Tribes
Sketch Map of Political Regimes of the Tang Dynasty

Shiwei
Uighur
Mohe
Persia
Turk
Silla
Japan
Chang'an
Tubo
Tang Dynasty
Sindhu
South China Sea
Islands of PRC
Ryukyu
Pyu
Chenla

Sketch Map of Territory of the Tang Dynasty (618–907).

areas and the consolidation of the nation. The decline of the Sui Dynasty started from the second monarch, Emperor Yang, who was a typical tyrant. Emperor Yang led a luxurious and corrupt life. He employed over one million laborers to build irrigation ditches, some half of them died within ten days. As a result, the regime of the Sui Dynasty became rather unstable, rebellions happened frequently, the national power declined, and finally collapsed.

The Sui Dynasty was succeeded by the Tang Dynasty. As one of the longest dynasties, which lasted 289 years, with Chang'an as the capital, the unified and centralized Tang Dynasty was an unparalleled powerful and prosperous period in China's history. This historic period is divided into the early one, having a powerful national strength and cultural prosperity, and the later one, featuring social unrest and people's declining livelihood. The first emperor of the Tang Dynasty, Li Yuan, a vassal in the Sui Court, seized the opportunity to take

Horse Herding drawn by Han Gan of the Tang Dynasty (618–907).

control during the rebellions at the end of the Sui, proclaimed himself emperor and changed the state title into Tang, still with Chang'an as the capital city. The nation thus was unified.

Taizong, Li Shimin, was the second of the Tang emperors. He was the second son of Emperor Gaozu, Li Yuan. He is considered to be one of the greatest of the Chinese emperors. Li Shimin led the army in a campaign to secure the whole of the empire for his father and finally created a united China in about four years. Li Shimin wasn't the Crown Prince. He launched a palace coup and killed his brother to seize the Crown Prince position. The emperor was forced to abdicate. Li Shimin became Emperor Taizong. He rethought the experience of the Sui's decline, listened to opinions and proposals from all sides, used able people, reduced the tax burden on people and encouraged and developed production. He successfully strengthened the relationship between the Han and minority nationalities. This era of peace and prosperity is called the Prosperity of Zhenguan in history. This peaceful time reached a summit during Emperor Xuanzong's reign, who was Taizong's successor. That period is called the Heyday of Kaiyuan in history. Taizong's capacity for recognizing a man's ability, regardless of his background was demonstrated by appointments he made. People who had been opposed to him even got positions. Taizong practiced the art of control. He looked at the people as water and the government a vessel, saying the water can both float and capsize a vessel.

During the Tang Dynasty, the achievements in ideology, culture and arts in ancient China was taken to new heights. Buddhism, Taoism and Islam coexisted. Many great poets and writers emerged, such as Li Bai, Du Fu and Bai Juyi. There were new developments in the aspects of astronomy, calendar, medical treatment and construction. During the Tang Dynasty, the business road was restored; as a result, envoys from over 40 countries came to Chang'an, to build relationships with the Tang Dynasty. The state, under the rule of the Tang Dynasty, became the most powerful and prosperous country in the world.

Life in Bianjing (present-day Kaifeng of Henan Province), then the national capital, as described in the *Riverside Scene at Qingming Festival*, masterpiece of Zhang Zeduan of the Northern Song Dynasty (960–1127).

In 755, two military generals of the Tang Dynasty, An Lushan and Shi Siming, launched a rebellion. Although it was put down, the central authority weakened increasingly from then on. A new local separatism emerged. The internal struggle for power grew. The national control was gradually lost. In the later Tang Dynasty, most parts of China broke out in a peasants' rebellion. The peasants seized the opportunity to fight. In 907, the Tang was replaced by the Liang Dynasty.

After the Tang Dynasty came to an end, ancient China stepped again into more than 50 years of division. Five dynasties of the Liang, Tang, Jin, Han and Zhou emerged sequentially in the central plain region in the north. In order to distinguish between them and the same names of former dynasties, the five dynasties were termed as the Latter Liang, the Latter Tang, the Latter Jin, the Latter Han and the Latter Zhou in history. The period of the five dynasties lasted for only 53 years, from 907 to 960. At the same time, some small separate states were built in the southern areas and some places in the north. As a total of 10, they were also called the Ten States in Chinese history. They lasted for 88 years, from 891 to 979. Thus The Period of the Five Dynasties and Ten States was named by China's historians.

The Song Dynasty (960–1279) succeeded the Five Dynasties and Ten States. By means of the capital and boundaries changing, the Song Dynasty consisted of the Northern Song Dynasty (960–1127) and Southern Song Dynasty (1127–1279), in China's history, also called the "two Songs". Its founder Emperor Taizu, Zhao Kuangyin, through a mutiny seized imperial power in 960 AD. He changed the state title into Song, and named Bianjing (today Kaifeng in Henan Province) as the capital. This period was known as the Northern Song Dynasty in history. In the early period of the Northern Song Dynasty, southern China had been basically reunified, and most parts of the country were under the control of the Song.

Emperor Taizu of the Song Dynasty, Zhao Kuangyin, was originally senior officer of the imperial guards in the Latter Zhou Dynasty. He was draped with the imperial yellow robe by his supporters and seized political power by launching a mutiny. To avoid the recurrence of his story, he decided to find ways to weaken the power of the generals. Carefully designed, he hosted a dinner inviting the generals who had followed him for many years, and had contributed a lot to the establishment of his reign. During the banquet, he lamented: "Thanks to you all, I will never forget that it is you who brought me today. But do you know that the emperor is not happier than a military governor?" The generals didn't understand his meaning, felt surprised and asked why. He replied: "The reason is easy, who does not want to be the emperor?" The generals said: "Your Majesty, Why did you say so? Now who will think and do that?" He calmly said: "May it be right. Even if you don't think so, there is no guarantee that your subordinates will not covet the wealth. Once they draped the imperial yellow robe on you, it could not be help." The generals were scared and answered quickly: "In our ignorance we

implore the guidance of Your Majesty to give us a way out." He said," You'd better relinquish the leadership of the military, and buy more fertile farmland and big houses to enjoy yourselves. There isn't any problem between us. Let's live in peace. Is it all right?" The next day, the generals handed in letters saying they decided to resign because of illness. He immediately agreed, and rewarded them large amounts of money. This is the famous story in China's history, called remove from military position by means of cups of wine.

In 1127, the Northern Song regime was defeated by the Jin in the north. And Southern Song Dynasty was established in Lin'an (present-day Hangzhou of Zhejiang Province).

With a prosperous economy, radiant arts, education and culture, developed science and technology and liberal governing, the Song Dynasty was one of the "golden age" periods in Chinese history, and also considered as another period of Renaissance and economic revolution by Western scholars. There were more than 50 countries with trade relations with China in the Song Dynasty.

Third Reunification
of Chinese Empire

When the Yuan Dynasty (1206–1368) succeeded the Song Dynasty, China entered its third empire reunification period. During the Yuan, Ming (1368–1644) and Qing (1616–1911) Dynasties, the empire creates greater glories, and went into its decline in the late 18th and early 19th centuries.

The Yuan Dynasty is the first central government in Chinese history established nation wide by an ethnic minority. In the 11th century, the Mongolian tribes emerged and came to the forefront in the Mongolia steppes in north China. In 1204, Temujin, born in an aristocratic family, reunified the Mongolian steppes. In 1206 Temujin was formally elected as ruler over Greater Mongolia, and he adopted the name and title of Genghis Khan, and the Mongol Khanate was

Ruins of the Yuan Dadu, Great Capital of Yuan Dynasty (1271–1368).

63

built. In the early times of the Mongol Khanate, relying on its strong military strength, it attacked Central Asia and Europe many times. Its territory constantly expanded, the Western Xia (1038−1227), Jin (1115−1234), Dali (ethnic minority regime in north and southwest China) and Tubo (ancient Tibetan regime in China) were defeated consequently. In 1271, Kublai, a grandson of Genghis Khan, adopted a dynastic title, that of Da Yuan (or "Great Origin") replacing the Mongolian title, and made Dadu (today's Beijing) the capital. He respected Genghis Khan as Taizu, and named himself Emperor Shizu. Since that time Beijing would become the capital of the Yuan, Ming and Qing Dynasties. China's political center was transferred from south to north. In 1279, the Southern Song Dynasty was destroyed by the Yuan. It ends the long-term situation of several governments existing side by side. China also achieved a new uniformity.

The Mandate of Heaven now shifted to Zhu Yuanzhang, historically known as Emperor Taizu of the Ming Dynasty (1368-1644), a peasant leader

Sculptures at the Ming Xiaoling Mausoleum: (left to right) Tang He, Liu Bowen, Zhu Yuanzhang, Empress Ma, and Xu Da.

who became eminent during the rebellions. After eliminating his rivals, Zhu Yuanzhang became the emperor in 1367, and established the state title Ming in 1368. The capital city first was in Yingtianfu (Nanjing in Jiangsu province) and later in Beiping (now Beijing), which was renamed from Dadu.

Emperor Taizu of the Ming Dynasty, Zhu Yuanzhang, was born poor. He used to be a beggar and a Buddhist monk when he was young. He was courageous, resourceful and was able to get followers to fight the Mongols. So he soon became a peasant revolt leader. He proposed "to construct high walls, to store grain everywhere, and to be the king gradually". After hard work, he founded a powerful army, by which he solved all obstacles and finally reunited China. After becoming the emperor of Ming, he formulated new laws, adopted a new system of government, and reformed the administrative agencies to strengthen the feudal centralization. In order to strengthen the supervision and control of his subjects, he also set up special officials, such as the Patrol Division

Bronze sculpture of Zheng He at the Nanjing Shipyard Ruins Park, Jiangsu Province.

Nanjing
Taicang
Ming Dynasty
Fuzhou
Quanzhou
Xiamen
Guangzhou
Qeshm
Bengal
Muscat
Chittagong
Dhofar
Cuttack
India
Duzhushan
Luzon
Aden
Siam
(Thailand)
Champa
Kingdom
Qui Nhon
Socotra
Andaman Islands
Bangkok
Calicut
Chania
(Cambodia)
Cochin
Quilon
Colombo
Nicobar Islands
Pulo Condore
(Con Son Island)
Sulu S
Male
Sri Lanka
Lumbri
Brunei
Mogadishu
Maldives
Malacca
Brava
Jubba
Temasek
(Singapore)
Burni
Malindi
Western Seas
Palembang
Mombasa
Sumatra
Java
Surabaya
Jeddah
Mecca

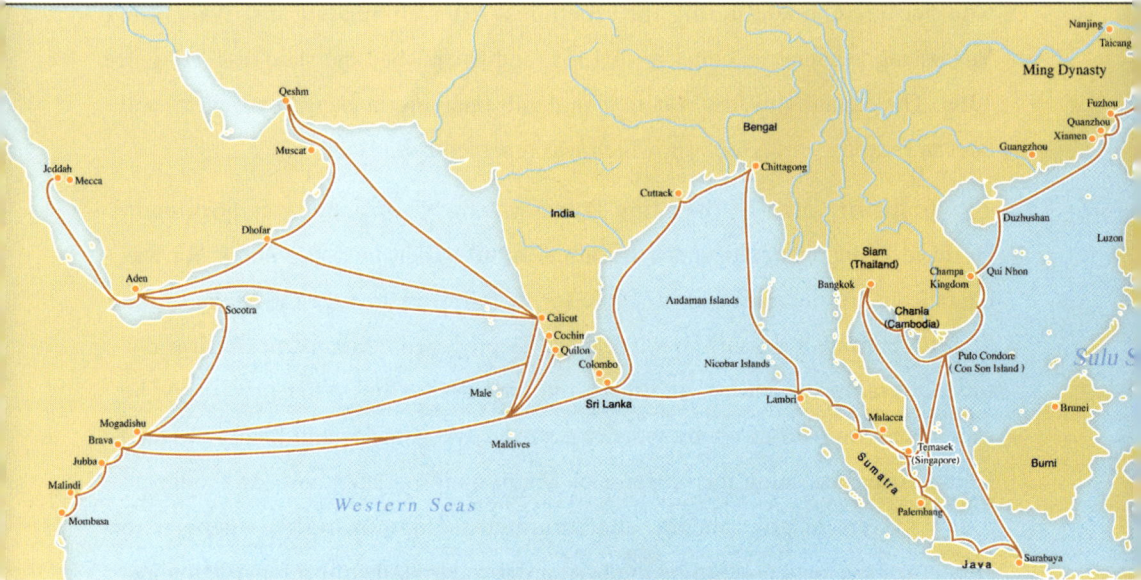

Route Map of Zheng He's Voyages to the Western Seas.

and the Imperial Guard. Zhu Yuanzhang was one of the cruelest emperors in China's history. To avoid others coveting the reign of his family Zhu, he killed more than 30,000 of his followers at one time, among which included the veteran generals who had made great contribution. According to historical records, he looked ugly. Because some honest painters could not paint him as a male beauty, they were killed.

In 1421, a great Ming Dynasty Emperor Chengzu, Zhu Di, changed the capital from Nanjing to Beijing, in order to facilitate the consolidation of the northern border, and further control the northeastern region. During the Ming, the Great Wall in the north was built, repaired and consolidated, and became a major barrier to defend against foreign invasion. Since the Yuan Dynasty, the city of Beijing had continued to be built. The Forbidden City was built in this period. Emperors who did not forget to build his palace used for after death. The Ming Tombs located in the northern part of Beijing were built in this period.

Zheng He's long voyages to Southeast Asia and the Indian Ocean produced an important impact on world navigation. It happened in the Ming period. To strengthen the friendly ties with overseas countries, emperor Chengzu sent Muslim Zheng He (1371–1433) as a Chinese ambassador to the West. From 1405 to 1433, Zheng He made seven navigations, visited over 30 countries and regions in Asia and Africa, with the farthest having reached the coast of the Red Sea and Africa. Zheng He's magnificent voyages occurred half a century earlier than European navigators.

The Ming Dynasty was a stage in history in which China's economy and culture became more developed. It also was the period of the Western Renaissance, geographic discovery and religious reformation. With some Western missionaries coming to China, the exchange of eastern and western cultures is in initial stage.

In the later years of the Ming, an ethnic minority living in northeast China, known as Manchu was rapidly developing. In 1636, the minority leader of the local government proclaimed himself Emperor Huangtaiji, renamed the dynasty as Qing, and the national title was changed to Manchukuo, which is the origin of the government "Manchurian". In 1644, a Ming commander stationed in Shanhaiguan Pass led the Qing army through the pass. The Qing Dynasty quickly secured rule of the whole country. It is the last feudal dynasty in Chinese history and ruled the country for 267 years. In the early and middle period of the Qing Dynasty, the unified multi-ethnic country was consolidated and developed. Emperors Kangxi, Yongzheng and Qianlong are the greatest ones in the Qing history. They put down rebellions and the achieved the reunification of Taiwan, Outer Mongolia, and Xinjiang. They also set up the Tibet Minister, to defend against invasion, and basically laid a territory the size of China today.

Emperor Kangxi was a very great and advanced emperor in late ancient society in China. His rule began at almost the same time as King Louis XIV ascended the throne of France, and they have many similarities: both being the

Image of Qing Emperor Kangxi Doing Readings.

emperor or the king very young, being gifted, being of the same talented and very high caliber, and firmly controlling the power under autocratic monarchy rule for half a century, and bringing their own country into a new historical peak of prosperity. Kangxi came to the throne at eight years old. He ruled the country for 61 years. He was the longest reigning monarch since there were written records in Chinese history. As well as rare in history, he loved reading books and studying. He is the first Chinese emperor to come into contact

Part of Portrait Showing Qing Emperor Qianlong Reviewing the Troops by Italian painter Giuseppe Castiglione,

Complete Library in the Four Branches of Literature (part) in the National Library Exhibition.

with western modern scientific knowledge and was most interested in western technology.

Qianlong was the last great emperor in ancient Chinese history. As Emperor Kangxi's grandson, Qianlong came to the throne at age 25, reigned for 60 years and was the overlord for four years after an abdication, and he died at the age of 89 as the oldest emperor in history. He ruled the country for over 63 years, and was the longest reigning monarch in Chinese history. In Chinese history, the Qianlong emperor is a cultural type as a learned man. He commissioned his officials to compile the well-known *Si Ku Quan Shu (Complete Collection in Four Treasuries),* which is a major contribution for the preservation of Chinese culture. This project took 20 years and 4,186 people worked on it. Many of the royal palaces and gardens of the Qing Dynasty found in Beijing were built or repaired by Qianlong, such as the Summer Palace, Yuanmingyuan Palace and

the Hall of Prayer for Good Harvest at Temple of Heaven, now mostly listed as world cultural heritage. The Emperor Qianlong was learned, cultivated, diligent, gifted and productive. He loved writing poems, essays, calligraphy and painting. In his free time, he must do three things: writing articles, painting and writing poems. He left more than 42,600 poems in his life; this achievement was and is unique.

In the middle and later period of Qing Dynasty, China's agricultural civilization comes to its end and the Western countries started to accumulate primitive capital and to grow their colonial expansion. The collision and conflict between China and Western countries lasted more than one century. With the agricultural empire eventually unable to match the powerful capital empires, autocratic monarchy was chosen to step off the stage of history.

A Multi-ethnic Country

China has fifty-six ethnic groups. It is this cultural diversity that distinguishes it from other countries of the world.

All the ethnic groups have made their own contribution to China's present territory. The ancient Cathay people first settled in Shaanxi and Gansu drained by the Yellow River and the Central Plains. The Dongyi people, who lived in the east of China, were the first to exploit the coastal areas. The ancestors of Miao and Yao were the pioneers who developed the basins of the Yangtze, Pearl and Minjiang Rivers. The Tibetan and Qiang ethnic people cultivated present day Qinghai Province and the Tibetan Autonomous Region. The Yi and Bai ethnic people fought to make a sustainable life for themselves in the remote and

The Qiankun Bay of the Yellow River, which situates between Linfen of Shanxi Province and Yan'an of Shaanxi Province.

unforgiving mountainous areas of southwest China. The Manchu, Xibo, Ewenki and Oroqen ethnic people were the first to occupy northeastern China. The Huns, Turks and Mongolian people first made the vast Mongolian grassland their home. The Li people first settled what we know today as Hainan Island, and the Gaoshan ethnic people first built their homes on the island of Taiwan.

Throughout history, the Han ethnic people have always constituted the major part of China's population. Most of them live in compact communities on the Central Plains, a basin area located at the middle and lower reaches of the Yangtze and the Yellow Rivers. This part of the world boasts a temperate climate and vast and fertile land the combination of which makes this a prime farming area. However, other, minority ethnic groups are mostly to be found in the border areas, where geographic conditions are more varied. Thus, instead of farming, they had to develop excellent skills of herding, hunting and fishing, based on

The portrait drawn by Yan Liben, noted painter of the Tang Dynasty (618–907), which shows how Tang Emperor Taizong met in 641 with Gar Tongtsan, envoy sent by Tubo King Songtsan Gambo for marriage with Tang Princess Wencheng.

the unique local conditions of grassland, desert, forest, plateau, mountains, hilly areas and lakes. Over time, the Central Plains, fabled as a land of milk and honey, became well developed in culture and economy. The economic development of most minority people living in the border regions, however, lagged behind. Thus they tended to engage in trade with the peoples of other regions, especially those of the Central Plains, resulting in economic and cultural ties, and a limited migration of some of the minority people to those Plains. As our history progressed, many ethnic groups which originated on the Mongolian grasslands moved southward in search of economic and cultural development, and subsequently dropped their nomadic way of life and took up farming. So successful were some that they even established dynasties of great historical significance, such as the Northern Wei Dynasty (386–534) established by the Sienpi people and the Yuan Dynasty (1206–1368) by the people of Mongolian origin. This would indicate that they became thoroughly assimilated into the culture and lifestyle of the Han people.

Throughout the years, the Central Plains have always been the center of China's territory, and their original settlers, the Han ethnic people, while assimilating many minority groups, have still dominated the cultural and ethnic makeup of the Chinese population. Ancestors of the Han ethnic people lived on the Central Plains some 4,000 to 5,000 years ago. From the Xia (about 2070 BC–1600 BC) to Zhou (1046 BC–256 BC) dynasties, they incorporated some minority peoples such as Yi, Qiang, Di, Miao and Man, and evolved into a new ethnic tribe, the Cathay. Then, during the Qin (221 BC–206 BC) and Han (206 BC–220 AD) Dynasties, the incorporation of smaller tribes with the majority Cathay people eventually led to the rise of the Han ethnic group. During the Sui (581–618) and Tang (618–907) Dynasties, some nomadic tribes, such as the Siepi, Qiang and Huns, migrated from their northern homelands and came south to settle on the Central Plains where, with time, they became assimilated into the local Han people. There were mutual benefits to be gained: while those minority groups adopted the language, costumes, customs and ideologies of

Historical Chronology of China	
Xia	About 2070 BC–1600 BC
Shang	1600 BC–1046 BC
Western Zhou	1046 BC –771 BC
Eastern Zhou	770 BC –256 BC
Qin	221 BC–206 BC
Western Han	206 BC–25 AD
Eastern Han	25–220
Three Kingdoms (Wei, Shu, Wu)	220–280
Western Jin	265–317
Eastern Jin	317–420
Northern and Southern Dynasties	420–589
Sui	581–618
Tang	618–907
Five Dynasties	907–960
Northern Song	960–1127
Southern Song	1127–1279
Yuan	1206–1368
Ming	1368–1644
Qing	1616–1911
Republic of China	1912–1949
People's Republic of China	founded on October 1, 1949

the Han people, the Han, for their part, also learned from their cooking, music, dance forms, and the style of their clothes. A good case in point is the emperor Xiaowen of the Northern Wei Dynasty (386–534), who carried out reforms in the Siepi regime. He not only encouraged his people to learn the Han language and wear Han clothes but also advocated the adoption of Han family names and intermarriage with members of Han society. Hundreds of years later, the Manchu rulers also followed the same idea when they established the Qing Dynasty (1616–1911). Having established their regime on the Central Plains, the following 300 years saw them wholly adapt to the local culture and their complete assimilation with the local people.

Feudal regimes followed from centralization. History shows us that every regime must have a set of policies to deal with the relationship between the Central Administration and regional powers. Here in China these policies and methods helped to safeguard the unification of the country. Among them, two major systems featuring either regional or semi-regional autonomy were commonly adopted by feudal rulers as the basic political systems by which they would unite their fiefdoms. One of them was characterized by conferring an official title on the regional state ruler. The other involved the establishment of the Jimi prefecture, which is exempted from State taxation. Irrespective of the political methods employed, however, Central Authorities tended to take a softly-softly approach when dealing with the alliances between different ethnic groups. Based on the actual situation of the minority tribes involved, the Central Government adopted a variety of measures. In some cases, they would send envoys to the local region, or even a member from the imperial family to marry the local ruler. In other cases, it would confer official titles on the most influential local figures or otherwise establish stronger and stronger economic links. Over the course of two thousand years, these methods promoted significant ties between regional powers and the Central authorities and unquestionably promoted the national solidarity of China.

Traditional Ideology, Culture and Society

When we speak of traditional Chinese ideology and culture, we are in fact referring to that which took shape before 1840, when the Opium War broke out. The traditional Chinese ideology and culture are unique in style. Throughout history, although they have drawn from other cultures, they have still preserved many distinct Oriental characteristics, which have been powerful enough to have a far-reaching influence on the culture of China's neighbors. The traditional Chinese ideology and culture are the foundation of the spirit and character of the Chinese people and lie behind all the achievements of China's historical development.

Confucianism and the Orthodox

A variety of schools of thought and their exponents emerged during the period from the pre-Qin period to the early Han (202 BC−220AD) Dynasty, including Confucianism, Taoism, Legalism and Mohism. Prominent figures emerging during that span of time include Confucius, Mencius, Lao Tzu and Zhuang Zi.

The three major schools of thought dominating the traditional Chinese ideology and culture are Confucianism, Taoism and Buddhism. Among them, Confucianism is the most influential. That influence can be found in many major concepts concerning the life of ancient Chinese people, such as the idea of how to be a successful ruler, the moral value of society, and the way one conducts oneself in that society. It has also greatly influenced schools of thought in other parts of East Asia, perhaps most significantly those of the Korean Peninsula and Japan.

The honorific adjective "Confucian" at first referred to people who presided over specific rites, but subsequently took on a broader application as it became an honorific title for scholars.

Confucius (551 BC−479 BC) was the founder of Confucianism. Born in the State of Lu in the Qufu area of Shandong Province, he is still revered as a thinker, politician and educator. Legend has it that he himself compiled six ancient classics, namely *The Spring and Autumn Annals, The Book of Music, The Book of Songs, The*

Portrait of Confucius.

Book of Rites, The Book of Changes and The Book of History. Confucius coined many wise phrases and expounded theories about the law, life and government. Our main access to his thinking is through *The Analects*, a work compiled by his disciples and considered the most reliable source of information about his life and teachings. Confucius heavily emphasized what he called "benevolence and rites" in his ideological system. In his opinion, benevolence, concentrating on "loving people", represents a variety of moral standards. He once said: "The humane man, wishing himself to be established, sees that others are established, and, wishing himself to be successful, sees that others are successful." And, on another memorable occasion, "Do not do to others what you do not want done to yourself". He lived in the second half of the Zhou Dynasty (1046 BC–256 BC), when the Zhou King was weak and the real power rested with local state rulers. Seeing rampant intrigue and vice, he deplored the contemporary disorder and lack of moral standards. He came to believe that the only remedy was to convert people once more to the principles and precepts of the sages of antiquity. He therefore lectured to his disciples on the principles of the "rites and music". He believed that rites give public display to social hierarchies and music unifies hearts in shared enjoyment. Both of them act as a form of communication between the citizen's humanity and his social context, and strengthen social relationships. To these ends he urged people from all walks of life to voluntarily follow social conventions, and to effect a balance between order and harmony.

In China's history, Confucius was the first to establish private schools and make it possible for common people to get access to education. He was worshipped by the Chinese people as Master Kong, the great educator. Legend has it that he lectured numerous students, of whom seventy-two turned out to be very successful. Many of his most famous ideas were expressed during these lectures and it is these ideas, often contained in wise sayings, that were subsequently compiled by his followers and gained wide acceptance in China. Today, these sayings are still part of everyday speech, and it is quite common to hear people quote such lines as "To study and not think is a waste. To think and

Portrait of Mencius.

not study is dangerous", "Isn't it a pleasure to study and practice what you have learned?" and "When three men are walking together, there is one who can be my teacher."

Another prominent figure who has made a great contribution to the Confucian ideal is Mencius (385 BC–304 BC). Also a great thinker, politician and educator, he is regarded as the true transmitter of Confucius's teachings. Chinese scholars worship him as the greatest Confucian thinker after Confucius himself. He developed Confucius' ideals and put forward a series of concepts expressing the principle that a ruler should govern his country with benevolence. He pointed out that only if the ruler were to adopt policies of benevolence, would he get real support from his people, this being a development of his belief that the people's support is more important than anything else for good governance. He was passionately opposed to oppression or misuse of force. He also believed that human nature is fundamentally good, a concept which deeply influenced ancient Chinese society. A statement of this belief is to be found in *The Three-Character Scripture*, which begins with the words "Men, at their birth, are naturally good."

But this view was challenged by another Confucian thinker, Xun Zi (318 BC–238 BC), who held the opposite opinion, proclaiming that "human nature is fundamentally bad". Xun Zi greatly emphasized the importance of rites and made a significant contribution to the development of Confucianism in this regard. In his opinion, rites represent social regulation and the estate system, which are essential for a well-ordered life, society and country. He described the relationship between the king and his people as that between a boat and water, once being quoted as saying "while the water can carry a boat, it can also overturn it."

Confucianism dates back to the pre-Qin period. However, it did not gain its prominence over other schools of thought until the Han Dynasty (206 BC–220 AD), when Emperor Wudi (140 BC–87 BC) designated it as Orthodox. Later, during the Song (960–1279) and Ming (1368–1644) Dynasties, Confucianism further developed into two schools, which respectively emphasize heavenly principles and consciousness. The rise of these two schools led to the formulation of what is known as Neo-Confucianism. Neo-Confucianism, the innovative

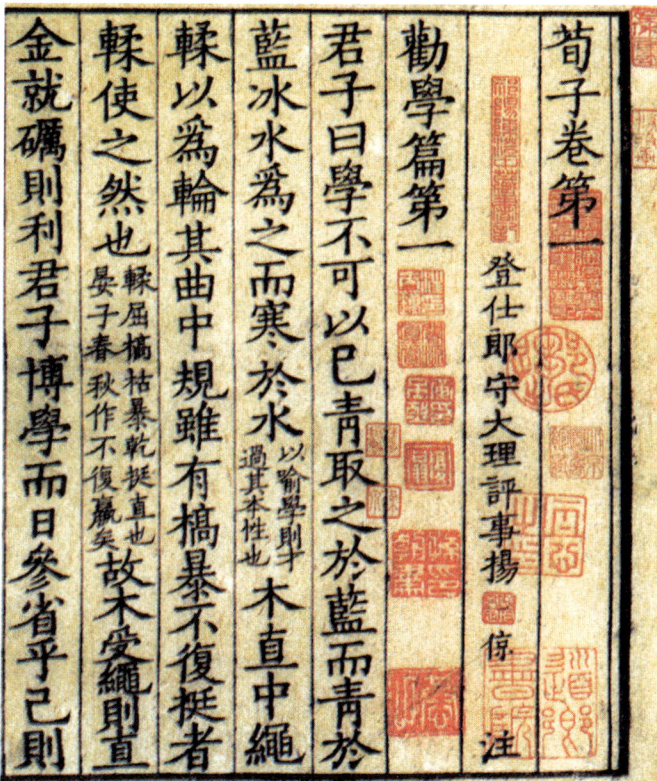

Photocopy of *Xun zi*.

Engraved portrait of Zhu Xi, science master of the Song Dynasty (960–1279).

reinterpretation of the traditional Confucian core, associates the moral standards put forward by Confucius and Mencius with the heavenly principles. It demonstrates human nature, the status of human beings in the universe, and the relationship between the two. It attaches importance to the pursuit of cultural and ideological promotion. Thanks to it, the moral principles of Confucianism have been much enriched.

Traditional Ideology, Culture and Society

The traditional Chinese ideology and culture refer to what took shape before 1840, when the Opium War broke out. The traditional Chinese ideology and culture are unique in style, and although they draw from other cultures, they still preserve distinct Oriental characteristics, which are powerful enough to have far-reaching influence on the culture of neighboring countries. Traditional Chinese ideology and culture are the foundation of the spirit and character of Chinese people and behind the achievement of China's development.

The founder of Taoist thought was *Lao Tzu* (about 600 BC–500 BC) who was a contemporary of Confucius. He wrote the book Lao Tzu, i.e. *Tao Te Ching,*

Statue of Lao Tzu at the Lotus Hill in Fangshan, Beijing.

called the Classic of the Way and the Natural Virtue by the Old Master by later generations, to clarify his philosophy. "Tao" is the most important concept among Lao Tzu's thoughts. He held that the essence of everything on earth was generated from "Tao". In view of Lao Tzu, "Tao" is a blend of two aspects, the unity of "not-being" and "being" which can mutually transform each other. Lao Tzu viewed "no-act" as the quality of "Tao" and "no-act" means complying with the original situation of all existing things. Lao Tzu also put forth the famous proposition that "all existing things are bound together in a universal context that is founded upon a principle called "Tao" and held that "Tao" is "nature" complying with all things existing on earth. Lao Tzu believed that "no-act" had a close relationship with "nature", and if rulers did "no act" people would be "natural".

The "Huang Lao School" was a major sect of the Taoist school during the Warring States Period (475 BC–221 BC). "Huang" refers to the forefather of the Chinese race, the Yellow Emperor or Huangdi, and "Lao" refers to Lao Tzu. The "Huang Lao School" explains Lao Tzu's thoughts with dependence on the Yellow Emperor. Literature left by the Huang Lao School mainly includes the *Medical Classic of the Yellow Emperor* and *Guan Zi*, which mostly discuss social political issues and self-cultivation. The Huang Lao School called Tao "the great void" and explained Tao as "qi", holding that the generation of all existing things relied on "vitality" which was the source of man's life and wisdom. The Huang Lao School attached importance to the idea of "temporization", stressing that "Tao" temporized the nature of all existing things. Regarding politics, monarchs should temporize the nature of officials and common people subject to them and remain tranquil and empathize with the role of officials and common people when managing state affairs. This school of thought was adopted and accepted by rulers of the early Western Han Dynasty (206 BC–25 AD) and served as the source of policies such as "managing state affairs by no act" and recuperating and multiplying the state.

Zhuang Zi (about 369 BC–286 BC) was the most influential ideologist of the Taoist school in the pre-Qin period (before 221 BC). As Mencius inherited and developed the thought of Confucius, Zhuang Zi inherited and developed the thought of Lao Tzu. Later generations often juxtaposed Zhuang Zi and Lao Tzu and called them together as Lao Zhuang. Zhuang Zi's thought is mainly manifested in his book *Zhuang Zi*. Zhuang Zi's thought focuses on seeking man's spiritual freedom. He held that the most difficult position for men was the loss of spiritual freedom. Man created wealth and culture and yet man was dominated by wealth and culture and became the slave of substance. In the view of Zhuang Zi, the fundamental way to break free of such a difficult position was to reach "no-self", meaning surpassing self and reaching the realm in which the "heart wanders about in Tao", i.e. the extremely beautiful and joyful realm of "unity of heaven and man".

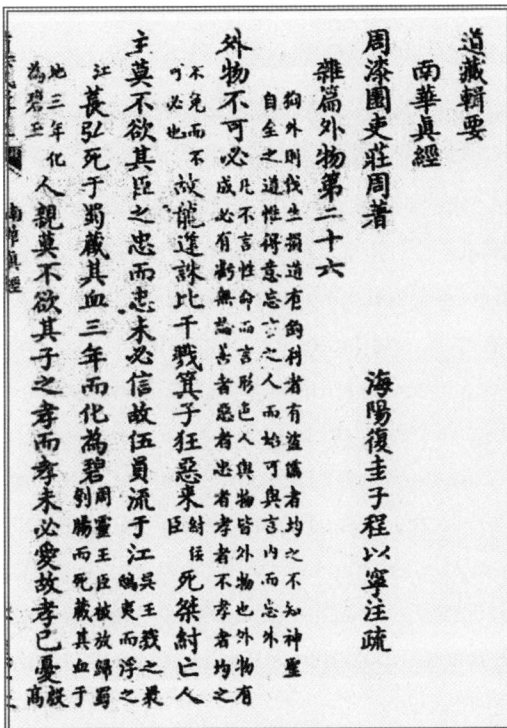

Photocopy of Zhuangzi.

Resident temple of Taoist Zhengyi School at Longhu Hill, Yingtan, Jiangxi Province.

During the Wei (220–265) and Jin (265–317) dynasties Taoist thought experienced a renaissance and the Wei Jin Metaphysics Sect (xuan xue in Chinese) came into being, and held the works *Lao Tzu, Zhuang Zi* and *Zhou Yi* (*The Book of Changes*) *as* its major classics. The system of a "new Taoist school" of thought was established by re-explaining these classics with a focus on "the fundamental and the incidental, and being and not-being". The *Lao Tzu* philosophy is the knowledge of universal profoundness and abstruseness, while the word "Xuan" (metaphysical) means profoundness and abstruseness and can be used to describe "Tao", the universal origin, so people at that time called the Taoist school adhering to the theories of Lao Tzu the "Xuan Sect". The Wei Jin Xuan Sect discussed many issues. Fundamentally it was to solve the relationship between the cosmology philosophy of the Taoist School and the idea of administration by the feudal ethical code of Confucianism, i.e. the relationship between Confucian thought and Taoist thought.

Under the influence of Taoist thought, Taoism came into being in the 3rd century. Taoism views *Lao Tzu* as the fundamental classic expressing its religious creed and Lao Tzu as its hierarch. Taoism, with the belief of seeking longevity and no death as its core, integrates the beliefs and arts of necromancy, astrology, medicine, etc. to preserve man's health. It makes use of Taoist thoughts, especially the thought of "qi" (using "qi" to show the existence of all living things on earth) to form a vast system of religious thought absorbing some thoughts of Buddhism and Confucianism. According to present knowledge, the earliest Taoist organizations were Taiping Tao and Wudoumi Tao at the end of the Eastern Han Dynasty (25–220). They were not accepted by the government at the time, but later after alteration, they gradually became the official religion. With the inclusion of Buddhist thought, in order to increase its acceptance in the local culture, Taoism was supported by governments for more than 1,000 years after the Eastern Jin Dynasty (317–420) and spread and developed very quickly. By the time of the Song Dynasty (960–1279) many schools and sects had formed across China, with Zhengyi and Quanzhen as the two most influential sects. In the middle of the Ming Dynasty (1368–1644), the government discontinued the policy of worshipping Taoism and the influence of Taoism began to decline.

Taoist thought had great impact on the development of aesthetics, literature and arts of China, such as imagist theory and the theory of artistic conception. The Taoist theory on "unity of falsehood and reality" became an important principle of classic aesthetics in China and had great impact on poetry and painting in ancient China.

Introduction of Buddhism

Buddhism was born along the Ganges River in India in the 6th century BC. At the end of the Western Han Dynasty (206 BC–25 AD), it was introduced into China via Central Asia and gradually penetrated into Chinese society, combined with Chinese culture and became an important part of Chinese culture.

As to the introduction of Buddhism into China, there is a record: During the reign (58–76) of Emperor Mingdi of the Eastern Han Dynasty (25–220), one evening Emperor Mingdi dreamed of a golden man in the west. The next morning he asked his ministers to explain the dream. A minister told him, "I have heard of Buddha in the west, you must have dreamed of Buddha." Emperor Mingdi immediately sent envoys to invite Buddha to China. Later his envoys

At the beginning of the new year, citizens in Qingdao, Shandong Province, go worshipping Buddha at the Zhanshan Temple.

brought back two monks and a number of Buddhist books and records. Emperor Mingdi built a temple in his capital Luoyang especially for the two monks.

The development of Buddhism in China has an outstanding feature-attaching great importance to the translation of Buddhist sutras. At the beginning the translation of Buddhist sutras in China was mainly done by monks from Central Asian and South-Asian countries, but their translation was not satisfactory. Then Chinese monks began to go to the Central Asian and South-Asian countries for Buddhist scriptures. The most outstanding representative of them was Xuanzang (602–664) of the Tang Dynasty (618–907). Born in a poor family, Xuanzang became a monk at 13. In the course of research and religious discussion over many years, he came to believe it difficult to have a thorough knowledge of Buddhist sutras due to different opinions from various sectors. So he made a decision to go to India for Buddhist scriptures. After experiencing innumerable trials and hardships he reached India, and devoted himself to research of various Buddhist sutras. His knowledge was respected and praised highly by Buddhist community. After completing his learning and coming home, Xuanzang refused the offer of Emperor Taizong of the Tang Dynasty (618–907) to leave the Buddhist circle and take a political position. He focused his attention on the translation of a great number of Buddhist sutras he had brought back from India and made great contribution to the development of Buddhism.

The acceptance of Indian Buddhism by Chinese people experienced a course of gradual deepening of knowledge. But Chinese people held the basic attitude of only taking things they could use instead of taking everything. The Buddhist thoughts accepted by Chinese people were mainly Mahayana (created in the 1st century in India and upholding the idea of giving lenity to all living things and responding to the merits of others). In the course of spreading and developing in China, Buddhism harmonized and mixed with Chinese society, and tried its best to suit Chinese society. During the period, there appeared Chinese Buddhist sects. Especially during the Sui (581–618) and Tang (618–907) dynasties from the 6th to the 10th century, owing to the prosperity of social economy, Buddhism

achieved unprecedented development in China and gradually several large Buddhist sects such as Sanlun, Tiantai, Faxiang, Huayan, Lu, Chan and Jingtu formed.

Although it was an exotic culture at the beginning, Buddhism had a very wide impact on the development of Chinese culture after its localization. Buddhism had great impact on the development of Chinese phonology, linguistics and philology. The use of Chinese pinyin was enlightened first by Sanskrit, a phonetic language. Many Buddhist words became Chinese words, such as "freedom", "equality", "world", "all living things" and "realm", which enriched the vocabulary of the Chinese. "Most of the famous mountains around are occupied by monks." Buddhism also created temple culture in China. Today on relevant festivals temples are crowded everywhere, which has become a special mass cultural phenomenon. Buddhist thoughts about empty, realm and soul, and theories of the Chan sect in particular, had great impact on Chinese culture, arts and architecture. Buddhism also played a role in accelerating the development of Confucianism and Taoism. Buddhist ideas such as leniency, being a Samaritan, getting rid of evil and accepting goodness influence the behavior of Chinese people.

Basic Spirits of Traditional Thought and Culture

American scholar Philip Lee Ralph and others set forth their thoughts in their book *World Civilizations* (first published in 1998 by the Commercial Press): "When the ancient Greek philosophers were discussing the quality of the substantial world and Indian ideologists were thinking about the relations between soul and god, China's sages were trying to find the basis of human life and the fundamental principles of wise and able government."

The traditional thought and culture of China has a long and rich history. It has added enormously to the spiritual wealth of succeeding generations, and is in many ways unique in the overall history of human thought and spiritual endeavor. Its findings can be summarized as follows:

—Fundamental is the principle of putting people first. China is the country where what we might describe as humanistic thoughts made their earliest appearance. The ancient ideologists in China mostly advocated the building up of a moral and orderly cultural society by means of a humanistic view of civilization. According to this philosophy, if heaven and earth are the father and mother of all existing things, human beings are the most intelligent and important among all existing things. As the ancient scholar Xun Zi put it, "water and fire have qi but no life, grass and trees have life but no awareness, animals have awareness, and human beings have qi, life, awareness, and also friendly sentiments, thus we can plainly infer that human beings are the most precious inhabitants of this earth." "Benevolence" is the core of Confucian thought. Confucius himself maintained that, "benevolence means loving others." When one of his disciples asked how to define those all-important attributes of wisdom and knowledge, Confucius replied that a wise person gave preeminence to other

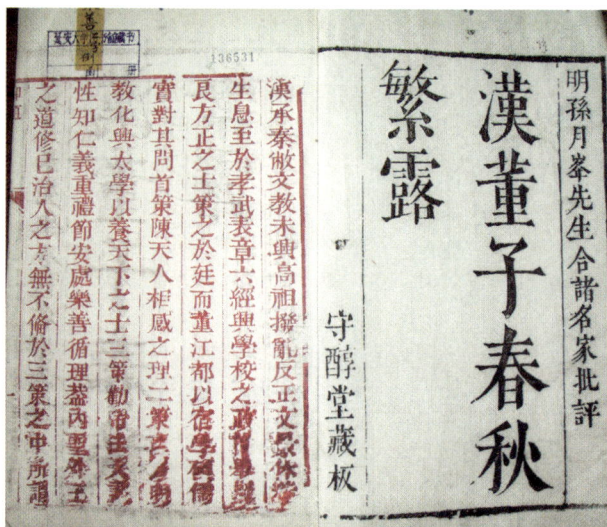

Chun Qiu Fan Lu by Dong Zhongshu of the Han Dynasty (202 BC−220 AD) promotes the theory of "unity of heaven and man" and "interaction between heaven and mankind".

people's affairs. In ancient China there was popular saying, "people are the root of a nation, and if that nation is solid then its people are able to live in peace with each other." Mencius put forward the thought that "people are most precious, the nation comes next, and monarchs are not important", which developed the Confucian philosophy of "putting the people first".

—Another important strand of thought is the concept of the unity of heaven and mankind. "Heaven" holds a special position in China's traditional culture; it refers to both the heaven in nature and the heaven of God's will. The former views sky and earth as the root of all existing things; the latter is subjective, imagined and irresistible. The proposition of "unity of heaven and man" in traditional Chinese culture is a natural outlook and an attitude to nature, i.e. human beings and all existing things on earth are an organic whole, despite the fact that the concepts of "heaven" and "man" have necessarily contradictory aspects. The concept of "heaven" is of the supreme, the most sacred and inviolable; heaven's force is far greater than that of man, and heaven's will decides man's will, so man must comply with heaven in order to realize and coordinate the unity of heaven and man. A distinctive character of Taoist thought is its emphasis on the idea that man should do things in compliance with nature, should develop alongside the development of all existing things, and should neither act in isolation nor seek to change nature in a random manner. This compliance with nature is also most strongly advocated in Confucian thought.

—The concept of peace is valued highly in Chinese thought. Peace is the inner spirit of Chinese culture and its importance is manifested mainly by the concepts "peace is valuable", "be harmonious but individual" and "benevolence". Confucius said, "anything, no matter how big or how small, must have peace as its starting point and peace as its end-result." Why is "peace" so important? According to ancient ideologists in China, all things on earth are produced and developed from "peace", i.e. "peace generates living things", and thus it is perfectly possible for the world itself to be continuously peaceful and prosperous. Meanwhile the traditional Chinese philosophers were also laying stress on "being harmonious but individual". On the one hand they viewed "harmony" as the supreme value for which one should seek, and on the other maintained that difference and diversity should be acknowledged, that each of us should respect and understand others and mutually forgive any wrongs arising out of that diversity. Thus "peace" can only be realized gradually by mutual and equal consultation, dialogue and cooperation. Traditional Chinese thought holds that "people must be divided according to stipulated regulations and laws" to prevent them from starting wars due to unsatisfied desires and unworthy ambitions. Hence, "benevolence and charity" should be followed by everyone, the ideal being a kind of universal benevolence to be attained by an education based on the precepts of kindheartedness, justice and morality. The resulting "benevolent people" are unassailable and will continue on the path that leads from "benevolence" to "peace".

—"Seek for the World of Great Harmony" is recommended by the ancient scholars, and yet what is this "World of Great Harmony" they would have us

seek? Confucius thought that the World of Great Harmony was a world where correct reasoning was universally adopted and all things were public. Lao Tzu also postulated an ideal society in which everyone could "enjoy sweet food, wear beautiful dresses, live in peace and maintain joyous customs." The so-called World of Great Harmony is in fact what modern commentators would refer to as a Utopian social ideal; a world without differences between classes, with neither oppression nor exploitation where people live equally and harmoniously and can enjoy the fruits of their labors. The direct result of this idealistic view of society was that in the history of China various peasants' uprisings were inspired by an ambition to establish a society in which there would be no distinction between the nobleman and the peasant, and where wealth would be equally shared. Kang Youwei (1858–1927), a revolutionary leader far closer to our own time, wrote a book, *On Great Harmony*, in which he put forward a society "where all things are public, there is no class distinction, all things are equal, and there is neither despot nor elected president above the people" as his personal vision of a "World

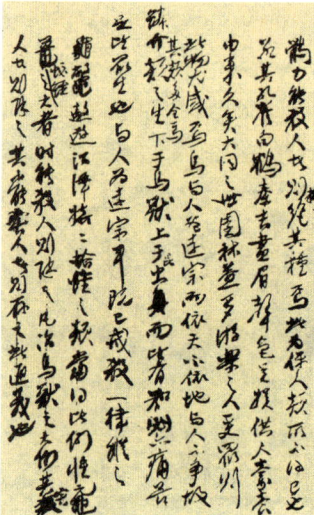

Manuscript of Book of Great Harmony by Kang Youwei.

Portrait of Kang Youwei.

of Great Harmony". Meanwhile his near contemporary Sun Yat-sen (1866–1925), a forerunner of China's democratic revolution, also took the view that "all things are public" as his political credo. In traditional Chinese culture, the idea of Great Harmony has its restrictions, both historical and political, but the simplicity of its message, its advocacy of public ownership, personal freedom, equality and philanthropy in fact reflect the longings of many people throughout the ages for a fairer and happier future society.

—Emphasize the spirit of going into society. The Confucian philosophy, which holds the leading position in traditional Chinese culture, required people to care about reality, and appreciate the internal moral cultivation which would lead to the benefit of real society. When one of his disciples enquired of him how he could discover more about the issues related to ghosts and gods, Confucius rebuked him sharply: "You cannot act properly in the world of men if you only want to talk of the things related to ghosts." So it was that Confucius himself only talked about things in this life, did not speak of ghosts, gods or an afterlife, and firmly stated that although he "respected ghosts and gods" yet he was "very far off from them". Going into society, he stressed, one must continuously enhance oneself by moral cultivation and become useful in the administration of public affairs. Everyone can accomplish great things if they do so from their innermost beings, basing their courses of action on the things around them and the simple realities of daily life. This method of achievement has as its starting point a just and sincere heart, and proceeds through studying the phenomena of nature, the acquisition of knowledge, the cultivation of personal morality, the good governance of one's family, and finally results in the ability to govern a state - and why not ultimately the whole world?

It is true to say that much of great value has been accumulated in the traditional Chinese culture, with an agricultural ideology as its base, but also that there exist within it a number of limits, some defects, and even aspects that are completely wrong. The principle errors inherent in this traditional Chinese

culture include: a lack of democratic spirit and excessive praise for rulers and the concept of rule; advocating hierarchy; making men more important than women; giving too great a prominence to collectivism and in consequence overlooking the value of the individual; and pursuing egalitarianism at the expense of creativity.

Society Steeped in Traditional Thoughts and Culture

Formed against a background of agricultural society, traditional Chinese culture took the form of a patriarchal clan system with families as its basic units. The concept of "the State" was rarely seen, in its place were usually such concepts as "under heaven" or "the god of the land and the god of the grain". In traditional Chinese culture, no family meant no state; family was both a group of living breathing beings as well as a unit of production. It is important to note, however, that the term "family" in this context does not simply refer to the family who live together under one roof but rather a whole extended family of multiple blood relations on both the male and the female sides, including uncles, aunts,

A happy family of four generations, with 41 members.

cousins, grandparents, great uncles, great aunts, etc. It was customary to refer to the paternal side of this extended family as "internal" members, whereas on the female side they were "external". It does not take a mathematician to calculate that after only a few generations this could result in a very large "family" indeed.

At grass-roots level in ancient Chinese village, communities, families and clans were organized according to the above-mentioned principles of distinction between men and women and the hierarchy of older and younger. Such families and clans often lived in the same region, used the same ancestral temple, and could trace their lineage back to a common forefather. Within a clan there would usually be men of superior knowledge, perhaps even one who had passed the imperial exams in old China, or who were simply older, or who held a higher position in the family hierarchy, who would be accorded greater prestige. In a clan, a person of noble character and high prestige took the position of clan chief; he would be charged with administering the clan, making decisions that affected

"Houbengtang" family temple of Shuiteng Shabian Village, Shunde, Guangdong Province.

the clan as a whole, organizing the offering of sacrifices to their ancestors, and punishing those who violated the clan's own laws and regulations. These grass-root social organizations with clans as the principle units played a vital role in establishing order and stabilizing the entire fabric of ancient Chinese society. It is the greatest single difference between ancient oriental society and that of the West.

Chinese society against the background of traditional culture founded a state based on morality instead of laws. Moral criteria became the rules of this society and everyone was constrained by morality. Confucian thoughts became the core values of traditional Chinese culture and formed the basis of the aforesaid moral criteria, perhaps the most famous being represented by the expression "three main-stays and five constant virtues", where the three main-stays are the king (main-stay of officials), the father (mainstay of sons) and the husband (main-stay of wives), and the five constant virtues refer to the relationships between the five

Performing dance to attract visitors at the Chentuan Temple Scenic Area in Anhui Province on March 2 or the second day of the third lunar month of 2014.

principal pairings in that society, i.e. the monarch and his officials, father and sons, husbands and wives, the old and the young, and bonds between friends. Thus, according to these precepts, there is "loyalty between the king and his officials, blood relation between fathers and sons, distinction between husbands and wives, order between older and younger, and trust between friends." Those betraying these moral criteria were considered, respectively, traitorous, disloyal, unfaithful, disobedient or unfriendly, and were rejected as such by their society. This ancient Chinese society viewed the above-mentioned Confucian morality and ideals as its most basic foundation by which the social order could best be regulated and maintained.

In order to found a state on the basis of morality, it is absolutely necessary to ensure that every member of society is himself a moral person, which involves the issue of enhancing the inner morality and cultivation of all the people.

During the lunar New Year's Day, people in Jiujiang of Jiangxi Province go worshipping the world's highest statue of Amitabha in Donglin Temple, the birthplace of the Pure Land Sect of Buddhism, at the foot of Lushan Mountain.

According to traditional Chinese culture, a man of good virtue should at first cultivate his own moral character, then seek to influence others by his speeches, and at last contribute personally to the general good of society. A virtuous man should gain knowledge, learn from direct inspection, think cautiously, distinguish clearly between right and wrong, and carry things out with boldness and vigor.

Under the influence of traditional culture, religion was not developed in ancient Chinese society. In fact, throughout the history of China religion has never held a prominent position in society, and so, during the ancient period under discussion, there was no dispute between religious and imperial power, nor was there conflict or outright war between different religious factions – another significant difference between ancient Chinese society and that of the west. In China there were not such books as the *Bible* and the *Koran*, or such propagators and preachers as Jesus or Mohammed.

The Confucian culture, the principle foundation of traditional Chinese culture, puts forward the virtues of going into society and living among mankind. It mainly discusses human and ethical relations, and does not involve the issues surrounding religious belief. Confucian thoughts were much respected as orthodox thoughts by rulers of past dynasties, thus severely restricting the development of religious thought in China. Another important part of traditional Chinese culture is Taoism. Although it later developed religious overtones, original Taoism focused on the discussion of natural rules and the cultivation of temperaments, which is greatly different from, say, the Christian belief in God. Classical Buddhism, quite contrary to all we have said about traditional Confucian thought, says that we should stand aloof from worldly affairs, but in ancient China it experienced a sort of make-over and eventually evolved into the Chan sect with its religious elements much weakened and its adherents given a great deal of liberty. In China there is a saying which goes, "one dies for a righteous cause and one stands to become a Buddhist," which vividly makes the point that it is not difficult to become a Buddhist disciple. Even today, if

you go into any of China's temples you will still see many people burning joss sticks and kneeling in worship. In fact, the majority of them are not genuine Buddhist disciples, but are only praying for peace or an end to some personal misfortune. In traditional Chinese culture Heaven is the greatest God, but people worship instead of believing in Heaven. At the very dawn of Chinese history the people performed totem worship activities, in which the dragon was often the object of worship, but these were more an expression of their awe and lack of understanding of the power of nature, not a religious belief. Today Chinese people maintain the tradition of offering sacrifice to ancestors, and each year there are several festivals at which ancestors are remembered in this way, but equally these are not religious activities and are simply a way for people to preserve their memories of, and pay their respects to, the departed.

Against the backdrop of this traditional cultural background, there were many other unique phenomena in old Chinese society still worthy of our continued attention today. Traditional Chinese society was one in which "men are noble and women are inferior," and it was customary for people to

The 100-year-old ladies with bonded feet.

undervalue women's role in society. This was the age of high-born women having their feet bound, also the period when a man would have both a wife and concubines. In fact, men could marry a concubine, and those men holding positions of wealth and power could even marry several. Take, for another example of how traditional society worked, the system of grass-root country gentlemen. Country gentlemen were not themselves government officials but they had special relations with the government. They were greatly influenced by Confucian schools of thought and made use of their cultural knowledge and social influence to serve the government in a disguised form and obtain benefits, it being the actual case that the government effectively implemented its administration over the grass roots population via them. And finally, let us not forget the system of eunuchs in royal palaces where the affairs in those royal palaces were managed by the eunuchs, some of whom achieved positions of great power and influence.

National Character Shaped by Traditional Thoughts and Culture

In the long course of historical development, the traditional Chinese thoughts and culture, as an ideology, were injected into the blood of Chinese nationality and had a profound impact on the shaping of the Chinese national character.

—Constantly strive to become stronger. "Heaven goes soundly, and man should constantly strive to become stronger." This famous exhortation to men of accomplishment encouraged them to follow the natural spirit of marching forward, working hard, contributing to society, and never ceasing, however hard

In Suriname's capital of Paramaribo, people of the Chinese origin perform lion dance, to celebrate the traditional Spring Festival.

the task. The sage Mencius viewed these precepts, combined with the ability to bear hardships and difficulties, as the only route to success. He said, "So, if God were to give an important task to a certain person, the first thing that person must do is to temper his will power, and thus be prepared to strain his muscles and bones, starve his stomach and lay waste his body…" Thousands of years of history have proved that the Chinese nation is full of toughness, that its population will never yield to the sufferings of natural disasters, will overcome domestic troubles and foreign invasion, and will persevere constantly until the task at hand is complete.

—Tolerance and harmony. The Chinese national character has a very strong degree of inclusiveness. Traditional Chinese culture makes great play of "harmony and peace" and "neutralization". It also recommends solving conflicts and differences by cooperation, does not advocate attacking or invading others, and is opposed to the idea of war. Such tolerance is manifested in the acceptance of other nationalities and the absorption of cultural achievements of other peoples. Several times in China's history the central plains were invaded, but on each occasion the cultures of these invaders were absorbed into the culture of the central plainsmen and became an important part of the Chinese national culture. Regarding the issue of morality, Chinese people pay attention to being "even-tempered and good-humored"; regarding governing a family, they believe that "a harmonious family makes everything prosperous"; regarding governing a state, they hold to the dictum that it is "peace and harmony which can make a state prosper"; and regarding foreign relations, they expound the ideal of "harmonizing millions of people". When dealing with the relations between men, families and states respectively, they attach importance to the pursuit of common interests, but while seeking them still preserve respect for other points of view, mutual tolerance and a continuance of common development.

—Diligence and frugality. They have long been an essential aspect of the Chinese character. In fact there is an ancient maxim which tells us that, "a state should be diligent and a family should be frugal." Here, "being diligent" means that a man should pursue his course with concentrated attention, with the utmost effort, and not allow remissness or weariness to deflect him from his task. This is because in Chinese culture the word "diligence" actually means a combination of the two concepts of "diligence" and "being hard-working". "Being frugal", on the other hand, means that a man should use his wealth reasonably, eschew extravagance and waste, persevere, and see things through to the end. Here we in fact have a combination of the ideas of "diligence" and "acting vigorously," often referred together as "frugality". In ancient times, due to primitive laboring methods, the fruits of such labor were hard-earned and people could only live by diligence and frugality. So Chinese ancestors learned to equate frugality with the public good and extravagance with the bad. There have been many popular apothegms throughout the long history of China, a number of which are

Luochengtou Power Community in Handan, Hebei Province, refutes waste of food to the welcome of its residents.

still relevant today: "When we look back we can see that the successful ones depended on diligence and frugality and the unsuccessful on extravagance and waste," is one such, "the way to have a family is by being frugal and diligent" another. Praising highly diligence and frugality and accumulating social wealth by honest hard work has always been regarded as the simplest but greatest virtue with which to make a state or a family prosperous.

—Be kindhearted and tolerant. Chinese culture emphasizes "the accumulation of good deeds in order to make virtue," advocating doing good deeds and holding that many such good deeds can make people capable of reaching a higher plain. In China Buddhism expounds the doctrine of standing aloof from worldly affairs, but it also contains a positive spirit of going out into society. The feelings of leniency and assistance advocated by Buddhism not only help people to be freed from the various sufferings of the real world but

When traditional Spring Festival comes, Nantong in Jiangsu Province donate to support local migrant workers from poverty-stricken families.

also strive to harmonize the relations between man and his fellow man, man and all other living things, and man and the very fabric of nature itself. It further attempts to mitigate various forms of conflict and encourages people to improve themselves and their lives by study. Many of China's popular folk sayings are concerned with the contrast between good and bad, the need to pursue the one and repudiate the other. Examples include, "Goodness necessitates a sharing of itself," "Sow the wind and reap the whirlwind," "We must do good rather than evil, on however humble a scale," "Those families doing many good deeds have endless luck and happiness, but the families doing many bad deeds have endless disasters." Consistent with being kindhearted, Chinese culture also stresses "tolerance", advocates "being lenient with an offender", believes in the "abandoning of former enmity", and opposes the "accumulation of rancor and mutual hostility". In traditional Chinese culture there are various ways in which one can follow the path of a good and virtuous life, such as "loving to do philanthropic work" and "showing sympathy towards the weak". There is one particular phrase which Chinese people like to repeat: "When one is in trouble, others will offer aid." Such aid will usually take the traditional form of solidarity, friendship and mutual assistance. Thus is kindheartedness and tolerance expressed in a typically Chinese way.

—Be optimistic and practical. The Confucian culture believes that it is proper to take one's place in day-to-day society. It advocates active participation in social activities and administrative affairs. The Confucian culture respects, confirms and faces reality, holds a positive and optimistic attitude to life, and opposes pessimism and disheartenment. Under the influence of this Confucianism, the Chinese people have always paid attention to reality and practicality, have pursued merit and opposed mere empty show, have scorned idle talk and empty thoughts. In the minds of the ordinary Chinese people, man should live to pursue reality, neither evading real issues nor embracing chimera, and most of all should keep actively pushing forward. Confucian culture stresses the value of self-study, not just for the simple accumulation of knowledge but as a way of enhancing one's self-cultivation and better enabling one to make contributions to social life. Another ancient saying makes a similar point: "Research both natural phenomena and human relations in society; thoroughly understand the changes from ancient times to today; ultimately form the theory of a school."

—Be Moderate. Now let's take a look at what is meant by moderation and "the golden mean". Due to the impact of traditional culture, Chinese people give great consideration to "the golden mean" when considering a course of action. This advocates not doing things excessively, but rather aiming for an appropriate moderation. For a simple illustration one can take eating. If one eats too much, one will feel unwell due to excessive fullness; if one eats too little, one will be hungry and undernourished. Or, again, consider the wearing of shoes. Shoes that are either too big or too small are uncomfortable and make walking difficult;

Some 1,000 people performing Taichi shadow boxing at the Tongyi Square in Xianyang, Shaanxi Province.

shoes of the correct size are an analogy of "the golden mean". In traditional Chinese business culture there is the thought that attempting to make more and more profit will eventually result in loss and in fact all things, when developed to extremes, will tend to produce the opposite of what is intended. Nothing should be done excessively; to do so is to develop in the opposite direction.

　　—The ideology of worry and disaster. Chinese people have a very optimistic attitude towards life, but at the same time are full of the ideology of worry and disaster. Mencius said: "Live in worry and disaster and die at ease." In different historical times, people with lofty ideals had different worries and disasters; some worried about the decline of monarch and state, some worried about the nation being in peril, and some worried about the sufferings of the common people, all of which meant that the ideology of worry and disaster became part of the essential character of the Chinese people. As a result we have been left a number of well-known sayings, handed down to us from antiquity, representing this facet of the national character. "Be the first to worry about the people's woes, the last to share the weal of the people"; "Although the age has not exceeded a hundred years, yet our minds contain the worry of ten-thousand"; "Every common man has his obligation to the rise and fall of the nation"; "I must care about my home, my country and even the whole world"; "Disregarding my humble position, I will not forget to worry about the nation"; "Without worry, a man is not wise"; "He does not have a penny in his pocket, yet must always have worry about the nation in mind." All of which are intended to encourage the people to attain a profound and lofty realm of "being both happy and worried in accordance with the whole nation".

　　Traditional culture has also had some negative impact on the shaping of the Chinese character. Due to an excessive emphasis on reality, there is a comparative lack of idealism; the ideology of the "golden mean" encourages the self-sufficient mind and makes people satisfied with the present situation, and has the tendency of producing people who lack the will to explore and take risks;

there is arrogance, and people, not believing that others might in some ways be superior to themselves, become inward-looking and conservative; others stick to conventions, excessively believe in the doctrines of their predecessors, and are unwilling to attempt to exceed those who came before them. These are just some of the negative traits of the traditional culture as it has shaped the Chinese character.

Exchanges Between Ancient Chinese and Foreign Culture

Influenced by such geographic features as high mountains, broad deserts, high plateaus and vast oceans, ancient China experienced a difficult exchange with the outside world, but that does not mean that there was no communication at all. The highly-developed ancient Chinese culture once had a profound impact on the cultural process of the outside world, and in the long course of its historical development absorbed other exotic cultures, especially those of Central and South Asia.

The Silk Road was the main passage by which ancient China was able to make exchanges with the outside world. Originally used to unite the Central

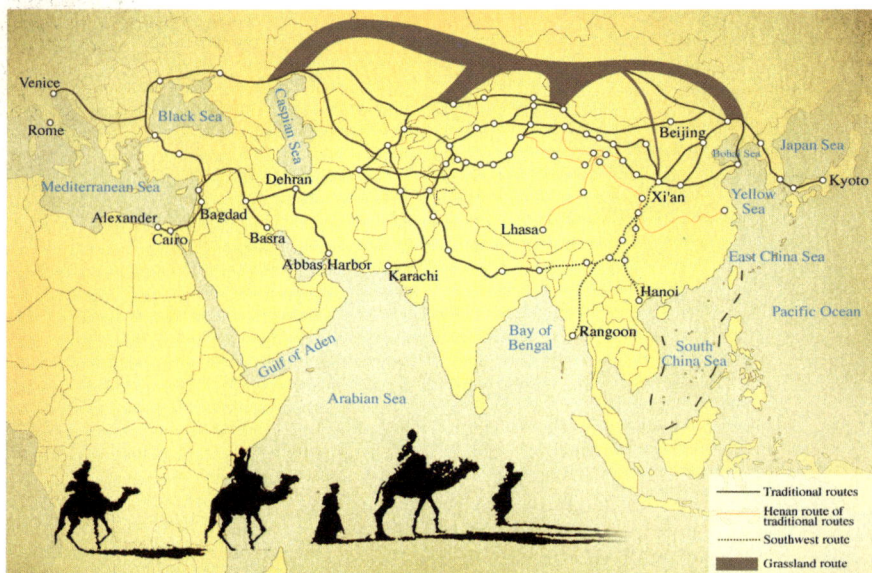

Sketch Map of Land Silk Road.

Asian states in resistance to the Hun powers on the northern grasslands, the Silk Road was opened during the Han Dynasty (206 BC–220 AD). Owing to the Silk Road, China opened up communications with the Central Asian and West-Asian states in regard to politics, economies, and cultural and military affairs. In the long period of more than 1,500 years from the Han Dynasty to the Ming Dynasty (1368–1644), i.e. from the 3rd century B.C. to the 17th century, the Silk Road carried the responsibility of developing relations with other states in Europe and Asia. It was the precious link between ancient Eastern and Western cultures and had a significant influence on the development of both. The Silk Road is still working. In recent years, China puts forward construction of the "Silk Road Economic Belt" to the benefit of peoples of countries involved. This will inevitably bring the role of the ancient Silk Road to full play.

In the long years of the Road it was usually merchants carrying bales of silk who trudged along its seemingly endless miles of often difficult terrain, thus giving a name to one of the most important thoroughfares in history. At that

Foreign envoys in Chang'an (Xi'an today) during the Tang Dynasty (618–907).

time the silk of China was well known in Central Asia, South Asia and Europe. The Roman writer Pali Aghatis said: "The precious colorful silk made in China looks like the beautiful blooming flowers in the fields and its fineness can bear comparison with the gossamer spun by spiders." The tea, perfume, porcelain, lacquer work, ironware and medicines of China, plus the knowledge in various fields such as astronomy, medicine, music and architecture, and most especially paper-making, printing and the making of colored inks, were transported or spread to Central Asia and the regions beyond by the Silk Road, thus influencing the cultural development of all the known world. Meanwhile, the Silk Road also introduced the culture west of Central Asia to China, especially religion and the arts, which greatly influenced the development of Chinese culture. Thus, for instance, Islam was introduced to northwestern China, which had a profound impact on the local social development. Acrobatics, operas, music and dancing from the regions to the west of Central Asia were also introduced via the Silk Road, and these were all catalysts for a great surge in the development of traditional Chinese art. The Silk Road's prosperity reached its summit during the Tang Dynasty (618–907) from the 7th to the 10th century, when the exchanges between China and foreign countries were most frequent and many envoys of countries from behind the western mountains came to the Tang Dynasty's ancient capital, Chang'an.

Regarding the exchanges between ancient Eastern and Western cultures, it is necessary to mention the introduction of Christianity and its subsequent influence on the future of East-West communications.

As early as the Tang Dynasty (618–907), Nestorianism (from the Nestorian sect of Christianity) was introduced to China by means of the Silk Road. It had a limited popularity and never achieved wide-scale recognition. Of far greater significance was Monte Corvino, who became the first person to propagandize Roman Catholicism in China. He landed on Quanzhou, Fujian in 1293, reached the capital of the Yuan Dynasty (1206–1368), Dadu in 1294 and began to preach the Catholic faith. Later he spread the word on the Roman version of Christianity for more than 30 years. During the Ming (1368−1644) and Qing (1616−1911) Dynasties, Jesus Penitent came to China by sea and tried to spread religion to the hinterland of China. In 1557 Portugal occupied Macao by force and turned it into an important base for the promulgation of Catholicism in the east. In 1583 an Italian Jesus Penitent Matteo Ricci (1552−1610) arrived in Guangdong in South China. A remarkable man, he harmonized Catholicism and Chinese culture, and persuaded the Chinese people to accept the faith of Catholicism. In return he accepted the costume of a Chinese Buddhist disciple granted to him by local officials of the Ming Dynasty (1368−1644), believing that by so doing he could integrate both himself and his religion into the mainstream of Chinese culture. Trading western sciences for Confucianism, he studied hard and wrote works in Chinese in order to preach western philosophy and Christian doctrines. In 1600 Matteo Ricci presented a mechanical chiming clock as a tribute to the Chinese

Portrait of Matteo Ricci.

emperor and was granted approval to live in Peking. While there he made a wide circle of friends among the city's scholar-bureaucrats and strove to gain their sympathy. By the time he died of illness in 1610 there were over two and a half thousand Catholic disciples across China. Early missionaries, under the influence of Matteo, played a very great role in spreading western knowledge in China. They translated many books on western science and technology in collaboration with the same class of Chinese scholar-bureaucrats who had aided Matteo.

It was a German, Johann Adam Schall von Bell (1592–1666), an academician of Roman Academy of Apostolic Sciences, who was the next most influential missionary in China after Matteo Ricci. Having accurately forecasted a solar eclipse, he was appointed as an astronomic official to the Chinese court. He and a fellow scientist, the Belgian Ferdinand Verbiest (1623–1688), made great efforts to promote the western calendar in China. Although stoutly opposed by some Chinese scholar-bureaucrats, they obtained support from Emperor Kangxi of the Qing Dynasty (1616–1911). According to statistics, by 1701 there were 130 Catholic missionaries and nearly 300,000 Catholic disciples in China.

Later, however, there occurred what became known as the "Argument on Rites". This concerned the questions of whether Catholicism should become part of Chinese culture, how to translate the concept of "Creator", and whether Chinese Catholics could still participate in such traditional ritual activities as offering sacrifice to ancestors and Confucius. The missionaries representing Matteo Ricci thought that "Heaven" in the Confucian classics had a meaning equal to that of "the Lord" in Catholicism; furthermore, that the activities of offering sacrifice to ancestors and Confucius by the traditional Chinese were only a kind of worship and were not contrary to the tenets of Catholicism. The opposition held an opinion exactly to the contrary. Both sides put forward vehement arguments, and at last the Vatican ordered that Chinese Catholics were henceforth banned from offering sacrifice to ancestors and Confucius. Not to be outdone, and in a classic case of tit for tat, Chinese Emperor Kangxi immediately imposed a ban on Christian preaching. This argument developed from within China to outside and from east to west, lasting for more than a hundred years, until at last Catholicism was banished once again from China. But the Argument on Rites achieved a rather unforeseen result: it aroused Europeans' enthusiasm for Chinese culture. Soon books on Chinese history, philosophy, geography, arts and customs were popular in Europe, and all of these branches of Chinese culture became topics of urgent debate among western scholars. Matteo Ricci himself had already introduced China's Confucianism, Buddhism and Taoism to a western audience in his book *A History of Christianity in China*, and had said, "The greatest philosopher in China is Confucius. He lived into his seventies and, throughout his life, was tireless in teaching through speech, action and writing. People respect him as the greatest sage the world has ever known. In fact, both by virtue of what he said and how he lived, he is never inferior to even the most

Portait of Johann Adam Schall von Bell (Before 1904).

revered of our ancient philosophers. Indeed, the majority of western philosophers cannot be compared with him."

Traditional Chinese thoughts and culture had their greatest influence on some of the countries in its neighboring regions, particularly the ancient Korean Peninsula and the many separate islands forming Japan. At the time of the Tang Dynasty (618–907) from the 7th to the 10th century, Chinese culture was particularly highly developed and during this period Japan sent thirteen separate envoys to review the culture and system of the Tang court. They also sent their brightest students to study at the Tang Imperial College. After returning to their homeland, these students were appointed by the Japanese court to various departments of education, medicine, criminal law and arts according to their studies. In the 6th century, Buddhism was introduced to Japan by China and soon became the largest and the most influential religion in that country. Japan also sent its own monks to study at the Tang court, where they learned Buddhist knowledge from China's acknowledged masters. In 753 an accomplished Tang Dynasty monk named Jianzhen was invited to Japan by Japanese monks and eventually completed the journey after 11 years of hardship and a perilous sea voyage. Jianzhen passed the last ten years of his life in Japan where, by dint of his great wisdom garnered over many long years of patient study, he made great contributions to their religion, architecture and medicine and became the symbol of friendship between China and Japan. In the middle of the Seventh Century Japan witnessed the famous "Taika Reform of 646 A.D." following the political and economic systems of the Sui (581–618) and Tang (618–907) dynasties, which led to an all-around reform of Japanese society, as a result of which Japan entered a whole new period of social, political and economic development.

No less important was the influence of traditional Chinese thoughts and culture on ancient Korea. In the Sui (581–618) and Tang (618–907) dynasties from the end of the 6th century to the beginning of the 10th, the Silla regime on the Korean Peninsula also sent students to study abroad in China just as they

Preaching Buddhism in Japan, which is a picture album depicting how China's Tang Dynasty eminent monk Jianzhen crossed the ocean to preach Buddhism in Japan.

sent monks to study among the learned at the Tang court. Regarding its political system, Silla followed the system of three ministries and six departments adopted by the Sui and Tang Dynasties to establish its central administrative organ and followed the local system of those same Dynasties when establishing their system of prefectures and counties. Silla also based its educational system on Sui and Tang models, opened the subject of Chinese national study with the teaching of such Confucian classics as *Lunyu (Analects of Confucius), Spring and Autumn Annals* and *Xiao Jing (The Book on Filial Piety)*, and adopted the Chinese system of imperial examinations in order to determine which scholars were worthy to become government officials.

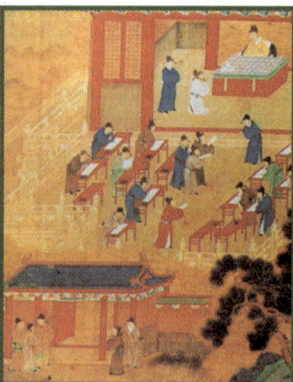

Developed Country of the Agricultural Civilization Era

China is written into the annals of history as a developed country in the era of agricultural civilizations. Both domestic and foreign historians are in consensus that ancient China represented the agricultural civilization, whose productivity and social development led the world for a fairly long time. For more than 2,000 years the Chinese ancestors worked hard and were creative, hence enriching and developing the civilization of human beings.

Progress in Agriculture and Development of the Handicraft Industry

In Sichuan Province in southwest China, a flood control and irrigation project designed and built in the Qin Dynasty (221 BC–206 BC) is still in service, which is the famous Dujiangyan Irrigation Project.

Ancient China took agriculture as the main economic model. The alluvial plains formed by major water systems such as the Yellow River, Yangtze River, Pearl River and Liaohe River provide favorable natural conditions for developing agriculture. All previous dynasties of China regarded agriculture as the

Fish Mouth Diversion Dyke, one of the three major scenic spots at the Dujiangyan Water Works.

foundation of the country and encouraged agricultural production with effective policy measures. For a rather long period of history, the agricultural technology level of China was at the forefront of the world.

As early as the Shang (1600 BC–1046 BC) and Zhou (1046 BC–256 BC) dynasties, Chinese people began to engage in farming. The main crops at that time included millet, barley, wheat, beans and rice. In the Spring and Autumn Period (770 BC–476 BC), ironware was adopted for farming tools. In addition, people began to plow using cattle and agricultural production gained further development. In the Qin (221 BC–206 BC) and Han (206 BC–220 AD) dynasties, with the improvement of tools and techniques of production, especially the adoption of irrigation systems and reclamation movement organized by the government enlarged the area suitable for farming. During the 70 years from the foundation of the Han Dynasty (206 BC–220 AD) to the enthronement of the Emperor Wudi of the Han Dynasty, because there were no severe wars and turbulences in the country and the weather was favorable without great natural disasters, people harvested adequate crops and barns in both rural and urban areas were full. Meanwhile, the finances of the State enjoyed a surplus. Some literature records that due to such good harvests of crops at that time, the accumulation of grains stored in the barns of the State was so great that they had to be stored outdoors, resulting in putrescence. However, people competed with each other for fortune. It was popular to raise horses, rich or poor. Groups of horses were commonly seen running in the lanes in the countryside. After the Eastern Han Dynasty (25–220), the agricultural economy in the Yangtze River areas began to develop quickly and in the vast southern areas of China rice was harvested twice a year and the level of agricultural production was further improved.

In the early Tang (618–907) Dynasty, the development of China's agricultural economy reached a new record high. With developed production and abundant grains, population increased and people became rich. The cultivated area spread from north to south China, with all the flat ground being utilized.

Estimated Population of China, Europe, Indian Subcontinent and Rest of the World in 50–1820 AD (Unit: million)				
Year	China	Europe	Indian Subcontinent	Rest of the World
50	40	34	70	250
960	55	40	–	300
1280	100	68	–	380
1500	103	72	110	425
1700	138	96	153	592
1820	381	167	209	1,049

Source: *China: Renaissance of a World Power* by Conrad Races (Germany), published by International Cultural Corporation in April 2007 (first edition).

In 732, China had a population of 45.43 million, doubling that of the early Tang Dynasty. In the Song Dynasty (960–1279), the country vigorously started using irrigation systems, making use of most rivers and lakes. The old channels were repaired and irrigated areas increased. Meanwhile, efforts were made to strengthen intensive cultivation, bringing about an increase in grain output. In the Kangxi and Qianlong Period of the Qing Dynasty (1616–1911), the policy of giving the people peace and security was put into practice, reducing the burden on peasants and encouraging agricultural production. As a result, the history of China saw a period with unprecedented development in agricultural production and rapid increase in population.

Ancient China set great store by agricultural production and summarizing the farming experience so as to popularize it and put it into application. Before the Qin Dynasty (221 BC–206 BC), articles on agriculture appeared, not only studying agricultural technology but also discussing agricultural policies. The important literature of the pre-Qin period, *Lu's Spring and Autumn Annals*, puts forth four thesis on agriculture. *The Book of Master Fan Shengzhi* was an important agricultural work of the Western Han (206 BC–25 AD), taking the central Shaanxi plain as experimental base. In the Eastern Han Dynasty (25–220), *Simin Yueling* recorded farm life in the present day Luoyang area of Henan Province. Another book *Qi Min Yao Shu* (*Essential Techniques for the Peasantry*) written by Jia Sixie in the Northern Wei Dynasty (386–534) is a key agricultural literature of ancient China, introducing agricultural production technology in the middle and lower reaches of the Yellow River. Statistics show that there are more than 300 literatures studying agriculture in the history of ancient China, which, in one aspect, reflects the advanced development of the agricultural civilization.

The handicraft industry was an important supplement to the agricultural economy, which gave impetus to the development of agricultural production and, at the same time, enriched the style and content of the agricultural civilization. In the period of the origin of Chinese civilization, the level of ceramic art, weaving and manufacture of jade articles was fairly high. In the Shang (1600 BC–1046 BC) and Zhou (1046 BC–256 BC) dynasties, the handicraft industry became mature, and was called as "all sorts of crafts". The jade articles and bronze

Tri-colored glazed pottery of the Tang Dynasty shown at the Nanjing Museum.

White glazed wine pot and heater.

vessels were of a high level. In the Spring and Autumn Period (770 BC–476 BC) and Warring States Period (475 BC–221 BC), the ironware foundry became a key handicraft sector, with various kinds of ironware being used in war, social production and life. The Han Dynasty (206 BC–220 AD) saw iron making and casting, steel making, textiles, lacquer manufacturing and paper making upgraded. In the Sui (581–618) and Tang (618–907) dynasties the castings industry developed quickly, the level of metalwork was greatly improved and the technology of manufacturing porcelain became more mature. The porcelain produced in the Tang Dynasty (618–907) featured pure and exact color. In the Song Dynasty (960–1279), the handicraft industry was enlarged in scale, with further compartmentalizing of division of labor. Meanwhile, technology and quality grew at an unprecedented rate. The famous Jingdezhen Kilns entered the golden period. The Ming Dynasty (1368–1644) witnessed fast progress in cotton weaving and metal smelting. The largest iron furnace had a capacity of more than 1,000 kg of ores, with a daily output of 500–plus kg. In the Qing Dynasty

Per-capita Income of China, Europe, World in 50 to 1820 (1990 international market rate: US$)				
Year	China	Europe	Indian Subcontinent	Rest of the World
50	40	34	70	250
960	55	40	–	300
1280	100	68	–	380
1500	103	72	110	425
1700	138	96	153	592
1820	381	167	209	1,049

Source: China: *Renaissance of a World Power* by Conrad Races (Germany), published by International Cultural Corporation in April 2007 (first edition).

(1616–1911), the scale of the handicraft industry was constantly enlarged, with even more distinct division of labor. Jingdezhen Imperial Kilns had an annual output of more than 100,000 articles.

The handicraft industry of the ancient China was mainly managed by governments. After the Song Dynasty (960–1279), especially in the Ming Dynasty (1368–1644), the private handicraft industry gradually developed. From the mid Ming Dynasty (1368–1644), due to blooming consumer demand, the private textile industry greatly exceeded the one controlled by the government. In addition, wage labour and handicraft shops came into being.

Top-Ranking Technologies

China "maintained a scientific knowledge level too far ahead for the western world to catch up with from the third century to the 13th century" is a comment of Dr. Joseph Needham, a famous expert on the history of Chinese science and technology, on ancient China in this regard. Ancient China's science and technology ranked at the forefront of the world for a long time, not only contributing the "four great inventions" for the human beings, but also leading the world in the fields of astronomy, aerography, medicine, agriculture, botany, zoology, irrigation, transportation, construction, garden design, metal smelting, watercraft manufacture, ceramic making, textiles and printing and dyeing.

The "four great inventions" of ancient China refer to paper making, printing, gunpowder and the compass, which changed the course of human civilization.

The adoption of paper as writing materials is undoubtedly revolutionary. The paper making technique was invented in the Han Dynasty (206 BC–220 AD), before which, people wrote on tortoise shells, bamboo and thin silk. However, those materials are heavy, expensive and hard to use. In the Eastern Han Dynasty (25–220), a eunuch named Cai Lun summarized experiences of predecessors and improved the paper making technique. Finally,

Portrait of Cai Lun of the Eastern Han Dynasty (206 BC–220 AD).

128

he invented the plant-fiber paper making technique, which greatly increased the output of paper. Through a long period of development, especially in the Song Dynasty (960–1279), paper making techniques grew more mature, widely adopting bamboo paper and grass paper. Furthermore, there appeared *Zhi Pu*, a book specially summing up paper making techniques. China's paper making techniques were first introduced to neighboring countries such as Vietnam, Korea and Japan in the 3rd to 4th centuries and then to the Central Asian areas around the eighth century and to North Africa and Europe in the period from the 11th century to 13th century.

The invention of paper facilitates writing; and that of printing provides access to knowledge for people, which is also revolutionary and promotes social development. In the early sixth century, several centuries after the invention of paper making techniques, China invented block carving printing, which carved characters on a wood block and then added ink to it to print. The Five Dynasties (907–960) saw the appearance of copper plate printing, and the printing of a large

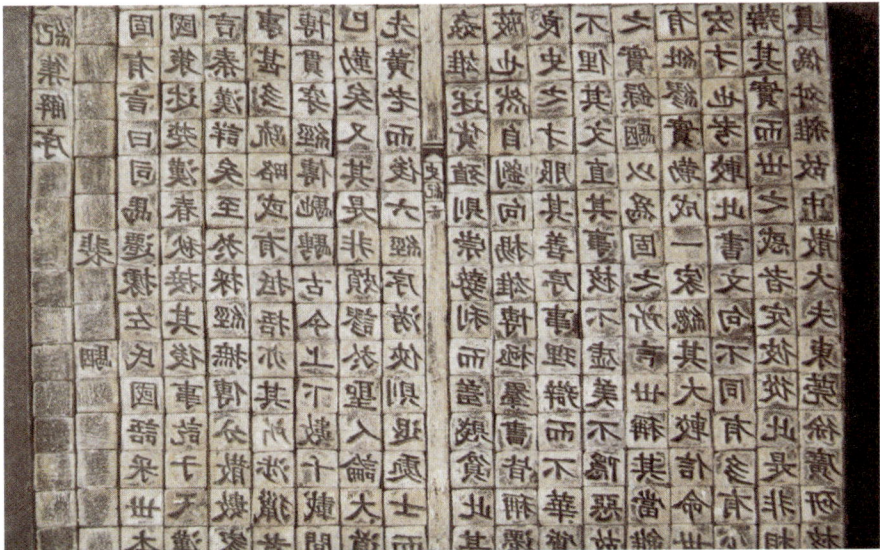

Bi Sheng mud Letter Press Plate (Model).

number of sutra books, historical records, medical books and Buddhist and Taoist books. In addition, chromatic printing was invented. However, moveable-type printing is no doubt a major revolution in printing history. In the Northern Song Dynasty (960–1127), a civilian called Bi Sheng invented the mud movable type technique. Therefore, people no longer used the whole block. In the Yuan (1206–1368) and Ming (1368–1644) dynasties, wood and metals such as tin, copper and lead movable types were invented. The printing technique was introduced to foreign countries from the Tang Dynasty (618–907), first to Japan, Korea and then to the states of East Asia, South Asia and West Asia and to North Africa and Europe via Persia. In 1456, Gutenberg of Germany printed the *Bible* in movable type. After it was introduced to Europe, it played an important role in promoting the Revival of Learning and religious reformation of Europe.

The ancient world suffered frequent wars. Hence, the adoption of gunpowder in wars was a major upgrade in the means of warfare, with far-reaching ramifications. The invention of gunpowder is related to the alchemy of China's Taoism. Alchemy is to abstract various medicinal and mineral substances so as to make a drug good for healthcare, with a purpose to make people live forever and never grow old. The Taoists gradually learned the chemical properties of sulfur and saltpeter, which are the materials of gunpowder. Gunpowder was invented in the Wei (220–266), Jin (265–420) and Southern and Northern (420–589) Dynasties and adopted in the military field in the Tang Dynasty (618–907). In the Northern Song Dynasty (960–1127), gunpowder was produced on a large scale and firearms such as bows with exploding arrows, crossbows with exploding arrows, jet exploding arrow and pipe-typed exploding arrow appeared. The technique of making gunpowder was introduced to Arabian states via India. European people learned to make gunpowder and firearms during their wars with Arabian people.

The invention of the compass informed people as to directions. As early as the Warring States Period, Chinese people discovered the polarity pointing

Compass of the Han Dynasty (202 BC–220 AD).

property of magnets and invented the magnetic directional instrument called "Sinan". In the Song Dynasty (960–1279), people discovered the method of artificial magnetization and further developed the compass and made it a tool for navigation. Hence, the celestial navigation method of "watching stars at night and watching the sun in the daytime" was gradually eliminated. Extensive adoption of the compass in navigation opened an epoch in this regard. Thanks to the mature technique of the compass, in the early Ming Dynasty (1368–1644), Zheng He made seven ocean voyages to the west, a feat in the history of navigation. Around the 12th and 13th centuries, the compass was introduced to the Arabian states and then to Europe. It played an important role in the opening-up of European navigation and the discovery of the new continent.

In many aspects of the astronomy such as astronomical observation, calendrical calculation and astrological instruments, ancient China also made world-recognized achievements. The earliest *Spring and Autumn Annals* of China records 37 solar eclipses, 33 of which were correct, and a lot of records in astronomical phenomenon such as eclipses of the moon, star showers, Halley's Comet, macula and polar lights. Ancient China attached great importance to the formulation of a calendar. As early as the pre-Qin period, China confirmed the year of to have 365.25 days, which was the most exact calendar in the world at that time. Most dynasties subsequent had their own calendar, of which, the most

famous one was the Shoushi Calendar, compiled by Guo Shoujing, an astronomer of the Yuan Dynasty (1206–1368), fixing the length of the year at 365.2425 days, exactly the same as the present-day calendar. There were numerous sorts of astrological instruments in ancient China. In the Han Dynasty (206 BC–220 AD), a scientist named Zhang Heng invented an armillary sphere, which adopts water drops from clepsydra to drive the gear equipment inside so as to make it rotate once at a uniform rate every day. The appearance of the stars is completely in accordance with the star images of observatories.

Ancient China is the earliest state which established a mathematics system. In the Eastern Han Dynasty (25–220), thanks to compilation, preparation and supplement by numerous people, *The Nine Chapters on the Mathematical Art* which collected all the achievements on mathematics since the Qin Dynasty (221 BC–206 BC) came out, setting up the mathematics system of ancient China. It mainly served the daily life, involving arithmetic, algebra and geometry and so on. Its concept and calculation of fractions, calculation of proportion, introduction of negative, algorithm for plus and negative and solution of setting up a linear equation group were all 800-odd years earlier than those of India and 1,000-odd years earlier than those of Europe. In the Southern and Northern Dynasties (420–589), mathematician Zu Chongzi calculated a pi, exact with seven significant figures, which was 1,000-plus years earlier than the world computing method.

Before the appearance of Western medicines in modern times, the development of Chinese medicines was at the forefront of the world, with a system of traditional Chinese medicines coming into being. *The Medical Classic of the Yellow Emperor*, or *Huang Di Nei Jing*, began to discuss Chinese medicine theories systematically. This is the earliest existing book of its kind, guiding the clinical practice of herbalist doctors for thousands of years. In the late Eastern Han Dynasty (25–220), a medical scientist called Zhang Zhongjing completed the *Treatise on Febrile Diseases Caused by Cold and Miscellaneous Diseases*,

Armillary sphere in front of the Shanghai Science and Technology Museum.

laying the foundation of therapeutics of Chinese medicines. Another medical scientist named Li Shizhen spent his whole life writing the *Compendium of Chinese Materia Medica*, systematically summing up the theories of traditional Chinese medicines before the 16th century.

Theories of the traditional Chinese medicines base on "Qi", which is divided into Yin and Yang. It was believed that the relative balance of Yin and Yang served as the basis to maintain the normal activities of the human body. If such a balance was disturbed, diseases occurred, thus affecting people's health. Another thought of the theories is the theory of the five elements. It tries to generalize the attribute of various things in the objective world by using the five philosophical categories namely wood, fire, earth, metal and water, and explains the interrelationships and transformation rule by using the dynamic mode of the promoting and restriction relation in the five elements. The promoting relation is wood promoting fire, fire promoting earth, earth promoting metal, metal promoting water and water promoting wood; the restriction relation is wood

restricting earth, fire restricting metal, earth restricting water, metal restricting wood and water restricting fire. Hence, only grasping the interrelationships of the whole could the doctor know the pathogeny and pathology and then make a prescription to cure diseases.

Sound Political, Legal and Official Selecting System

China had a set of complete political, legal and official-selecting systems in conformity with an economic system with agriculture as the main part. Different from those of western countries, these systems have ancient Oriental characteristics.

Political System

Beginning from the Qin (221 BC–206 BC) and Han (206 BC–220 AD) dynasties, the centralized system and the autocratic monarchy system were established, consolidated and developed.

Throne for emperor in the Palace of Heavenly Purity of the Palace Museum in Beijing.

135

The Qin and Han dynasties established the Yamens in the central government, namely the Three Excellencies and Nine Ministers to implement policies and administer affairs. Three Excellencies refers to the Prime Minister (Chengxiang), the Great Commander (Taiwei), and the Censor-in-chief (Yushi Dafu). Nine Ministers are the Keeper of the Rites (Fengchang), Chief of Retainers (Langzhongling), Keeper of the Imperial Chariot (Taipu), Chief of Honor Guards (Weiwei), Grand Diplomat (Dianke), Chief of Justice (Tingwei), Grand Agriculturalist (Zhisu Neishi), Censor of the Imperial Bloodline (Zongzheng), and Keeper of the Imperial Wealth (Shaofu). The system of Three Excellencies and Nine Ministers made the division of power among organs systemically and enforced the imperial power, and this system was used by following dynasties. The whole country was divided into two tiers, namely the commanderies (Jun) and counties (Xian), and later changed to three tiers, i.e. prefectures (Zhou), the commanderies (Jun) and counties (Xian).

China's autocratic monarchy which began in the Qin Dynasty is the core of China's ancient political system. The emperor was regarded as the Son of Heaven, with special status and unbounded power. The emperor differed from the common people even in his title. Beginning from the Han Dynasty, each emperor had his special temple name, posthumous title and reign title. In general, the temple name of the founding emperor of a dynasty was called Zu (ancestor), such as Emperor Gaozu of the Han, and Emperor Gaozu of the Tang. The Chinese character which most expresses the achievements of an emperor was used as his posthumous title, such as Wen, Wu, Yuan, and Jing. A phrase with a special meaning was used to outline the title of an emperor's reign, such as Jianyuan, Zhenguan, Tianbao, Kangxi, and Qianlong.

In order to ensure the smooth inheritance of the imperial throne, the crown prince system was established during the Han Dynasty. The crown prince may be the son of the emperor or the younger brother of the emperor. If the emperor could not handle the state affairs by virtue of his youth, his mother would do so for him. This is the system of the empress holding court. This system caused an unforeseen problem in that the empress and her trusted followers contended for imperial power with the emperor and his trusted followers. The empress's trusted followers who have consanguinity with the empress are called the waiqi (relatives of a king or an emperor on the side of his mother or wife). The emperor's trusted followers who were castrated and lived in the imperial house were called eunuchs. In Chinese history, incidents in which the waiqi or eunuchs seized power often took place, and competition between crown princes also happened.

China's autocratic monarchy was perfected in the Sui (581–618) and Tang (618–907) dynasties. The prime minister system also was improved in those dynasties. In ancient China, the prime minister was the highest-ranking chief executive who assisted the emperor in handling government affairs and led other officials of all ranks and descriptions. The position of the prime minister was thought to be "below one person, above 10,000 people" among the common people. The prime minister differed in the way to address in different dynasties. When the prime minister assisted a ruler in governing the country, there was sometimes a contradiction between him and the emperor in power. The Sui and Tang dynasties reformed this system. They let the officials discuss official business collectively, thus weakening the power of the prime minister. This also eliminated the contradiction between imperial power and the power of the prime minister and forced the latter to submit to the former. The central organs serving the emperor were also improved, namely the "three departments and six ministries". Three departments refers to the Department of State Affairs (Shangshusheng), the Imperial Secretariat (Zhongshusheng) and the Imperial Chancellery (Menxiasheng). The Department of State Affairs was the highest administrative organ with its Six Ministries (Liubu) for Personnel (Libu), Population (Hubu), Rites (Libu), War (Bingbu), Justice (Xingbu) and Works (Gongbu). The Imperial Secretariat was the highest decision-making organ and the Imperial Chancellery was the highest deliberative organ.

China's Sui Dynasty (581−618) established "Three Departments and Six Ministries"

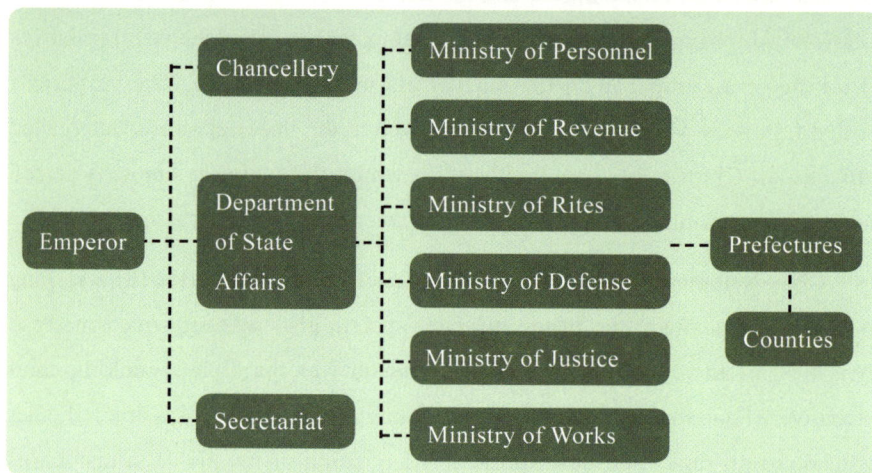

Emperor — Chancellery; Department of State Affairs; Secretariat

Ministry of Personnel, Ministry of Revenue, Ministry of Rites, Ministry of Defense, Ministry of Justice, Ministry of Works

Prefectures — Counties

During the Ming (1368–1644) and Qing (1616–1911) dynasties, the autocratic monarchy was further strengthened and redeveloped. In order to prevent powerful and imperious officials from seizing power, Emperor Taizu of the Ming Dynasty abolished the position of prime minister and directly controlled the six ministries of government affairs, thus intensifying imperial power. The Ming Court also set up the Eastern Depot (a secret police organization), Western Depot, Jinyiwei imperial guards and other secret agent organs run by the eunuchs to protect imperial power and to strengthen supervision over officials of all ranks and descriptions, thus taking the autocratic system to the extreme. The Ming and Qing dynasties followed the provincial administration systems of the Yuan Dynasty. The Ming Court divided the whole country into 13 provinces and two Zhili (meaning "directly ruled by the Imperial Court"), namely south Zhili and north Zhili. The Qing Court divided the whole country into 18 provinces and directly ruled five regions, i.e., northeast China, Inner Mongolia, Outer Mongolia, and Tibet. In the late Qing Dynasty, the Court also set up Xinjiang Province,

Taiwan Province, Northeastern China's Fengtian Province, Jilin Province and Heilongjiang Province.

Legal System

The purpose of the ancient Chinese legal system was to guarantee the imperial power. Its basic frame was the combination of courtesy and punishment, with no division between justice and administration.

The Qin Dynasty put rule by law at a premium. It formulated the *Law of the Qin Dynasty*, which in content covers 29 aspects, such as politics, military affairs, agriculture, market administration, currency flows, traffic, administrative management, case trying and judicial proceedings, etc. The Qin Dynasty adhered to severe punishment for people committing misdemeanors as well as serious crimes. There were a dozen kinds of death penalty. The strict laws did not help the Qin Dynasty last long, but triggered the dissatisfaction of the people, thus accelerating the subversion of the Qin Dynasty. At the beginning, the Han Dynasty drew the lessons from the downfall of the Qin Dyansty due to cruel and complicated laws and made lenient and simple laws. It formulated the *Nine Basic Laws* of the Han. After the rule by the Han Dynasty became stable, the articles of law became increasingly complicated and numerous. The law of the Han Dynasty was grouped into four varieties, which refers to the legal articles, imperial decree, application of law, and case analogy. The law of the Han Dynasty puts more emphases upon imperial power, takes Confucian classics as the basis for legal principle, adheres to the principle of combination of courtesy and law, turning courtesy into law, primary virtue & accessory punishment, and virtue being prior to punishment, thus laying solid foundation for the later legal system of "combination of courtesy and punishment".

The building of the legal system witnessed new developments during the Sui and Tang dynasties. The Sui Court formulated the *Kaihuang Codex*, while the Tang Court, on the basis of it, enacted the *Law of Wude*, the *Law of Zhenguan*,

the *Code of Yonghui* and compiled the Interpretation of the *Laws of the Tang Dynasty* and China's first administrative corpus juris - the *Six Corpus Juris of the Tang Dynasty*, all of which together formed a perfect legal system. The law of the Tang Dynasty followed the principle of "turning courtesy into the law", and definitely stipulated, "Virtue and courtesy are the root of ruling a country while punishment is the way of ruling a country". The punishment was divided into five categories. In the aspect of law enforcement, the death penalty review procedure in particular was improved. Legal supervision was enforced and the system of "three interdependent judicial departments", i.e. first trial, review, and supervision was implemented.

The legal systems of the Ming and Qing Dynasties are similar systems. The Ming Court formulated the *Collected Statutes of the Ming Dynasty*, while the Qing Court worked out the *Criminal Laws of the Qing Dynasty*. The two dynasties both made up for the insufficiency of the law by enacting regulations. By the late Qing Dynasty, about 2,000 regulations had been added to the *Criminal Laws of the Qing Dynasty*. In the Qing Dynasty, juridical practice was carried out in light of regulations prior to the laws. The Ming and Qing dynasties were different in governing the country. The Ming Dynasty was strict while the Qing Dynasty lenient.

18 Decrees of the Qing of the Qin Dynasty.(221 BC–207 BC).

Official-Selecting System

The perfect official-selecting system which met the requirement of the autocratic monarchy system

140

was set up in ancient China. It experienced many stages of development, such as recommendation, family background and examination.

The Han Dynasty formed a complete official-selecting system. This system was composed of the methods adopted by local and central court to promote officials. These include the method for the emperor to directly appoint the special talent to an official position, for the prefect to directly appoint his subordinate to a position, for the children of high-ranking officials to enjoy special consideration in promotion, and for the officeholders to have restricted amount of assets.

The Nine Rank System became the only official-selecting system in the period From the Wei and Jin dynasties to the early Sui Dynasty. Under this system, the Court set up the post of the Talent Rater (zhongzheng) in various prefectures and counties, who was responsible for judging the talents. The Talent Rater (zhongzheng) classified the talents into upper-upper, upper middle, upper-lower, middle-upper, middle-middle, middle-lower, lower-upper, lower-middle, and lower-lower ranks, in light of the judging standard and his perception of the talents, in order for their future selection. With the right to judge but no right to appoint, the Talent Rater (zhongzheng) needed to submit his opinion to the government agency, and this was regarded as the basis for the government agency choosing someone for a job. Although having the right to appoint, the government agency had to do so in accordance with the judgment by the Talent Rater (zhongzheng) and could not make bold decisions. This formed the separation between the Talent Rater (zhongzheng) and government agency. Apparently this system was reasonable, but it met the needs of the politics of powerful families. In fact, the position of the Talent Rater (zhongzheng) was mostly controlled by the families of officials for generations.

Ke Ju, or Imperial examination system, was instituted to select officials in ancient China. This system began in the Sui Dynasty, developed in the Tang Dynasty, was standardized in the Song Dynasty, and was improved in the Ming and Qing dynasties. The Sui Dynasty abolished the old method of selecting

talented people, and gradually set up the system of examination in three subjects, i.e., Xiucai, Mingjing, and Jinshi. The Tang Dynasty developed the imperial examinations set up by the Sui Dynasty, especially the ones in Jinshi and Mingjing subjects. The examination was held annually with dozens of talents being selected each time. The examination covered knowledge and theory on Confucian classics, political comment and literary talent and grace. The Song Dynasty made adjustment to the imperial examination system and set forth strict provisions regarding the examination procedure and methods, so that the imperial examination tended toward standardization. More than 50,000 scholars were recruited. The imperial examinations in the Ming and Qing dynasties were more standardized and complete. Compared with the Song and Yuan dynasties, the new imperial examinations adopted the eight-part essay to choose scholars as officials. The eight-part essay is a type of writing, which assigns a topic focusing on the Four Books (*The Great Learning, The Doctrine of the Mean, The Confucian Analects*, and *The Works of Mencius*) and the Five Classics (*The Book of Songs, The Book of History, The Book of Rites, The Book of Changes and Spring and Autumn Annals*) annotated by the Confucians of the Song Dynasty. The candidates needed to model after the manner of speaking and expound their ideas for the sage in a special style in writing. An imperial examination was held every three years during the Ming and Qing Dynasties, which was divided into three levels, namely, the imperial exam at the provincial level, the metropolitan examination, and final imperial examination. The

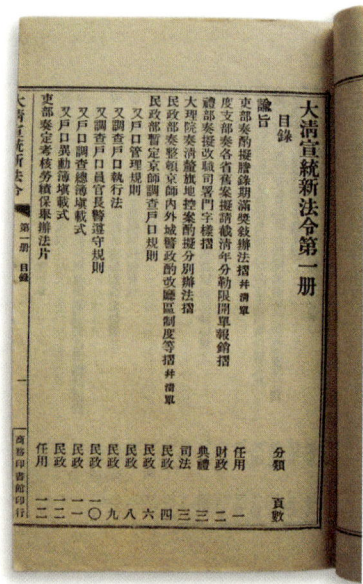

Law of the Qing Dynasty (1644–1911).

Chart of Imperial Examinations created during the Song Dynasty (960–1279).

successful candidates in the imperial examinations at the provincial level were called Juren. The successful candidates in metropolitan exams were called Huiyuan. The successful candidates in the highest imperial examinations were called Jinshi, and were divided into Sanjia (three ranks). The first rank includes three persons, i.e. zhuangyuan (title conferred on the one who came first in the highest imperial examination), bangyan (second place in the palace examination), and tanhua (number three in the palace examination), on whom the title jinshi would be conferred. There were no restrictions on the origin of the candidate in the imperial examination. One could be "a common farmer in the morning and ascending in the emperor's hall in the evening." In feudal Chinese society, imperial examinations were almost the only opportunities for intellectuals from all walks of life to realize their political ambitions.

The political, legal and official-selecting systems set up in Chinese ancient times are the outcome of an agricultural civilization. Historically, these systems helped the court stabilize the ruling order, admit outstanding persons, enhance the quality of officials, and still be in conformity with the imperial autocracy.

Language and Characters

China is one of the countries in which language and written characters appeared earliest forming the Chinese language and alphabet.

In the Spring and Autumn Period before the Qin Dynasty, the common Chinese language appeared. Since the 12th century, the Beijing dialect has become the representative of northern dialects. The modern standard language used by the Han people is called Putonghua (Mandarin) in Hong Kong and Macao, the Chinese national language in Taiwan and Chinese among the overseas Chinese. It takes the pronunciation of the Beijing dialect as standard pronunciation, the northern dialect as the basic dialect, and the model works in modern vernacular Chinese as grammar standards. Chinese language underwent three development stages, namely Chinese ancient language, modern Chinese

Chinese characters dictation test in a primary school.

and contemporary Chinese language. Chinese ancient language is the wording used in ancient times with the written language being the classical style of writing. Contemporary Chinese language is the one formed in the past 100 years, including the spoken and written language. Compared with the Chinese ancient language, contemporary Chinese language is easier to understand and use. Chinese language, belonging to the Han-Tibetan family, is the language with the most native speakers in the world. It is one of the official languages in Singapore. It is also one of the official and working languages of the United Nations.

The Chinese language has its own features. As far as the syllable structure, the Chinese syllable structure is regular. A Chinese syllable is composed of the initial consonant, and simple or compound vowel. For example:

Syllable	Initial consonant	Vowel
dong	d	ong
xi	x	i
nan	n	an
bei	b	ei

The same Chinese syllables are differentiated from each other by the tones. In Chinese Mandarin, the syllables of the four characters " 酣 (han), 韩 (han), 喊 (han), 汗 (han)" are the same, but different in tones, so each expresses a different meaning. In Chinese, there are some homonyms. Although they are of the same pronunciation, they have different shape and meaning and usage of expression. Cases in point include: " 红 "(red), " 宏 "(macro) and " 虹 "(rainbow). They all pronounce "hong", but they are obviously different words.

The Chinese word is composed of the morpheme, which is the smallest linguistic unit that has semantic meaning. For example, the word " 国 (nation)" is composed of a morpheme, the word " 宇宙 (universe) " two morphemes, and the word " 人民币 (RMB)" three morphemes, while the word " 窈窕 (gentle and

graceful)" consisting of two Chinese characters is a morpheme and word, and the word " 巧克力 (chocolate)", composed of three Chinese characters, is also a morpheme.

Quite different from many western languages such as the English language, the Chinese language does not pay attention to the morphological change of a sentence, but instead the word order, namely the order of the words in a sentence. It shows the grammatical relation and expresses different meaning through changing word order. For example, the sentence " 我要学 (I want to learn)" differs from the one " 要我学 (want me to learn)".

Just as from Chinese ancient language to contemporary Chinese language, Chinese language is constantly developing. As a whole, its development trend is simplification. Words and phrases of the Chinese language obviously develop from more monosyllabic words to more polysyllabic words and disyllabic words are in the majority. For example, 曾 - 曾经 (ever), 可 - 可以 (OK), 但 - 但是 (but), 宾 - 宾客 (guest), 目 - 眼睛 (eye), and 日 - 太阳 (the sun).

Any foreigner who has been to China will find that in North, South, East or West China, Chinese people always communicate in different accents. These spoken languages are different from each other in sound, words and phrases and expression. They are called the Chinese dialects. Due to historical and geographical reasons, they can be roughly classified into one of the seven large groups, i.e., Northern dialects (Putonghua, Mandarin), Wu dialect (Jiangzhe dialect), Gan dialect (Jiangxi dialect), Xiang dialect (Hunan dialect), Kejia dialect (Hakka), Min dialect (Fujian dialect), and Yue dialect (Cantonese). The speakers of the northern dialect live in most areas of China to the north of the Yangtze River. The speakers of the Wu dialect are generally distributed in southern Jiangsu Province and Zhejiang Province. The speakers of the Gan dialect live in most areas of Jiangxi Province and parts of Hubei Province. The speakers of the Xiang dialect are distributed in Hunan Province. The speakers of the Kejia dialect are scattered in Guangdong, Guangxi, Fujian, Jiangxi and Sichuan provinces. The speakers of the Min dialect are found in Fujian, Taiwan and Hainan provinces and parts of Guangdong Province. The speakers of the Yue dialect live in most areas of Guangdong Province and part of Guangxi Zhuang Autonomous Region.

Chinese characters have more than 3,000 years of history, which makes it one of the oldest writing systems still in use in the world.

The most sophisticated and earliest Chinese characters are Jiaguwen, inscriptions on bones or tortoise shells of the Shang Dynasty (16th–11th century BC). To date, China has unearthed more than 100,000 pieces of animal bone and tortoise shell, including over 3,500 distinctive Chinese characters, among which one third have been identified. Jiaguwen is a kind of Chinese characters that resemble drawings very much. Another kind of Chinese characters which appeared after the Jiaguwen is the Jinwen, inscriptions on ancient bronze objects. After the Emperor Qinshihuang unified China, he also unified Chinese language and introduced xiaozhuan (lesser seal script). Since the xiaozhuan script was very time consuming, people of the Qin further improved the characters and created a new style, lishu (official script). During the stages of xiaozhuan and lishu, the character font and structure underwent great changes with little hieroglyph color. Kaishu came into being in the Eastern Jin Dynasty and was based on Lishu. After Kaishu appeared, the block-shaped Chinese characters were finalized and Kaishu has been used ever since. Kaishu is the standard calligraphy that has been used for the longest period of time.

Evolution of Chinese Characters			
Inscriptions on bones or tortoise shells of the Shang Dynasty			
Inscriptions on ancient bronze objects			
Small seal style			
Official script			
Regular script			

Chinese characters differ from English words. The basic units of English are letters, which have tone but no meaning. However, those of Chinese are separate characters, with both tone and meaning. Hence, the Chinese character is an ideogram. English has only 26 letters, and the words are comprised of various combinations of the letters, while Chinese characters are comprised of strokes, some having scores of strokes.

Though the structure of a Chinese character is complicated and difficult to grasp, there are mainly four types. The first one is a hieroglyph, made by depicting the shape of the object. For example, the Chinese character "yu (referring to fish)" is in the shape of a fish and "shui (referring to water)" is in the shape of water. The second is a self-explanatory character, made by adding abstract symbols to the hieroglyph. For example, the Chinese character "mu (referring to mother)" is made by adding two points to the character "nu (referring to woman)", which indicates the character of a nursing woman. Another Chinese character "zu (soldier)" is made by adding a left-falling stroke to the character "yi (clothes)", meaning that soldiers wear clothes with symbols. The third is an associative compound, made by combining several ideographs. For example, the Chinese character "yi (spill)" looks like water spilling from a vessel. Another character "jian (reflect)" looks like one is looking into a vessel of water, with a meaning of looking into a mirror. The fourth is a pictophonetic character, with one element indicating meaning and the other sound, such as the Chinese characters "ling", referring to bell, and "jiang", referring to river.

The number of Chinese characters is one of the largest in the world. It is hard to accurately count the number of Chinese characters, which is estimated to add up to over 60,000. However, only 3,500 of them are commonly used and only 2,500 are the most common ones. This figure is generally equal to the number of common English words. In this regard, it is not an extremely difficult thing to learn Chinese.

Incomparable Achievements in Literature

Ancient Chinese literature is of long standing and boasts brilliant achievements. With its unique style it has enriched the civilization of human beings. Ancient Chinese people committed themselves to creating literature, resulting in various styles of literary works, including ci (lyric poetry), qu (a type of verse for singing), fu (prose-poetry), prose, rhythmical prose characterized by parallelism and complexity, fiction and drama. Numerous excellent works were produced.

The Book of Songs and *The Songs of Chu*

Poem is an important style of ancient Chinese literature, and possesses a prominent place among the ancient literary works. The oldest extant literature is *The Book of Songs*, the first collection of poems in the history of Chinese

The Painting drawn by Ma Hezhi of Song Dynasty (960–1279) according to The *Book of Songs.*

literature. It includes 305 poems collected over a span of 500 years, from the early years of Western Zhou (1046 BC–771 BC) to the middle of the Spring and Autumn Period (770 BC–476 BC). The works were originally sung with music, but the music book was lost, and only the lyrics remain. There are three sections, namely Feng, Ya, and Song. Feng contains local ballads; the contents of Ya include praying for a good harvest and nobles praising the monumental contribution of the forefathers; Song is comprised of songs of sacrifice. The book mainly consists of four-character poems, with rich contents and diverse artistic approaches. Many poems especially those in the section of Feng provide true and vivid depictions on people's lifestyles such as working, every-day life, wars and feasts. There is a passage describing a soldier who was on expedition for a long time, which tells about army life, the grief of leaving home when returning home. It reads like this: "When I left here, willows shed tears. Now I come back on a snowy track. Long, long is the way, hard, hard the day. My grief overflows, who knows? Who knows?" Moreover, there are a large number of poems with the theme of love and marriage. One which depicts a young man missing his sweetheart reads like this: "By riverside are cooing a pair of turtledoves. A good young man is wooing a maiden fair he loves. Water flows left and right of cresses here and there. The youth yearns day and night for the good maiden fair. His yearning grows so strong, he cannot fall asleep. He tosses all night long, so deep in love, so deep!" The realistic writing and awareness of unexpected development expressed in *The Book of Songs* exerted great influence on the creation of subsequent literature.

Another style of poetry originated in the State of Chu in south China in the late Warring States Period (475 BC–221 BC), namely Qu Yuan, a great ancient patriot and poet, is a representative writer of the literature of this style. His magnum opus, *The Sorrow of Separation*, which is the longest lyric among the Chinese classical literatures, depicts his grief and wrath because there was no way to save the nation and realize his ideal during the period when he was exiled. *The Sorrow of Separation* adopted the artistic approach of romanticism, such as,

"In the morning I drank dew drops on the lily magnolia, and in the evening I ate fallen flowers of the autumn chrysanthemums... I used waternut leaves to make my coat, and used lotus flowers to make my skirt." Those became the direct source of the romanticism of Chinese literatures. Some enterprising verses are still recited by people today that "The road ahead is long and long, I will seek truth in the heaven and on the earth."

Poems of the Tang Dynasty (618–907)

After experiencing fu (prose-poetry) of the Han Dynasty (206 BC–220 AD) and rhythmical prose characterized by parallelism and complexity prevailing in the Jin Dynasty (265–420) and the Southern and Northern Dynasties (420–589), Chinese literature saw the Tang (618–907) become the dynasty of poems. During those 300 years, poets came forth in great number, creating a vast quantity of poems. The *Complete Poetry of the Tang* compiled in the Qing Dynasty (1616–1911) contains more than 48,900 poems by more than 2,300 poets. The authors were of different statuses, including emperors, nobles, officials and men of letters as well as monks, nuns and geishas. It is obvious that poetry became a common literary style in the Tang Dynasty (618–907).

The poems of the Tang Dynasty (618–907) feature the maturity of "modern style" poetry, which is categorized into lushi (poem of eight lines), long lushi and jueju (poem of four lines). The eight-line poem with five characters to a line and a strict tonal pattern and rhyme scheme and eight-line poem with seven characters to a line and a strict tonal pattern and rhyme scheme are two common types among lushi, the former totaling 40 Chinese characters and the latter 56. The lushi which have more than eight lines are called as long lushi. The jueju only have half the number of characters as lushi, the one with five characters to a line totaling 20 characters and the one with seven characters to a line totaling 28.

Yellow Crane Tower in Wuhan, Hubei Province.

Lushi stresses rhyme. The first, third, fifth and seventh lines do not rhyme, but the second, fourth, sixth and eight lines do rhyme. Moreover, lushi also attaches great importance to antithesis, matching both sound and sense in two poetic lines. For example, "heaven matches to earth, cloud to wind and land to sky". The middle couplets are required to have neat antithesis. In addition, lushi stresses tonal patterns, which are divided by tones of Chinese characters. In the Southern and Northern Dynasties (420–589), the four tones of Chinese came into being, of which, the first tone was designated as the level tone, and the other three as oblique tones. They are used in line with a certain scheme, making the poem suitable for reading aloud and fluently.

A five-character regular verse of the Tang Dynasty (618–907) by Wang Bo:

Farewell to Vice-Prefect Du Setting out for His Official Post in Shu

By this wall that surrounds the three Qin districts, through a mist that makes five rivers one.

We bid each other a sad farewell, we two officials going opposite ways.

And yet, while China holds our friendship and heaven remains our neighborhood.

Why should you linger at the fork of the road, wiping your eyes like a heart-broken child?

A seven-character-regular-verse of the Tang Dynasty (618–907) by Cui Hao:

The Yellow Crane Terrace

Where long ago a yellow crane bore a sage to heaven, nothing is left now but the Yellow Crane Terrace.

The yellow crane never revisited earth, and white clouds are flying without him forever.

Every tree in Hanyang becomes clear in the water, and Parrot Island is a nest of sweet grasses;

But I look toward home, and twilight grows dark with a mist of grief on the river waves.

A jueju with five characters to a line of the Tang Dynasty (618–907) by Wang Zhihuan:

On the Stork Tower

The sun beyond the mountains glows, the yellow river seawards flows.

You can enjoy a grander sight, by climbing to a greater height.

A jueju with seven characters to a line of the Tang Dynasty (618–907) by Li Bai:

Leaving White Emperor Town at Dawn

Leaving at dawn the White Emperor crowned with clouds, I've sailed a thousand li through canyons in a day.

With monkeys' sad adieus along the riverbanks are loud; my skiff has left ten thousand mountains far away.

As literary works, Chinese ancient poems have strict standards for creation, being required to not only follow strictly the composing rules of rhyming and having neat antithesis and tonal patterns, but also stress the artistic conception of poems. Chinese ancient poets set great store by dealing with the relation between the connotation and description, the former lying in explaining the truth of matters and the latter depicting phenomenon of matters. Only by unifying the two organically could the poem be excellent. It is "a successful blend of scenery and sentiment". In this process of seeking the best poetic conception and background, it is hard to image how hard the ancient Chinese people worked on composing poems. "Unless my words are shocking I'll not let it rest till death" and "Only by revising a poem thousand times do I feel comfortable" were the determinations of the ancient poets. One poet of the Tang Dynasty (618–907) expressed his painstaking work in composing poems: "Two lines at last! It's been three years; reciting them, I let fall tears. If for you, still, they don't ring true, I'll go back to my autumn hills".

Of the Tang poets, Li Bai, Du Fu and Bai Juyi are the most outstanding ones. Li Bai, reputed as the "fairy poet", lived in the most prosperous time of the Tang Dynasty (618–907). His poems are of both grand and elegant flavors, which find full expression in his poem depicting the fall of Lushan Mountain in Jiangxi Province, "The sunlit Censer Peak exhales a wreath of cloud; like an upended stream the cataract sounds loud. Its torrent dashes down three thousand feet from high, as if the Milky Way fell from azure sky." Du Fu is equally famous to Li Bai, enjoying the title of "poet of high attainments". He lived in the declining period of the Tang Dynasty (618–907); hence most of his poems were concerned about the country, with rich social contents and full of humanism. For example, "Behind the vermillion gates meat and wine go to waste while out on the road lie the bones of those frozen to death", "In the boundless forest, falling leaves swirl and twirl all around; On the endless Yangtze, rolling waves crash and splash all along", "Oh, for a great mansion with ten thousand rooms where all the poor on earth could find welcome shelter". His poems unified art and thought highly. Bai Juyi is a great poet in the Tang Dynasty (618–907). His poems bravely face reality and reveal and criticize the abuses of society, representing a genre. His two famous long poems *Song of Enduring Sorrow* and *Song of the Pipa* harmoniously combine narrating and expressing sentiment, and are time-honored masterpieces. Verses like "The boundless sky and endless earth may pass away, but this vow unfulfilled will be regretted for aye", and "Both of us in misfortune go from shore to shore. Meeting now, need we have known each other before?" are deeply loved by later generations.

Ci Poem of the Song Dynasty (960–1279)

In the middle of the Tang Dynasty (618–907), another literature style namely ci, equally famous to the Tang poems, sprung up and entered into its golden age in the Song Dynasty (960–1279). It is a kind of lyric adding words in line with a musical score, with a fixed number of Chinese characters and a stress on rhythm. Meanwhile, it has a fixed tune, also called tonal pattern, such as *Sunset on the River, Reminiscing Princess Tender* and *Buddhist Dancers*. Like poems, ci also stresses structure and rhythm. The Song Dynasty (960–1279) saw large numbers of outstanding ci poets, with masterpieces emerging continuously. Different styles and genres were also formed. *The Complete Ci-Poetry of the Song* is a collection of some 20,000 ci poems from close to 1,330 ci poets.

Before the mid-Song Dynasty (960–1279), the ci poems sought to be graceful and exquisite as well as connotative. *The Beautiful Lady Yu*, written by Emperor Li Yu of the Southern Tang Dynasty (937–975) expressed missing his homeland and the past like this:

When will there be no more moon and spring flowers, for me who had so many memorable hours? My attic which last night in vernal wind did stand reminds cruelly of the lost moonlit land.

Carved balustrades and marble steps must still be there, but rosy faces cannot be as fair. If you ask me how much my sorrow has increased, just see the over-brimming river flowing east!

Ci poet Liu Yong introduced it to the ordinary citizens. He expressed a scene that a pair of young lovers parted in the *Bells Ringing in the Rain*, reading sad and restrained:

Magnificent view of the Three Gorges of the Yangtze River.

Cicadas chill and drearily shrill, we stand face to face at an evening hour before the pavilion, after a sudden shower. Can I care for drinking before we part? At the city gate where we're lingering late, but the boat is waiting for me to depart. Hand in hand, we gaze at each other's tearful eyes and burst into sobs with words congealed on our lips. I'll go my way far, far away on miles and miles of misty waves where sail the ships, evening clouds hang low in boundless Southern skies. Parting lovers would grieve as of old, how could I stand this clear autumn day so cold!

The mid-Song Dynasty (960–1279) saw a turn in ci poetry's development, which was brought about by Su Shi, a great poet. He changed the gorgeous, graceful and restrained flavor of ci, introducing materials, sentiment, interest, artistic conception and techniques of poems into ci so as to diversify its styles. His ci poems are both graceful and inspiring. He established a school of heroic abandon for ci, new and fresh both in content and form. All of those can be found in his *Reminiscing the Ancient Times at Chibi Cliff* in the tune of *Reminiscing Princess Tender*.

Eastward the Yangtze River flows, its waves washing away traces of giant people of all times old. West of the ancient stronghold is said to be Chibi of Three Kingdoms, glory of Zhou Yu's. The disorderly peaks piercing the sky and splashing waves splattering the bank produce foams like piles of snows. What a great quantity of heroes came to the picturesque land. How splendid and heroic, imagine I, Zhou was at the time when Little Qiao became his wife. When Zhuge and Zhou talked and laughed, Cao Cao's warships and masts were burnt and sank. Touring the old land is my mind; how sentimental and laughable you may find me, on whose head early gray hair grows. Human lives are dreamlike; back to the moon my respectful cup of wine goes.

Another ci poet of the school of heroic abandon is Xin Qiji. He lived in the Southern Song Dynasty (1127–1279), a hero with great talent but having no room to maneuver. Hence, he used ci poems to express his thoughts, overwhelming

and inspiring. In the history of ci poetry, he was paid equal attention to Su Shi. His famous sentences include:

"Young I was, and ignorant of the taste of care, alone I loved to mount the stairs", "The rice fields' sweet smell promises a harvest good; I listen to the frogs croak in the neighborhood", "For, everywhere, no trace of her can be seen, when, all of a sudden, I turned about, that's her, where lanterns are few and far between" ... *"Blue hills can't stop water flowing, eastward the river keeps on going."*

The Tang (618–907) and Song (960–1127) Dynasties saw not only the brilliant development of poems and ci poetry but also plentiful results in the creation of prose. Litterateurs, represented by Han Yu and Liu Zongyuan launched the "Classical Prose Movement", renovating the rhythmical prose characterized by parallelism and complexity and advocating to learn the prose of the Qin (221 BC–206 BC) and Han (206 BC–220 AD) with odd numbers of lines. They created a large number of excellent literary works, leading prose to a new realm. In the Song Dynasty (960–1279), Ouyang Xiu, Su Xun, Su Zhe, Wang Anshi, Zeng Gong and others further developed prose. They are the well-known "eight great men of letters" of the Tang (618–907) and Song (960–1127) Dynasties in the history of Chinese literature.

Verses of the Yuan Dynasty (1206–1368)

Verse is comprised of sanqu (a type of verse popular in the Yuan (1206–1368), Ming (1368–1644) and Qing (1616–1911) dynasties, with tonal patterns modeled on tunes drawn from folk music) and Yuan-Dynasty zaju plays. The former originates from the folk people, mostly from ethnic minorities of north China; the latter is also a kind of Chinese classical poetry, freer than ci poetry. A Yuan-Dynasty zaju play is a kind of drama sung according to Northern Opera. Famous playwrights of the Yuan Dynasty include Guan Hanqing, Ma Zhiyuan and Wang Shifu, with their magnum opuses being *The Injustice Done to Dou E*, *Sorrow in the Han Palace* and *The Western Chamber* respectively. *The Injustice*

Done to Dou E reveals the seamy side of the officialdom and injustice of society. Guan Hanqing criticized the society with expressive techniques in a simple and natural way. The following is the melody sung by Dou E when she was taken to the execution ground, full of grief and indignation:

Rolling Embroidered Ball

The sun and moon give light by day and by night; mountains and rivers watch over the world of men. Yet Heaven cannot tell the innocent from the guilty, and confuses the wicked with the good! The good are poor, and die before their time; the wicked are rich, and live to a great old age. The gods are afraid of the mighty and bully the weak; they let evil take its course. Ah, Earth, you will not distinguish good from bad, and, heaven, you let me suffer this injustice! Tears pour down my cheeks in vain!

Novels of the Ming and Qing Dynasties (1368–1911)

The late period of ancient Chinese society namely the Ming (1368–1644) and Qing (1644–1911) Dynasties saw continued development of various styles

Illustrations for *A Dream of Red Mansions*.

of literatures, represented by fiction and plays. Fiction is divided into novel and short stories. All the novels are comprised of many chapters, each headed by a couplet giving the list of its content and telling a story of certain length. The story has a beginning, middle and end. It is derived from the folk story-telling. Hence, all of them were vernacular, easy to understand and spread quickly. The Ming (1368–1644) and Qing (1616–1911) Dynasties boast large numbers of novels, including the famous *Romance of Three Kingdom*s, by Luo Guanzhong; *The Outlaws of the Marsh*, by Shi Nai'an; *The Golden Lotus; Records of a Journey to the West*, by Wu Cheng'en; *Unofficial History of Officialdom*, by Wu Jingzi and *A Dream of Red Mansion*, by Cao Xueqin. *Romance of Three Kingdoms* is a historical novel about the Wei, Shu and Wu States fighting for dominion of the country in the late Eastern Han (25–220). It creates a large number of characters such as Zhuge Liang, Guan Yu and Cao Cao. *The Outlaws of the Marsh* is a hero-legend novel, portraying a number of insurrectionists fighting against the wicked, getting rid of the cruel, helping others and doing chivalrous things, and the novel succeeds in creating a large number of vivid heroic characters. *Records of a Journey to the West* is a supernatural novel of evil spirit characteristics. It is created on the base of the story that Xuan Zang, a hierarch of the Tang Dynasty (618–907), went to India to obtain sutras. With magnificent images, it successfully portrays Sun Wukong, a reincarnation of justice. *The Golden Lotus* is a novel revealing the ways of people and the world. It tells the story of Ximen Qing's family, from their becoming rich to their decline. It marked a transition in the development of Chinese novels. From then on, humanism and realism began to appear in novels. *Unofficial History of Officialdom* is a satiric novel, profoundly portraying the face and ugly deeds of a number of men of letters, business people, officials and country gentlemen under the system of imperial examinations and the cannibalistic feudal ethics.

A Dream of Red Mansion is a collective work and the crest of ancient Chinese literature. Cao Xueqin, with his experience as background, told the story of a feudal family from being flourishing to being in decline to eventual ruin. It is a masterpiece full of humanism and realism, reflecting the social visage and human relationships in the early Qing Dynasty (1616–1911) in an unprecedented extent and depth. It creates numerous characters each with a special meaning such as Baoyu, Daiyu, Baochai, Xiangyun, Tanchun, Xiren, Wang Xifeng and Jia Zheng. Cao Xueqin collects all the traditional cultures of China in the novel, establishing a literary monument with extensive and profound wisdom and culture. It enjoys a title of encyclopedia of Chinese traditional culture. Hence, it will help you know more about Chinese traditional culture if you read it carefully.

Compared with the western novels, Chinese traditional novels stress story and plot and feature fast rhythm, but are comparatively weak in mental description of characters.

Unique Artistic Style

Compared with arts in other countries, Chinese traditional arts, i.e. calligraphy, painting, music, dance, architecture and gardening, have a unique style, featuring colorful Chinese culture.

Calligraphy

Calligraphy is a traditional artistic form with Chinese characteristics, displaying oriental aesthetic value.

Calligraphy may be understood as the method or rule of writing Chinese characters. Calligraphy, as an art, refers to the art of writing Chinese characters. Chinese calligraphy serves the purpose of conveying thought and aesthetic tastes but also shows the abstract beauty of the line. Calligraphy takes the Chinese character as the vessel. And the Chinese characters, which feature the complex combination of lines and spots, may be written in many different forms. This makes it possible to create art through calligraphy. At the same time, Chinese characters still remain the main feature of hieroglyphic, symbolic and ideographic writing, which provides the conditions for the calligraphers to create aesthetic imagery. The tools are the brush pen, ink, paper and ink stone, which are commonly referred to as the four treasures

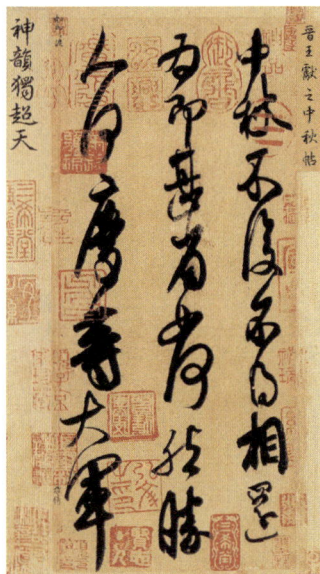

Mid Autumn Festival by Wang Xizhi.

of calligraphy. The brush pen made of animal hair is soft for soaking up ink, but also has strong retractility. Using it to write Chinese characters consisting of dots and lines makes Chinese characters appear complicated and changeable, thus forming different styles. When practicing calligraphy, one should pay attention to three basic elements, i.e. the technique of writing calligraphy (the written lines need to have an aesthetic feeling), the form of Chinese characters (strokes collocation need to be reasonable), and layout (Many characters are arranged in one through artistic conception).

Chinese calligraphy dates back to the early ages of China. When Chinese characters were created, people took note of the variation of their lines and graphs. The inscriptions on bones or tortoise shells, and inscriptions on ancient bronze objects, seal script and lishu (official script) all take on their different features in the form of a Chinese character, application of technique of writing and layout, displaying different aesthetic feelings. Starting from the Western Han Dynasty (206 BC–25 AD), people pursued the art of calligraphy. The *Zhangcao* (an early form of cursive script) of the Han Dynasty (206 BC–220 AD), a great contribution to calligraphy, is an elegant cursive script integrating cursive script and the official script. In the Wei and Jin period, Chinese calligraphy entered into a new age in which *kaishu* (regular script) and *xingshu* (running script) came into being and there were two calligraphist masters Zhong Yao and Wang Xizhi. Zhong Yao was the originator of *kaishu* (regular script). Most calligraphists came from the Wang family which made great achievements in the history of Chinese calligraphy. Wang Xizhi and his son Wang Xianzhi, known as the "Two Wangs" in Chinese calligraphy history, pushed the art of *xingshu* (running script) to a new phase. Of the *xingshu* (running script) works by Wang Xizhi, the *Preface to the Poems Composed at the Orchid Pavilion*, which is known as the "First *Xingshu* Work Under Heaven", is the most famous. During the same period, there was a kind of *kaishu* (regular script) called "Wei Monumental style" in North China, which was inscribed on steles.

In the Tang Dynasty (618–907), there appeared famous calligraphists such as Ouyang Xun, Chu Suiliang, Yan Zhenqing and Liu Gongquan, and the *kaishu* (regular script) reached its peak. In the Tang Dynasty, *Caoshu* (cursive script) experienced development to some extent, and kuangcao (highly cursive script) appeared. In the Song Dynasty, calligraphy began to convey the feelings and interests of calligraphers, instead of pursuing the esthetic values which ideally featured moral standards, so that calligraphy began to embody artistic quality. Su Shi, Huang Tingjian, Mi Fu and Cai Xiang are the most famous calligraphists of the Song Dynasty (960–1279), known as the "Four Calligraphist Masters of the Song Dynasty". Their calligraphy works, vivid and natural, do not follow the set rule, but instead develop a school of their own. Zhao Mengfu is the most well-known calligrapher of the Yuan Dynasty (1206–1368), whose *kaishu* (regular script), well-knit and graceful, is known as the "Zhao Style". Calligraphy continued to undergo development in the Ming (1368–1644) and Qing (1616–1911) dynasties. Dong Qichang is the most influential calligraphist of the Ming Dynasty. He learned from his predecessors and took nature as method and he made great achievements in *kaishu* (regular script), *xingshu* (running script) and

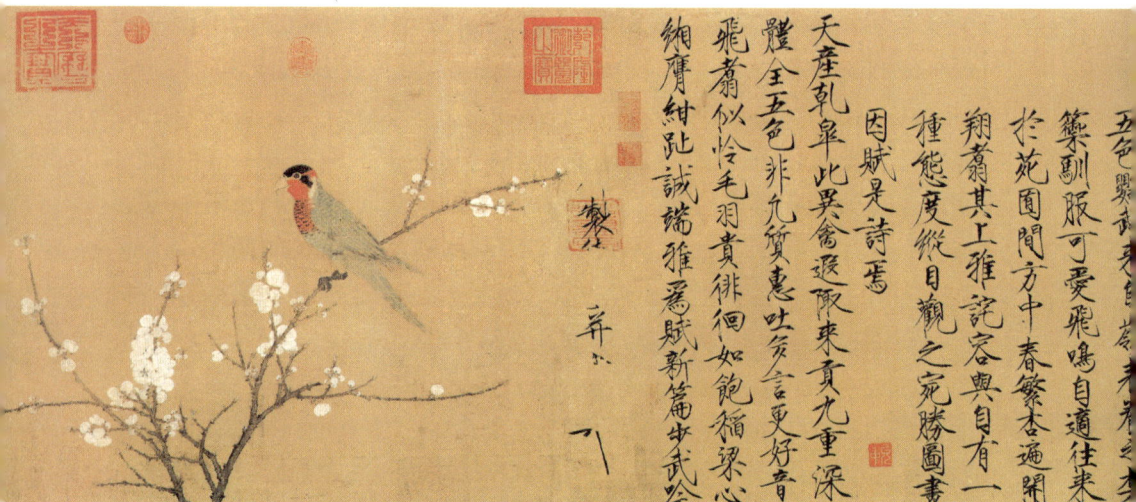

Portrait of Five-color Parrots by Song Empeor Huizong.

Caoshu (cursive script), which were praised highly by the later generations. In the early Qing and late Ming period, there appeared a number of calligraphers preferring a style featuring romanticism, which broke the rules of traditional calligraphy and created peculiar romantic works.

Chinese calligraphy was introduced into the Korean Peninsula in the 2nd–3rd century. In the 7th century, Korean calligraphy entered into a period of great prosperity, in which a great number of calligraphists and calligraphy works appeared. Of them, many still exist today. In the 7th century, Chinese calligraphy was introduced into Japan from the Korean Peninsula. In the 8th century, the Tang Dynasty conducted frequent cultural exchanges with Japan, and Chinese calligraphy became prominent throughout Japan.

Painting

Painting and calligraphy are the twin arts of Chinese traditional culture. Like calligraphy, Chinese traditional painting has unique and bright artistic features, giving it a style different from that of other countries.

Chinese painting pays attention to both painting realistically and freehand brushwork, and more attention to catching the spirit rather than shape. The basic method of Chinese painting is the application of lines and ink color. Pen and ink are the core tools for Chinese painting. Chinese painting substitutes ink for color, which is the big difference from western paintings. Traditional Chinese paintings are mainly ink-wash paintings. Ink-wash paintings mainly include landscape paintings, flower-bird paintings and figure paintings.

Chinese painting has a long history. Before the Qin Dynasty, many kinds of painting such as painting on silk, mural painting and lacquer painting were common. In the Wei, Jin, Southern and Northern dynasties, painting began to pursue independent aesthetic value, a number of figure paintings and landscape paintings appeared, and systemic painting theories began to form. Chinese traditional painting blossomed in the Sui (581–618) and Tang (618–907)

Playing Games in Autumn Courtyard by Su Hanchen of the Song Dynasty (960−1279).

dynasties. Zhan Ziqian, the outstanding painter of the Sui Dynasty, was good at painting horses and landscapes. Yan Liben and Wu Daozi, painters of the Tang Dynasty excelled in figure painting, Li Sixun and Wang Wei were good at landscape painting, and Xue Ji was good at painting flowers and birds. Starting from the Tang Dynasty, the technique of washing with water colors replaced painting with dark green. It is the method of ink-wash painting, which gradually developed into the mainstream of Chinese painting from the late-Tang period.

From the Five Dynasties (907−960) to Song Dynasty (960−1279), figure painting, flower-bird painting, and landscape painting underwent great development. Jing Hao, Guan Tong, Dong Yuan and Ju Ran were famous landscape painters during this period. Li Gonglin, a painter of the Song Dynasty created the line drawing method, pushing figure painting to new heights. It was said that the *Vimalakirti Figure* was painted by Li Gonglin, which is an elaborate work of line drawing of a figure. Zhao Ji, the Emperor Huizong of the Song Dynasty was good at painting flowers and birds, and the *Peach and Cooer*

Painting is his most famous work. The ink-wash paintings of plum blossoms and bamboo attained perfection in the Song Dynasty. *The Ink Bamboo Painting* by Wen Tong and the *Dead Wood and Grotesque Stone Painting* by Su Shi are from this period. The ink-wash landscape painting also witnessed great development, with the father and son painters, Mi Fu and Mi Youren, as the representatives. They adopted techniques such as the ink work including splash-ink, thus enriching the technique of washing with water colors. During the Yuan Dynasty, many changes took place in painting. The literati paintings held the dominant position. Most literati painters were also poets and calligraphers, thus integrating the paintings with the poems and calligraphy. Huang Gongwang, Wang Meng, Ni Zan and Wu Zhen are the most famous painters from the Yuan Dynasty, known as the "Four Masters of the Yuan Dynasty".

In the Ming and Qing dynasties, Chinese paintings, especially the ink-wash paintings paid more attention to the general expressive force. Dong Qichang, a great calligrapher and painter of the late-Ming period, learned from his

Night Revels of Han Xizai (part) by Gu Hongzhong of Nantang (937–975)of the Five Dynasties (907–960).

predecessors' strong points and formed his clean, elegant painting style which exerted important influence upon painting during the Qing Dynasty. Among the paintings of the Qing Dynasty, paintings by the Four Wangs, a group of painters, (including Wang Shimin, Wang Jian, Wang Hui, and Wang Yuanqi), the Four Monks (including Shi Tao, Badashanren, Hong Ren and Shi Xi), and the Eight Eccentrics of Yangzhou (a group of painters in Yangzhou during the years of Qing Emperor Yongzheng's and Emperor Qianlong's reign, Zheng Banqiao was one of the members) made the greatest accomplishments. The Four Wangs represented the so-called "orthodox school" of ink-wash painting with deep force and skill and their works are elegant and graceful. The Four Monks refused to follow the orthodoxy, stressed original creation, and argued against the bigoted beliefs of the ancients. The Eight Eccentrics of Yangzhou not only inherited the tradition, but also set store by life experiences, making their personality widely known. Their ink-wash paintings, the perfect combinations of poem, calligraphy, painting and stamp, exerted great effect upon modern Chinese painting.

Music and Dance

Chinese traditional music and dance, with a long history featuring the culture of the orient, obviously differs from those of western countries.

According to historical documents, there were as many as 70 varieties of musical instruments in the Western Zhou Dynasty (1046 BC–771 BC). The bayin system used in those days classified Chinese musical instruments into eight categories by their materials (i.e. metal, stone, skin, gourd, bamboo, wood, silk and earth). In 1978, some 124 musical instruments were unearthed from the Tomb of Marquis Yi of the Zeng State of the Warring States Period (475 BC–221 BC) in what is now Hubei Province in central China, showing the world China's splendid musical heritage. The unearthed bell set, exquisite, covers approximately five octaves, which means it can produce melodies in seven musical scales. In the Han and Tang dynasties, the musical instruments underwent constant development. Some instruments such as Pipa (four-stringed lute with 30 frets and pear-shaped body), Sanxian (a long necked lute with three strings without frets), Erhu (a two-stringed fiddle), Yue Qin (a moon-shaped lute with shorter neck and four strings) which are still popular today, were the main ones introduced from Central Asia into the Central Plains and experienced renovation during that period. Music in the ancient Chinese court was very developed with numerous persons were involved. There were tens of thousands of persons involved in making music in the court, and there was a special music institution in charge of the management of the performers and organizing, researching and creation of the music.

Chinese traditional dance originated from the performances in the totem, sorcery and sacrifice offering activities and later evolved into the dance with musical accompaniment. In the Western Zhou Dynasty, the musical dance performed by the female performers especially engaging in song and dance appeared. This kind of dance reached a fairly high level in the Han Dynasty and played an important role in ancient Chinese dance for a long period. Performers of this kind of dance received special training, so that the artistic level of ancient Chinese dance was enhanced constantly. Feast music and dance performed by the musical dancers represented the highest level of dance in the Tang Dynasty. Musical dance is a kind of large scale performance combining instrumental music, dance and song. In the Song Dynasty, another unique dance performance form—Team Dance appeared. This dance required numerous performers, each with one's own specific role. With regular procedure, it integrated song, dance, recitation, dialog and other artistic techniques that alternate, being a comprehensive artistic form.

Sculpture

The art of Sculpture holds an important position among Chinese traditional arts. Featuring oriental culture it is very different from that of other countries with ancient civilizations such as Greece, Egypt and Rome.

Terracotta Warriors and Horses of the Qin Shihuang Mausoleum in Xi'an, Shaanxi Province.

The origin of Chinese civilization has close links with sculpture. After the Neolithic Age, China produced rich and brilliant sculpture art. Pottery Sculpture appeared first. The bronzes of the Shang (1600 BC−1046 BC) and Zhou (1046 BC−256 BC) dynasties show excellent sculpture technique. After the Qin and Han dynasties, Chinese sculpture art experienced continuous development and a large number of sculptures were left in mausoleums, grottoes and temples. Chinese traditional sculpture absorbed and integrated foreign techniques in its development, thus forming its own characteristics. The Terra-cotta Warriors and Horses discovered in Lintong, Shaanxi Province in 1974 are affiliated with the Mausoleum of Qin Shi Huang, the first emperor of the Qin Dynasty (221 BC−206 BC) and the first unifier of China, and features life-sized sculptures of warriors and horses all with different facial expressions and postures. It became recognized universally as one of the Eight Wonders in the World. There were sculptures of high artistic value in the mausoleums of the emperors of the dynasties after the Qin Dynasty.

After Buddhism was introduced into China, the Buddhist Statue gradually became popular and combined with Chinese traditional sculpture to form a new sculpture style. Most of the Buddhist statues are distributed in the grottoes, of which the most well-known are the Yungang Grottoes near Datong City, Shanxi Province, the Longmen Grottoes near Luoyang, Henan Province, the Mogao Grottoes in Dunhuang, western Gansu Province, and the Maijishan Grottoes near Tianshui City, Gansu Province. With beautiful moulding, uncommon temperament and different styles, these Buddhist statues reached the peak of perfection, and are of high artistic value. Chinese temples and monasteries still house many statues of Buddha, Bodhisattva and Arhat.

Garden

Ancient Chinese gardens express the humanistic spirit through pursuing the beauty of the natural landscape and are in harmony with the thought "a perfect integration of man and nature".

The Chinese garden is divided into two categories: the royal garden and the private garden. Through long development, the two categories of garden building reached a peak in the Ming and Qing dynasties. After the Ming Dynasty moved its capital to Beijing, it increased input into the building of the royal gardens. Besides the Imperial Garden (Yuhuayuan) inside the Forbidden City, there were the Beihai, Zhonghai and Nanhai Lakes, together known as Sanhai (Three Seas), to the west of the Imperial Palace. With long and narrow waterways and natural and comfortable layout the Sanhai contrasts finely with the grand and majestic Imperial Palace architectures. Looking around on the Jade Flowery Islet in the center of the Sanhai, the Sanhai, Imperial Palace, Jingshan Hill, and hills in the distance undulate with clear arrangement, presenting a splendid sight and showing the royal strength and grace. The Qing Dynasty rebuilt the Sanhai on the basis of the Ming Dynasty and constructed several royal gardens in the west of Beijing, of which the largest, Yuanmingyuan, tried to include all the beautiful

sceneries under the heaven. In addition, the Qing Dynasty also built the Summer Resort in Chengde, Hebei Province, which covers an area of 560 hectares. The Summer Resort creates a quiet atmosphere by maintaining the natural features of a mountain forest, and constructing some small buildings.

While the royal gardens were built, some officials, rich merchants, celebrities and gentries set about building their private gardens. Chinese private gardens date back to the Han Dynasty and in the Wei, Jin, and Northern and Southern Dynasties, focused on natural landscapes. There were some 1,000 private gardens with the natural landscapes as the theme in Luoyang during the Tang Dynasty, which had an elegant and secretive style. In the Song Dynasty, the view borrowing, view in opposite place and other techniques were adopted in building the private gardens and ornamental stones were also applied. In the Ming and Qing dynasties, Chinese private gardens reached their zenith. They are mainly distributed in Beijing, Nanjing, Suzhou, Yangzhou, Hangzhou, Wuxi

Summer Palace in Spring, with various peach blossom and winter jasmine in full bloom.

Humble Administrator's Garden in Suzhou, Jiangsu Province.

and other places. There were as many as over 150 private gardens in Beijing, with the Banmu Garden, Yimu Garden, Cuijin Garden and Tsinghua Garden as representatives. A great number of private gardens were built in Suzhou, and at one time there were as many as 270. Of them, the Humble Administrator's Garden, the Lingering Garden, the Lion Forest Garden and the Canglang Pavilion are most well-known. These gardens are characterized by the combination of dwelling house and garden, making them perfect for habitation. And they were constantly enhanced culturally to be a synthesis including various hills and pools, flowers and trees, architecture, engravings, calligraphy, paintings, and handcrafts. Private gardens in Suzhou, as the representative of Chinese classical private gardens, are the cream, featuring the combination of culture and life. The gardens follow the principle of adaptation to nature and tactically encapsulate diverse natural views through limited spaces so that people can see big things through small ones and a quiet place in a noisy environment.

Colorful Social Life

Clothing, food, housing, travel, birth, aging, sickness and death, not to mention various customs and habits, are all essential parts of social life reflecting the level of civilization of a specific society. Influenced by the teachings of Confucianism, ancient Chinese people strove to improve the quality of their life filled with interest and happiness.

Marital Culture

The concept of marital life developed from the inherent reproductive need of humankind to multiply and develop. In China, this began with a group

A foreign groom lifts the cover for the Chinese bride during a traditional wedding ceremony in Pingtan, .Fujian Province.

marriage system practiced by primitive society. In the Xia (about 2070 BC–1600 BC) and Shang (1600 BC–1046 BC) dynasties, monogamy commonly prevailed, although polygamy was widely practiced among nobles. In the Qin (221 BC–206 BC) and Han (206 BC–220 AD) dynasties, the traditional marriage pattern of China was established, strictly adhering to the principle of "non-marriage between persons with the same family name". Apart from members of the imperial family, some aristocrats and persons holding high positions who engaged in polygamy, monogamy was the rule among ordinary families. Traditional Chinese culture regarded marriage for both boy and girl as proper upon coming of age. Chinese people usually regard a happy marriage and successful career as the two major goals in life, and that, once married, a couple should love each other and remain in harmony throughout their lives by assuming various obligations and responsibilities. The traditional Chinese wedding is extremely complicated with much stress on formality. It is divided into six stages known as the 'six etiquettes'. The first stage is the proposal. The boy's family asks a matchmaker to propose a marriage and then, if the other side agrees to negotiate, they will visit the girl's family with prepared gifts to make a formal proposal. Originally, the gift was a wild goose, but a domestically-raised goose, or even a wooden carved wild goose, were substituted in modern times. The second stage is then the 'birthday matching' to ensure the couple's compatibility. If the couple's birthdays and birth hours do not conflict according to astrology, the marriage formalities can then proceed to the third stage, which is the presentation of betrothal gifts. The boy's family should send such gifts as a ring, various other pieces of jewelry and colored silk as a keepsake of the engagement. The fourth stage is the presentation of wedding gifts. These should be sent to the girl's family accompanied by a band of drummers, and it is an important part of pre-nuptial etiquette. The fifth stage requires the two families to select a suitable wedding date, which strictly speaking, requires the boy's side to fix the month and the girl's family the day (especially to avoid the bride's menstrual period). The last step is for the bridegroom to set out to receive his bride.

Catering Culture

Chinese catering culture has a long history and rich content well-known to the world. The developed agriculture of ancient China provided the natural conditions for the development of the profound catering culture. In the Xia and Shang dynasties, catering ware was categorized into cooking, drinking and table ware. Most were ceramic in the Xia Dynasty and bronze in the Shang Dynasty. Chinese catering culture came into being in the Western Zhou Dynasty (1046 BC–771 BC), featuring a profound etiquette. In the Spring and Autumn Period (770 BC–476 BC) and the Warring States Period (475 BC–221 BC), exquisite and convenient lacquer ware replaced bronze and became widely used in daily life. The nine major tastes of Chinese cuisine, namely sour, sweet, bitter, spicy, salt, fresh, fragrant, tongue-numbing and light, were completed by the time of the Jin (265–420) and Southern and Northern (420–589) dynasties. The Sui (581–618) and Tang (618–907) Dynasties saw the creation of numerous edible

On the evening of November 12, 2013, the China Cooking Association sponsored the China Food in the United Nations activities at the headquarters of the United Nations. Foreign diplomats testing the Chinese food.

vegetables in people's daily life with a stress on daintiness. The Song Dynasty (960–1179) witnessed great development in catering culture. The national capital was the center for the exchange of southern and northern culinary techniques in numerous varieties. Ceramic table ware was also widely used. In the Ming (1368–1644) and Qing (1616–1911) dynasties, people in southern China began to eat mostly rice, while wheat predominated in northern China. In addition, corn and tomato were introduced from America. The Qing Dynasty witnessed the peak of Chinese catering culture, forming Jiangsu, Shandong, Sichuan and Guangdong cuisines. The representative of the Qing catering culture is the Feast of Complete Manchu-Han Courses, comprising a vast array of refined Manchu and Han dishes including delicacies of every kind. In ancient China, the daily dietary habits of the ordinary people were two meals in autumn and three meals in summer. They ate porridge in slack seasons and cooked rice during busy times.

Wine Culture

Wine is widely enjoyed around the world and China has its own great drinking culture. The earliest wine in China made from fruits can be traced back to the Stone Age. As the most developed country in agricultural civilization, China was able to brew liquor from corn more than 5,000 years ago. After the Western Han Dynasty (206 BC–25 AD), wine came into being. Among the liquor made from corn, 'yellow wine' prevailed before the Tang Dynasty with a rather low alcoholic content. Potent distilled spirits made their debut in the Song Dynasty. There was also 'medicinal liquor' containing herbal medicines used to cure disease. Beer was introduced into China from the West in modern times. In the Xia and Shang and Western Zhou dynasties, wine was mainly used for worship but gradually began to be enjoyed by the people, thus enriching Chinese culture. After drinking, one becomes braver and more high-spirited and vigorous, and there are many stories related to drinking in Chinese history. On the occasion of festivals, lucky days, gatherings and departure, or just to ward off the winter chill, people turned to wine. A lot of wonderful verses have been left by great

poets, such as "wait till we empty one more cup", "if you drink with a bosom friend, a thousand cups are not enough", "never tip an empty golden cup towards the moon".

Tea Culture

Differing from wine culture, the tea culture of China stresses weak instead of strong. Tea originated in China and was first grown on the Yunnan-Guizhou Plateau in the southwest China before spreading east along the Yangtze River via the Sichuan Basin during the Western Han Dynasty. The Yangtze River Valley has soil and climate suitable for planting tea. In the Wei and Jin dynasties, the prevailing culture stressed mildness, if not insipidity. Hence, the custom of drinking tea emerged. A family with position would offer a guest with tea. Certain literati, people of elegance, as well as hermits and monks, with much

Lao She Teahouse in Beijing: Teahouse staff guiding foreign friends to make centuries-old Puer tea cakes.

time for leisure and contemplation, developed the tea-drinking habit. In the Tang Dynasty, the work *Tea Classics* was published, spreading the culture further afield. People at this time cherished clarity and sense and this was considered to be fully embodied in the art of making and drinking tea. In the Song Dynasty, tea became popular both in the imperial court and among ordinary people, and the tea culture was continuously enriched in the following dynasties. Scholars of the Ming Dynasty attached great importance to personal integrity and they saw drinking tea as epitomizing moral refinement. The bitterness of the tea also reminded them of the harsh life experienced by the masses. Many people of letters in the Qing Dynasty sought mental liberation and balance and felt that slowly sipping tea induced great calmness. But, in traditional Chinese culture, there is a great difference between "tasting" and "drinking" tea, with the former becoming strongly associated with mental behavior. "Tasting" is the act of appreciating, enjoying, meditating and commenting on such aspects as color, fragrance and taste. It is favorable for the tea to be green in color, light in fragrance and moderate in taste. Famous teas such as Dragon Well Green Tea, Biluochun Tea, Dahongpao Tea and Junshan Silver Needle are highly prized. In regard to water, that drawn from a mountain stream is best, that of the river of moderate value and that drawn from a well decidedly inferior in making tea. With regard to tea ware, this should be worthy of appreciation and collection. Finally, the environment in which one savors the tea should be elegant, quiet and clean.

Housing Culture

Housing in ancient China was categorized into four types, including fence style, crypt style, house and tent style. Fence-style architecture was a kind of dwelling common in southern China in ancient times. It was raised from the ground and hence was most defensible and sanitary. Crypt-style architecture existed in northern China in primitive times and involved digging holes in the loess soil to create a dwelling. The soil layer in the north is deep and straight with low water content favorable for digging. Cave dwellings of this kind are

A Beijing Siheyuan style Turist hotel.

economical and simple, warm in winter and cool in summer. Houses replaced the crypt-style dwelling as the ancient people of northern China emerged to live on the surface. They featured a distinct culture of agricultural cultivation. The hard walls of houses were built by stamping earth between board frames to create a structure that was warm in winter and cool in summer, with good ventilation and natural lighting and convenient for movement in and out. In order to ward off winter cold, a heated adobe sleeping platform, the *kang*, was invented in northern China. Finally, the tent-style dwelling was created by nomads of northern China as most suitable for their life of constant movement. *Siheyuan* (a compound with houses on all four sides) is an old architectural style that still exists. Those in northern China differ in style from those in the south. The *siheyuan* of Beijing eventually became the chief representative of the north China style. Chinese people attached great importance to the location of dwellings from fairly early times, forming geomancy in the Qin and Han dynasties, commonly known as *feng shui*. A geomancer would always be called in to choose the best location for a house for the living and burial place for the dead, and many Chinese continue this practice today. Geomancy refers to making an overall evaluation on various architectural conditions such as climate, landform, ecology and view.

Costume Culture

Clothing made constant headway throughout human development, moving from primitive leaf and bark coverings to sophisticated textile materials. Correspondingly, shoes, embroidery, hats and various ornaments and hairstyles appeared. People wore different clothes on diverse occasions and in various seasons, thus forming a diverse costume culture. In the Xia, Shang and Western Zhou dynasties, the decorative function of clothes was prominent, and a clothing system in accordance with the hierarchy emerged. In the Western Zhou Dynasty, clothes differed by grade in terms of texture, shape, size, color and decorative patterns. There were strict grades for the robes of kings, feudal princes and

Night Revels of Han Xiza: Women in Tang style attires.

181

ministers. Uniformity in costume culture, however, emerged in the Qin and Han dynasties. People generally wore *shenyi*, a kind of full-length, one-piece robe. The Jin and the Southern and Northern dynasties stressed the beauty of clothing, with garments, hats and footwear displaying typical decorative patterns. The clothing in the Sui and Tang dynasties included officials' robes, civilian apparel, men's and women's clothing. The officials' robes showed were strictly delineated by rank in terms of style and color. Women's clothes of the Tang Dynasty mainly comprised a frock, skirt and cape. The skirt was big enough to cover the ground, and the cape hung over the shoulders and fell to the waist. Women of the Song Dynasty commonly wore a frock and skirt. A pomegranate-red skirt was most popular at that time. In the late Song Dynasty, the custom of binding feet began to prevail among noble women. In the Qing Dynasty, people of the subjugated Han ethnic group were compelled to tonsure their hair and meet various clothing requirements. Hence, great changes took place in costumes and a costume system with not only characteristics of the Manchu but also the traditional grading symbols of the Han was finally formed. A long gown and mandarin jacket were typical male apparel in the Qing Dynasty. Han women's costumes were the same with those of preceding dynasties, but the Manchu wore the cheongsam, which is still quite popular today. Han women mostly bound their feet, but Manchu women did not.

Major Traditional Festivals of China		
Time	**Festival**	**Activities**
First day of first lunar month	Spring Festival	This refers to the first day of a new lunar year. It is the most important traditional festival for the Chinese. During the festival, people put on their holiday's best, pay New Year's call to congratulate each other, family members and friends, worship ancestors, and gather for family union. Fireworks are set off, and lion and dragon dance is performed.
15th day of the first lunar month	Lantern Festival	This takes place on the first full-moon day of the first lunar month. People eat glutinous rice balls, meaning reunion. They hang lanterns, guess riddles written on lanterns, walk on stilts, and perform Yangko dance.
Second day of the second lunar month	Dragon Head Festival, also known as Second Day of Second Month	Worship Dragon God to pray for good weather and bumper grain harvest

April 5 or the day before or after	Qingming Festival	Toward the end of the spring, life returns and many go out for an outing. Friends gather to drink and recite poems, and fly kites. Sweeping tombs is one of the most important thing to do.
Fifth day of the fifth lunar month	Dragon Boat Festival also called Duanwu or Chongwu Festival	This festival is said to commemorate the great patriotic poet Qu Yuan by eating zongzi (glutinous rice pudding), hanging the Chinese mugwort leaf, drinking realgar wine and holding dragon boat race.
Seventh day of the seventh lunar month	Seventh Evening of the Seventh Moon also called Begging Festival	Legend has it that Cowboy and Weaver stars meet that night on the bridge formed by magpies. Women place incense burner table, on which are melons and fruits, and work line through needle holes to pray for wisdom.
15th day of the 8th lunar month	Mid-Autumn Festival	This festival is next only to Spring Festival in terms of importance for the Chinese. When the full moon rises, the whole family gathers for dinner, eat moon cakes while enjoying lanterns and guessing riddles. Various kinds of melons and fruits are displayed to worship the moon.

Ninth day of the ninth lunar month	Double Ninth Festival	On that day, people climb mountains, enjoy chrysanthemum, and wear cornel. Gradually, it expands to include love for the elderly.
29th or 30th day of the 12th lunar month	New Year's Eve	At the turn of a lunar year, the Chinese gather for family union. No matter where one goes, he/she will manage to come back for evening union dinner that day. They paste poetic couplets, post gate god, and paste New Year paintings, as well as worship ancestors. The elderly gives the younger generation the gift money. On the New Year's Eve some people stay up all night, which is called staying-up.

End of Feudal Power and Establishment of a Modern Country

After 1840, China, which had remained in the world forefront since the 2nd century BC, went into decline, suffering one catastrophe after another.

It was invaded and plundered by big powers with strong ships and cannons. Subsequently, advanced Chinese people began to seek ways to save the nation and achieve modern development. China experienced Westernization in the aspects of technology, social system and culture until the neo-democratic revolution led by the Chinese Communist Party. Thanks to more than 100 years of unremitting efforts, the nation finally found its way onto a new road of development.

Closed Doors and the Decline of the Qing Court

From the 17th to the 19th century, the world underwent a tremendous transformation. Britain became the modern country politically via its "Glorious Revolution" and economically through the "Industrial Revolution"; the French Revolution overthrew the decadent monarchy and created a republic; America became powerful after the War of Independence and Civil War; Germany rapidly prospered through unification and industrialization; and Russia and Japan also progressed by copying Western ways. In sharp contrast, the Qing Dynasty gradually declined after more than 100 years of its prime period.

Foreign Envoys Celebrating Empress Dowager Cixi's Birthday in 1903, a New Year picture of the late Qing Dynasty (1644–1911).

The Qing court repulsed foreign civilization. Before the Opium War in 1840, the Qing court regarded itself as the "Celestial Empire" as well as the largest and most powerful country in the world. In its eyes, other countries were all vassal states, which should submit to and learn from China. During the reign of Emperor Qianlong in the 18th century, the West was going through periods of great upheaval that created the various modern powers. However, the emperor paid no attention to these developments. In 1793, when meeting a Britain envoy, he portentously declared: "My Celestial Empire governs all other states in the world" and "we have abundant products of all kinds, so there is no need for us to trade with foreigners." He was blinded by the visionary Celestial Empire. Meanwhile, despite numerous achievements epitomized by the "four great inventions of ancient China" (papermaking, gunpowder, printing and the compass) that had a huge impact on the entire world, traditional Chinese culture ignored invention as it came under the influence of Confucianism stressing "cultivate one's morality, organize your own family, father your kingdom and conquer the world". Moreover, it regarded the means for improving production techniques as fanciful tricks and evil skills. Hence, when some missionaries took chronometers and guns to China, most officials of the Qing court learnt no long-term lessons from them.

A closed-door policy was adopted. Though Admiral Zheng He's voyages had penetrated to Arabia and Africa scores of years earlier than the first appearance of Western explorers, the Ming court did not take advantage of this to continue to develop the foreign relations. Contrarily, the mandarins banned ocean voyages, in order to prevent depredations by pirates and other states, and strictly restricting contact with external world by sea. It lost China a good chance to develop valuable contacts with emerging powers elsewhere. From the 16th century, China initiated virtually no maritime trade with outside world and it was left to others, like Portugal, Spain and Netherlands to seize the advantage. The Qing court enforced a ban even more strictly than the Ming. Previously, there were at least 100 ports in Fujian, Guangdong, Jiangsu and Zhejiang provinces

Small traditional shop managed by all family members during the Qing Dynasty (1644–1911).

that engaged in external trade, but eventually, the only contact point with foreign merchants became the port of Guangzhou lying far up the Pearl River in Guangdong Province. Furthermore, strict restrictions were imposed on the commercial activities of foreigners in Guangzhou. Foreign businesspeople were restricted to a small area of the city and could only trade through Chinese agents. This not only lost China the trading initiative but weakened its ability to resist aggression, while greatly limiting the views of Chinese people and enlarging the distance between China and the world.

Cultural authoritarianism was carried out. Imperial government itself is a kind of cultural autocracy, implementing obscurantism, which reached the peak in the Qing Dynasty. In the mid-17th century, for example, the Qing court prohibited scholars from establishing colleges, a free press was forbidden and only books related to imperial examinations were allowed to be published; those who published "anecdotes and obscene words" would be severely punished. In order to strengthen its cultural control, the Qing court regulated that the

Confucian classics should be instructed on the base of the annotations of the scholar Zhu Xi (1130–1200). Examinees for imperial examinations were required to write doctrinaire, priggish eight-part essays in accordance with these annotations. There was also a "literary inquisition" conducted in a large scale, which would sentence someone to death with book-phrases. During the reign of Emperor Kangxi, a man of letters named Dai Mingshi wrote a book *Collection of the South Mountain*, containing disguised anti-Qing sentiments. The book was suppressed and Dai and his lineal and collateral relations of three generations at or above the age of 16 were beheaded, in all several hundred people.

People are interested in the reasons why China declined in modern times just like the great Roman Empire. Of course, there are many reasons, but the followings are a few of the most commonly recognized.

The existence of a small-scale peasant economy fettered the development of productivity is a fundamental reason. The ancient civilization of China was a typical agricultural one, taking land ownership as the economic base and the autarkic natural economy as the main form. Peasants received land to cultivate from the landlord and turned in ground rent in either cash or crops. At the same time, they also engaged in cottage industry in order to make a living. This kind of production organization taking the household as the unit and an economy closely combining small-scale agriculture and a handicraft industry alleviated social contradictions and maintained low level development for a certain period; but, fundamentally, it went against the optimization of social division, expansion of production scale and elevation of the level of production techniques. The small-scale peasant economy meant people were conservative and lacked entrepreneurial spirit.

The long existence of an autocratic monarchical system is another important reason. In a certain period, the centralized autocratic monarchy system can accelerate social development, but it contains extremely obvious abuses that finally impede social progress. Among all the countries in the

Harvesting Rice, created during the Song Dynasty (960–1279).

world, the autocratic monarchical system of ancient China lasted for the longest time because the small-scale peasant economy provided fertile soil for it and Confucianism served as its moral pillar.

One noticeable phenomenon is that many ideologists emerged repeatedly through the various dynasties, but they worked to interpret Confucianism and merely served to entrench the autocracy rather than creating another school of thought. The monarchical power system had reached its peak in the Qing Dynasty, centered on the emperor supported by a rigid central bureaucracy. Hence, individuals could not gain full development and the whole of society lacked creativity and enterprising spirit for progress.

The policy of stressing agriculture and repressing commerce failed. There is a Chinese saying: "Food is the first necessity of the people and grains are the sources of food". During the Qing Dynasty, the population increased at a fast rate, reaching 250 million in 1750, surpassing 300 million in 1800 and hitting 430 million in 1850. With such a large population, agriculture was regarded as the foundation of the country and commerce as a mere supplement. The social status of business people was extremely low and they were despised for a long time. A person engaging in farming for a lifetime would be regarded as a good citizen, but a person in business was a shifty individual almost certain to be engaged in fraudulent practice. Due to this policy adopted by all previous dynasties, the government usually monopolized all industry that might have ordinarily been the preserve of merchants, such as salt, iron, wine and even the carrying trade and the handicraft industry. As a result, growth of folk commerce was painfully slow. Meanwhile, the commodity economy of China could not gain much development, so capital, technologies and talented people could not be properly utilized. This was the biggest difference in social development between China and the West.

Disasters Brought by Opium

Opium is not only addictive and a difficult habit to stop, but also endangers people's physical health, making them unable to work and can cause their death. Unfortunately it is this drug that has been closely linked with the fate of China in modern times. The developing course of China's history was impacted by opium and the relations between China and the outside world changed due to opium. The opium brought wars between China and Western countries such as the United Kingdom. Due to defeat in the wars, China ceded territory and gave compensation to Western countries and gradually fell into a semi-colonial and semi-feudal society.

Expansion by colonization in overseas areas was common among Western powers after geographic discovery. It was the United Kingdom which first

Opium smokers.

launched expansion by colonization in China and made use of opium as its tool. In the scores of years before the Opium War in 1840, China had always held a favorable balance of trade according to normal China-UK trade. At that time the products exported from China to the UK were mostly tea leaves and raw silk, and the goods imported from the UK to China were mainly wool fabric and metal products. In order to plunder more properties from China and obtain staggering profits, the British merchants came up with an idea involving this drug. They actually trafficked in large quantities of opium in China through illegal channels and attempted to further open the market in China.

Early in the 18th century the British merchants started to import opium to China and began their villainous drug trading. By the 1830s opium accounted for more than half the goods imported to China from the United Kingdom and its amount kept increasing year by year. In 1823 the amount was 9,035 boxes (about 65 kg of drug form each box), in 1830 the amount was 19,956 boxes, in 1836 the amount was about 30,000 and in 1838 the amount was about 40,000 boxes. It is estimated that by 1835 the people abusing opium across China were more than 2 million, and later with the increase in import, more and more people used opium.

The serious unchecked spread of opium seriously damaged the development of social economy in China and damaged the health of people, which aroused serious attention from the government of the Qing Dynasty (1616–1911). Emperor Daoguang of the Qing Dynasty (1616–1911) appointed Lin Zexu as an imperial envoy to Guangzhou, a center of foreign trade in southern China, to ban opium. Lin Zexu expressed his decision to ban opium, "If the opium is not banned, I will never return back. I swear to deal with the matter from beginning to end and there is absolutely no reason to pause the ban." With the support of the local government and people, on June 25, 1839, Lin Zexu destroyed opium captured from drug traffickers by burning it in public on the beaches of Humen. It is the "Destroying Opium at Humen" which is famous in the modern history of China.

Dashuifa SiteDashuifa Site of the Yuanminyuan Ruins.

The fight to ban opium in China aroused strong dissatisfaction from the United Kingdom. The British merchants required their government to launch a war immediately against China and force by arms the Chinese government to accept their conditions to open the market in China. In April 1840 the parliament of the United Kingdom passed the resolution to launch war against China and dispatched forces to brazenly invade China. It was the first Opium War and the Empire of the Qing Dynasty (1616–1911) was finally defeated. On August 29 1842 in Nanjing of Jiangsu, a city in the lower reaches of the Yangtze River, the representatives of the government of the Qing Dynasty (1616–1911) signed the first unequal treaty in the modern history of China, the *Nanjing Treaty*, with the British government. By means of this Treaty, the United Kingdom acquired many rights from China: China ceded Hong Kong to the UK (which was returned to China in 1997); China opened the five ports of Guangzhou, Fuzhou, Xiamen, Ningbo and Shanghai as trading ports; and China compensated 21 million tael to the UK (equal to one third of the financial revenue of the government of the

Qing Dynasty (1616–1911) in a whole year), etc. The UK also acquired consular jurisdiction, unilateral most-favored-nation treatment, inhabitation rights and renting-land rights in China by means of the *Humen Treaty*. After this, the United States and France also acquired the same rights as the UK by signing treaties with the government of the Qing Dynasty (1616–1911).

The Opium War was the first war in modern times between China and Western countries, as well as the beginning of the modern history of China. In the period of more than 100 years after this, China got in the position of falling behind and being beaten. Wars, ceding territory, compensation came endlessly. The major ones are shown as follows:

—The Second Opium War in 1856. In order to further open the market in China, the UK and France launched another invasion and China was defeated again. The allied forces of the UK and France attacked Beijing, the imperial town of China, occupied the Yuanmingyuan where they plundered without restraint and set fires. In June 1858 China was forced to sign the China-UK *Tianjin Treaty* and China-France *Tianjin Treaty*, mainly containing: foreign envoys residing in Beijing; opening ten additional ports as trading ports, i.e. Yingkou, Yantai, Tainan, Danshui, Shantou, Qiongzhou, Hankou, Jiujiang, Nanjing and Zhenjiang today; and compensating 4 million tael to the UK and 2 million tael to France. After this, China also signed the China-US *Tianjin Treaty* and China-Russia *Tianjin Treaty*, and the United States and Russia got the same benefits as that of the UK and France.

—The first Sino-Japanese War took place in 1894. China's next-door neighbor, Japan, launched an invasion of China and China was defeated. According to the traditional way of counting years in China, the year was Jiawu as called by the Chinese traditional calendar, so it is sometimes called the Jiawu War. The war was fought on the Yellow Sea in northern China and it was something rarely-seen at that time - a large-scale naval war. During the war the Beiyang Naval Fleet, which was thought to be an advanced navy run by

the Qing government was almost totally overwhelmed. This was an important historical moment for Japan and its modernization after the Meiji Restoration in 1868. It was a shocking moment for China - the first time that a neighboring island country, one which had learned and devolved from Chinese culture, defeated China. The whole country of China was astonished. In April 1895 in Shimonoseki in Japan, the representatives of the Qing government were forced to sign the Sino-Japanese *Shimonoseki Treaty*. This Treaty stipulated that: China would cede the Liaodong Peninsula, the whole island of Taiwan and its attached islands and the chain of islands of Penghu to Japan. After this unequal treaty, Japan would control Taiwan for half a century and the island would only be taken back by Chinese forces in 1945 when China won the second Sino-Japanese war. The *Treaty of Simonoseki* also stipulated that China pay an indemnity of 200 million tael to Japan (equal to three times the annual revenue of China at that time, and four times the annual revenue of Japan); that four additional trading ports be opened, i.e. Shashi, Chongqing, Suzhou and Hangzhou; and that Japanese people be allowed to operate factories in trading ports in China. The *Treaty of Shimonoseki* further emphasized the semi-colonial status of China.

—The Eight Powers Allied Forces War of invasion against China in 1900.

Eight-Power Allied Forces Invading Beijing (painting).

Eight countries of Russia, the United Kingdom, the United States, Japan, Germany, France, Italy, and Austria launched the war in order to maintain and expand their profits in China and the war ended with China's defeat again. The eight powers put about 100,000 troops together in the war; they not only occupied Tianjin and other important northern cities and regions but also occupied Beijing and forced Qing Government to escape to Xi'an. The Eight Powers Allied Forces slaughtered Chinese people unscrupulously in Beijing, plundered properties, burned down houses and made common people destitute and homeless, suffering from disaster. A great number of national classics, cultural relics and treasures were looted. In September 1901 the representatives of Qing Government signed treaties formally with representatives of 11 countries, i.e. the countries of the Eight Powers Allied Forces and Spain, Belgium and the Netherlands. As the year was Xinchou year in the traditional Chinese calendar, the treaty was also called the *Xinchou Treaty*. It involved China's compensation, establishment of "embassy regions" in Beijing and stationed forces inside embassy regions, allowing foreign stationed forces in 12 key strategic places along the railway from Beijing to Shanhaiguan, forever prohibiting Chinese people from founding organizations opposing foreigners, and changed the departments exercising general supervision over foreign affairs into the ministry of foreign affairs. The *Xinchou Treaty* further strengthened the Western powers' forces and impact on China. Regarding compensation, the Treaty stipulated that: the Qing Government make compensation of 450 million tael to all the involved countries, with customs duty and salt tax as guarantee and pay it off in 39 years. The annual interest was 4 percent and the total amount of principal and interest was 982 million tael. It is customarily-called the "Boxer Indemnity" (Gengzi Indemnity) (as the year when the Eight Powers Allied Forces launched the invasion was the Gengzi Year in the traditional Chinese calendar) and was the biggest indemnity since the Western powers invaded China. Hence the Qing Government's finances were exhausted, and the burden on Chinese people was greatly aggravated.

War Reparation Imposed by Foreign Powers on China	
1841	China paid 6 million taels of silver to the British threatening security of Guangzhou
1842	China paid 21 million taels of silver to the British
1858	China paid 4 million taels of silver to the British China paid 2 million taels of silver to France
1860	China paid 8 million taels of silver to the British and another 8 million taels of silver to France
1862–1869	China paid 400,000 taels of silver as compensation for the conflicts between missionaries and Chinese residents.
1870	China paid 490,000 taels of silver to France as compensation for the conflicts between missionaries and Chinese.
1873	China paid 500,000 taels of silver to Japan following Japanese occupation of Taiwan.
1878	China paid 9 million taels of silver to Russia
1881	China paid 9 million taels of silver to Russia for the recovery of part of Yili River area.
1895	China paid 200 million taels of silver to Japan following China's failure in war with Japan.
1897	China paid 30 million taels of silver to Japan for Japanese pullout of Liaodong Peninsula.
1901	China paid 450 million taels of silver to Western allied forces.
1922	China paid 66 million gold francs to Japan for its withdrawal from Jiaozhou of Shandong.
Source: *China Social History* by *Jacques Gernet*, published by China Tibetology Press in 2006 (first edition).	

During the September 18 Incident, the Japanese army attacked the Chinese armed forces in Shenyang.

—During the 1930s and 1940s Japan launched an all-around invasion of China. On September 18, 1931, the Japanese forces stationed in northeastern China attacked Shenyang City, which was the "September 18th Incident". In the following months, they occupied the three provinces of Liaoning, Jilin and Heilongjiang in northeastern China. On July 7, 1937, the Japanese invaders fabricated the Lugouqiao (Marco Polo Bridge) Incident outside Beijing City with the excuse that a soldier was lost. They launched an all-around invasion of China, large pieces of Chinese territory fell into the enemy's hands, the Chinese nation faced a crowning calamity and people suffered miserably. Once occupying a piece of land, the Japanese fascist invaders would adopt various brutal and outrageous methods and exerted their control by burning, killing, plundering and raping to the utmost. The Japanese invaders implemented a colonization policy in China, supported a puppet regime, carried out the exploitation by migrating,

and developed a cultural invasion and plundered resources and properties. Before the butcher's knife of the invaders, Chinese people did not submit but shared a bitter hatred of the enemy, united and attacked back. The Communist Party of China and the Chinese Kuomintang as well as various patriotic political powers and groups organized a broad anti-Japanese national united front, associated with the world anti-fascist forces of the United States, Soviet Union and the United Kingdom to conduct an anti-Japanese war of 14 years. On August 15, 1945 the Japanese invaders declared their surrender and Chinese people won the anti-Japanese war. It was the first victory won by Chinese people in opposing foreign invasion after 1840. China paid a huge national sacrifice to strive for the victory in the anti-Japanese war. According to statistics the casualties of Chinese people were more than 35 million and the property loss and battle consumption reached more than US$ 500 billion.

Seeking for Self-improvement

From the defeat in the Opium War, Chinese people had new understanding about the Western world. The defeat in the Opium War made some advanced Chinese people keenly feel that China had fallen behind the Western countries in aspects of technology and had to catch up and strive for self-improvement.

Lin Zexu was the first man to open his eyes to see the world in modern China. Before the Opium War, like most officials in the Qing Dynasty (1616–1911), Lin Zexu had little knowledge about the outside world. After being appointed to deal with the affairs related to opium, he began to learn and research the situations of the Western countries in order to find methods of resisting enemies, and then his idea changed and he proposed the idea of "learning the

First group of children sent by the Government of the Qing Dynasty (1644–1911) to study in America.

203

strong-points of enemies to overwhelm them." He organized people to translate foreign newspapers and books, including *Records on Four Continents* (the original book was published in London in 1836) written by a British man Hugh Murray, and introduced the Chinese people to the history, geography, economy, laws, military technologies, sciences and culture of the Western countries. Wei Yuan was another official of the Qing Dynasty (1616–1911) who advocated learning technologies from the Western countries after Lin Zexu. He opposed blind arrogance, criticized the conservative idea of refusing to learn the "good technologies" of the west, advocated using the Western technologies as reference, and definitely proposed the opinion of "learning good technologies of foreigners to overwhelm foreigners." On base of *Records on Four Continents* which the translation and compilation of was directed by Lin Zexu, he added a great deal of information and completed the famous *Records on Overseas Countries* which introduced in detail the geography, history and current situations of all the countries in the world and had a comparatively big impact on opening Chinese people's ideology and field of vision.

In the 1850s and 1860s a new crisis occurred in the rule of the Qing Dynasty (1616–1911). In 1851 a farmer movement leader Hong Xiuquan led the "Taiping Forces" in an armed struggle in Jintian Village, Guiping County, Guangxi in southwestern China and established the "Taiping Heavenly Kingdom" which grew quickly. In 1853 the "Taiping Forces" occupied Nanjing, changed the name of Nanjing to Tianjing, established a capital there, and formally established a power opposing the Qing Government. After 1860 the Qing Government suppressed the Taiping Heavenly Kingdom. In 1864 the Qing forces captured Tianjing and the Taiping Rebellion was defeated.

After the 1860s in the suppression of the Taiping Rebellion, a group of important officials of the Qing court such as Zeng Guofan, Li Hongzhang, Zuo Zongtang and Zhang Zhidong implemented the ideas of learning Western technologies proposed by Lin Zexu and Wei Yuan in order to maintain the power

Modern capitalist firms.

of the Qing court. They operated "foreign affairs", started the "self-improving new power", and defined the developing mode as "Chinese knowledge is the main part while the Western knowledge is put into practice." As they studied the West which was thought of as the world of "foreigners", this movement in the history of China is also called the "Westernization Movement" which lasted for more than 30 years.

——Establishing foreign-affairs organizations dealing with foreign countries. In January 1861 the Qing government formally established "yamen (government office) exercising general supervision over affairs of all countries" (Ministry of Foreign Affairs of the Qing Dynasty (1644–1911), in charge of such affairs as foreign negotiation, having trade relations and customs duty. Later Minister of Nanyang Trade Relations and Minister of Beiyang Trade Relations were established to take charge of the trade and foreign negotiations in the south (the region to south of the Yangtze River and the Yangtze River drainage area) and the coastal provinces in the north respectively. Meanwhile the Qing government

established the General Bureau of Taxation Affairs in 1861, appointing one main official and one deputy official. The positions were taken by Westerners who took charge of managing all customs duties. A British man named Robert Hart was in charge of the General Bureau of Taxation Affairs for 48 years.

—Running schools and sending students to study abroad. The modern education in China started from the "Westernization Movement." Since the 1860s the Qing Government had run a group of new-style schools teaching "Western languages" (languages of Western countries) and "Western arts" (technologies of Western countries) to cultivate various talents dealing with foreign affairs. In 1862, a school called "Tong Wen Guan" (School of Combined Learning) was founded in Beijing, and an American man Ding Weiliang (W.A.P. Martin) was appointed as its first president, and managed the school affairs for 32 years. According to statistics, officials of foreign affairs opened more than 20 new schools and cultivated a group of persons with abilities in foreign languages , engineering, telegraph, ships, mining affairs, weapons and medicine. The first group of students of modern China studying in Europe and the United States were sent in the course of the "Westernization Movement".

—Training new-style armies and building up military industry. It was held by foreign affairs officials that the ancient laws and regulations of China were much superior to the west, and only the "firearms" were inferior. By studying advanced foreign military technologies, China could become stronger. From 1861 to the 1890s, officials advocating the Westernization Movement operated more than 20 military factories (bureaus) across China, mainly producing guns, artillery and ammunition, as well as steel and iron and ships. The modern industry of China started from there.

—Running modern civil industries. Officials advocating the Westernization Movement combined "striving to become stronger" and "striving to become wealthy" with the latter one as the tenet. From the 1870s to 1890s officials advocating the Westernization Movement ran more than 20 civil enterprises, mainly in industries such as mining, metallurgy, and textiles and such causes as shipping, railway and telecommunication.

The Westernization Movement was the first time China studied the west after experiencing two defeats in the Opium Wars in modern times, as well as an industrialization movement within the system of the ruling group. As this movement was limited to the aspect of technologies, its limitation was very obvious. With the defeat of China in the First Sino-Japanese War, the Westernization Movement was declared bankrupt. The history made it clear that it was impossible to find the fundamental solution for China only by operating the Westernization Movement.

After the Westernization Movement, Chinese people really changed their views on the world. Before the Opium War in 1840 when Westerners came to China, the officials of the Qing Government were disdainful of them and would not want to have contact with them. They only ordered merchants to contact them. And those people contacting with foreigners were held in disdain by people. Due to lack of knowledge about outside world, no person of the Qing Government was willing to deal with foreign affairs outside of the country. The Qing Government did not send Chinese people to the United Kingdom and France as envoys until 1876. After scores of years of the Westernization Movement, the contacts between the East and the West increased and Chinese people changed their views on the outside world. In eyes of common Chinese people, Westerners gradually became "Yangren" (with a meaning of holding foreigners in esteem) from "Yiren" (with a contemptuous meaning).

Establishment of a Modern Country System

The Beiyang Navy operated by officials advocating the Westernization Movement with painstaking efforts was almost completely destroyed in the First Sino-Japanese War in 1894, and the Chinese nation was confronted with a severe crisis, which made some advanced Chinese people have further consideration on the developing direction of China: it was hard to become prosperous and strong only by learning Western technologies which could not change the fate of China from being beaten by others. It was a necessity to start with a system and carry out reform to establish an advanced country, hence the Hundred Days Reform and the Revolution of 1911 at the end of the 19th century and the early 20th century.

Liang Qichao.

The Wuxu Reform (Hundred Days Reform) got its name as its major activities occurred in the lunar Wuxu Year (1898) of the traditional Chinese calendar. It was an imperialistic reform and it tried to reform the autocratic system of the Qing Government to a certain degree like the "Glorious Revolution" in the United Kingdom and the "Meiji Restoration" in Japan. The decorum of monarchism was maintained while the parliamentarianism was carried out to divide imperial power and administrative power.

The leaders of the movement were Kang Youwei and his student Liang Qichao. They publicized the theory of Western society and politics, held evolutionism in esteem, and solemnly contradicted the feudalist obstinate thoughts and the people advocating the Westernization Movement which only advocated studying Western technologies without carrying out reform. It was hard for traditional Chinese culture and society to accept the reform of the thousands of years of an autocratic system. In order to make the theoretic basis for reform, Kang Youwei said in his works that the thoughts of civil rights, democracy and equality of the modern West and the political rules of parliaments and election were created by Confucius and dressed himself up as the true inheritor of Confucian orthodoxy.

In April 1895, Kang Youwei collaborated with the more than 1,300 successful candidates in the imperial examinations at the provincial level in Beijing to submit a written statement to Emperor Guangxu proposing to develop modern industry and implement the constitutional monarchy system, which was the event of "Gongche Shangshu" which had important impact on the modern history of China. The occurrence of the event showed that the intelligentsia started to become the mainstream in the movement to save the nation from extinction. The reforming proposal by Kang Youwei and others was supported by the Emperor of the Qing Dynasty (1616–1911) but was opposed by the obstinate and fogyish school of Empress Cixi who held the real power. The obstinate school represented by Cixi persisted in that "ancestral regulations cannot be changed", claimed that "they would rather the nation was subjugated than reform was carried out", and thought that "the theory of civil rights had a hundred harms without a benefit." On June 11, 1898 Emperor Guangxu issued the imperial decree of "Ming Ding Guo Shi" to declare the starting of reform. The reform lasted for 103 days until September 21 when Empress Cixi started a coup d'etat to abolish the "reform", so it was called the Hundred Days Reform.

The Hundred Days Reform ended in failure, but after the movement the modern democratic theory of the West began spreading in China. The failure of

the Hundred Days Reform also declared that in China it was impossible to carry out a constitutional monarchy like the United Kingdom or Japan, and the only choice was to put down imperialism by revolution in order to save China from extinction and establish a modern state. It was Sun Yat-sen and his revolutionary school that shouldered this historical duty.

Strictly speaking, the revolutionary movement to found a modern country in China started from Sun Yat-sen. It was the Revolution of 1911 led by Sun Yat-sen that put down the absolute monarchy controlling China for more than 2000 years and made a democratic republic the political choice of China.

Sun Yat-sen was born in 1866 in Xiangshan County (Zhongshan, Guangdong today) in Guangdong Province in southern China. This region was open to foreign countries very early and people had more contact with the outside world. The elder brother of Sun Yat-sen once went to Hawaii to develop and became an overseas Chinese capitalist. In his youth, Sun Yat-sen went to his brother and accepted a complete Western education supported by his brother, including natural scientific knowledge and social political theories. A will of "reforming China" came into being in his mind. In 1894 Sun Yat-sen associated with some revolutionary persons with ideals and integrity to found a revolutionary group, revive Chinese society, put forth the revolutionary proposal to "drive out foreigner aggressors, revive China and found a united government", and took an oath to put down the autarchy of the Qing court and establish a democratic republic.

From the end of the 19th century to the early 20th century, the movement to save China from extinction gathered force like a raging storm. "Guang Fu Hui (Restoration Society)", "Hua Xing Hui (the Society for the Revival of the Chinese Nation)" and other revolutionary societies emerged one after another and there came into being a requirement to found a national revolutionary party. In August 1905 Sun Yat-sen collaborated with Huang Xing and Song Jiaoren who were leaders of revolutionary societies to found "China Tong-meng Society

Portrait of Sun Yat-Sen.

(United League)" ("United League" for short, and the Chinese Kuomintang evolved from it) in Tokyo, Japan with "driving out foreigner aggressors, renewing China, founding a democratic republic and averaging land ownership" as its guiding principle. They set up a headquarters and nine branches inside and outside China, making it become a national revolutionary party. In his foreword to the official periodical of the Tong-meng Society, *Min Bao* (*Civic News*), Sun Yat-sen summed up the guiding principle of the Tong-meng Society and elucidated it to "the Three Principles of the People dealing with the questions of nationalism, democracy and people's livelihood". Nationalism covers two aspects, i.e. "driving out foreign aggressors and renewing China," to put down the court of Qing and make China an independent country; democracy covers "founding a republic", i.e. putting down the autocratic system and founding a modern Western democratic republic; and Principle of People's Livelihood covers "averaging land ownership", by which the land price was appraised and decided, after the success of revolution, the increased land price due to development of social economy was taken back by the state, and gradually the state would buy land from landlords. As the above-mentioned idea of "the Three Principles of the People" proposed by Sun Yat-sen aimed at putting down imperialism and founding a republic, it is also called the "old Three Principles of the People".

The founding of Tong-meng Society and the proposal of the idea of the Three Principles of the People indicated that a new stage of China's revolution was coming. After years of preparation in organization, thoughts and public

The first congress of the Republic of China (1912–1949) opened in Beijing on April 8, 1913.

opinions, at last on October 10, 1911 an armed uprising broke out in Wuchang (a part of Wuhan City), an important town in the middle of southern China, which aroused then the Revolution of 1911 across China (the year was Xinhai Year in the traditional Chinese calendar). The Revolution of 1911 broke down the domination of the Qing court by its swift and violent torrent. On January 1, 1912 after the election by representatives of 17 provinces, Sun Yat-sen took his oath in Nanjing and took the position as temporary President. He declared the founding of the temporary government of the Republic of China, viewed the year 1912 as the first year of the Republic of China and changed the Chinese calendar to the Gregorian calendar. Then a temporary senate was established as a legislative organ. At that time northern China was still controlled by the forces of the Qing court. In order to end the opposing situation between the north and south and establish a united republic state soon, the south conceded to the north and transferred the position of temporary president to an important minister of the

Qing court Yuan Shikai with the abdication of the Emperor of the Qing Dynasty (1616–1911) as the precondition. On February 12, 1912 the Emperor of the Qing Dynasty (1616–1911) declared his abdication. On April 1, Sun Yat-sen formally relinquished his leadership as temporary president. On the 2nd, the temporary senate decided to move the temporary government to Beijing instead of Nanjing as expected by Sun Yat-sen. At this point, in this old oriental country of China the absolute monarchy lasting for more than 2,000 years collapsed at last and a democratic republic with modern meaning began.

Then the south and north of China were under the control of different forces. The persons of the revolutionary party had their activities basically in south (with Guangdong as the center) and the warlord forces changed from the army men of the Qing Dynasty (1616–1911) were basically in the north (also called as Beiyang Warlord). In 1928 the Nanjing National Government united the whole country.

New Cultural Enlightenment Movement

The progress of any society is actually the progress in thoughts and culture. The development of thoughts and culture in modern China was accompanied by the movement of saving China from extinction. The course of saving the country from extinction was also the course of enlightenment.

The ancient thoughts and culture established on a base of natural economy had their rationality in previous history and played an active role in social development and progress, but fundamentally they did not suit the demands of the development of modern social productivity. In the society of absolute monarchy, people were oppressed gravely by regality, divine power, clan authority and husband authority, with no mention of freedom and equality. To break the old culture and advocate the new culture is the necessary demand for the modernization of China.

侯官嚴幾道先生

Portrait of Yan Fu on title page of his *Theory of Natural Selection.*

The Enlightenment of modern China started from the Hundred Days Reform at the end of the 19th century. The persons of the Hundred Days Reform viewed the introduction of modern Western thoughts and culture as an important content in publicizing the thoughts on reform and hoped to change the unenlightened situation of Chinese thoughts and views and cultivate people's intelligence. They translated and published a large number of books to introduce the Western theories on social politics and the most influential one was the book *Tian Yan Lun* translated by Yan Fu. The book's original name was *Evolution and Ethics* by a British biologist Huxley. In the book Huxley made use of Darwinism to explain the social development rules and the relations between people and held that the biological evolution rule of "survival of the fittest in natural selection" could also be used to explain the development of human history. In human society like living things, there are competitions between peoples and nationalities, and only the fittest one can survive. Such theory became the basis for promotion of overseas expansion policies adopted by Western powers, but in view of the position to save the nation from extinction, at the time of facing the crisis of being divided by powers, it could urge Chinese people to save the nation from extinction and survive. According to the theory, China can become strong instead of being weak only by reforming, or else it would be eliminated through selection.

During the Revolution of 1911, the revolutionists represented by Sun Yat-sen pursued the modern Western democratic thoughts as criterion and made efforts to publicize the thoughts, which aroused the cultural enlightenment movement with publicizing democratic republic thoughts as the core. They firmly pointed out in the historical condition that abolishing the autarchy and establishing a republic had become the general course of development and the popular sentiment, the revolution in laggard nationalities and states would select the advanced democracy out of necessity, and held in mind with confidence that the Chinese nation with thousands of years of history would never lack of the capability of adopting a democratic republic. Sun Yat-sen developed the Western

theory of separation of powers and proposed "constitution of five authorities" (adding examination and supervision authorities on the base of administrative, legislative and judicial authorities), with emphasis on selecting officials by means of examinations and on supervision of officials. After the founding of the Republic of China in 1912, Sun Yat-sen and other people made use of the state political power to make great efforts to publicize such ideas as freedom, equality and philanthropy publicly and legally and tried to establish a series of democratic constitutional government principles of the Western countries in the form of national fundamental laws by stipulating the *Provisional Constitution of the Republic of China* and made the democratic republic become the will of all citizens in the new country.

The Revolution of 1911 put down the monarch imperialism and put the thoughts of a democratic republic deeper in people's minds, but in a country with an autocratic cultural tradition of more than 2,000 years the way to a democratic republic was impossible to be smooth. In 1916 Yuan Shikai who had taken the position as President of the Republic of China publicly called himself Emperor of the "Chinese Empire" and went backward in history. He was suppressed by the national people and died upon apprehension after 83 days of dreaming of being emperor. It fully showed that it was still an important historical duty to completely eliminate the impact of old thoughts and culture.

With the May 4 Movement of 1919 as the symbol, before and after it, a group of radical democrats represented by Chen Duxiu, Li Dazhao, Lu Xun and Hu Shi held high the banners of "democracy" and "science" and launched a New Culture Movement to attack fiercely the old culture by running the magazine of *New Youth*. Then the enlightenment movement of modern thoughts and culture in China reached a peak.

During the New Culture Movement in the 1920s, radical democrats counted the dark aspects of Chinese society at that time one by one, stated the crimes of the autocratic system with profound grief and called on a generation

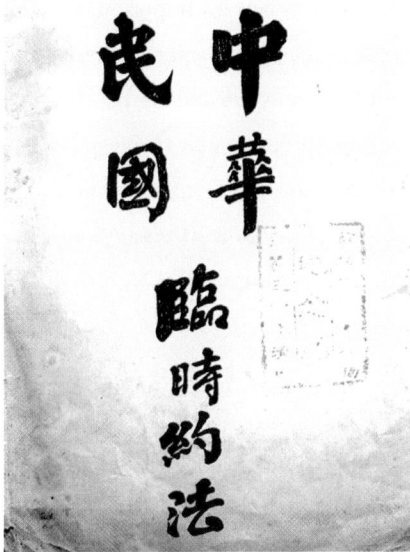

Photocopy of Provisional Constitution of the Republic of China (1912–1949).

Photocopy of *New Youth*.

of youth to fully understand the position held by China in the world and strive with self consciousness and the spirit of being realistic and continuing to forge ahead to conquer the evil in society. The soldiers of the New Culture Movement mentioned together the "human rights" and "science", advocated equality between human rights and scientific spirit, denied such fallacies as "regality was granted by gods" and "misfortune and fortune are decided by heaven god", and opposed the obscurity adopted by rulers. Aiming at the adverse current of worshipping Confucius and restoring ancient ways, Chen Duxiu pointed the critical cutting edge directly to the Confucianism, the supporter of an autocratic system. He thought that officials, sons and wives—all were attached to these things and had no independent personality according to the theory of "three cardinal guides", so such a feudalist system as a patriarchal clan and the "three cardinal guides and five constant virtues" were incompatible fundamentally with the democratic republic system.

Opposing old culture and advocating new culture was an important content of the New Culture Movement. Hu Shi and other scholars proposed the calling of "cultural revolution", put forth reforming on literary types and forms, opposed the classical style of writing and advocated writing in vernacular Chinese. Writer Lu Xun made use of his literary works to criticize the old Confucian ethic and morality. He published such stories and essays as *Diary of a Madman* and *True Story of Ah Q*, which made the anti-feudalism struggle of the New Culture Movement reach an unprecedented profundity.

Just at the time when the New Culture Movement in China showed its momentum like a raging fire, there came the news that the October Revolution of 1917 in Russia won victory and common people liberated themselves. It undoubtedly provided timely help for Chinese people who were seeking for truth in saving the nation eagerly, and it was not hard to imagine their happiness. So praising highly the October Revolution of Russia, publicizing Marxism and advocating taking the way of the October Revolution of Russia by China became the developing direction of the New Culture Movement. A group of intellectuals with initial Communist ideas emerged such as Li Dazhao, Chen Duxiu, Mao Zedong and Zhou Enlai.

Ups and Downs of National Revolutionary Movements

Although the Revolution of 1911 put down the absolute monarchy of the Qing court, the Western powers still colonized China and people's rights were not yet safeguarded.

The incidents damaging the republic occurred one after another. First there occurred the incident that the premier of the No.1 Party in the council of ministers was assassinated (in March 1913 Song Jiaoren, principal of the Kuomintang was assassinated and died in Shanghai), and Sun Yat-sen launched the "Second Revolution" (meaning completing the causes that had not been fulfilled by the Revolution of 1911); then in 1916 there occurred the incident that Yuan Shikai restored the imperialism and Sun Yat-sen and others launched the movement of protecting the country, meaning safeguarding the system of the Republic of China; and later there occurred the incident that Beiyang Warlords annulled the *Provisional Constitution*, and Sun Yat-sen and others launched the movement to protect the Constitution for the second time. In a short while, the systems of parliament, president and cabinet embarked upon a political venture, but they did not solve the issues of China and became the excuses used by warlords and politicians.

The above-mentioned facts made Sun Yat-sen feel the duties of Chinese revolution had not been finished and they should keep on striving. He summed up the lessons of revolution failure, used the successful experience of the Russian Revolution as reference and thought that the reason for the repeating emergence of revolution was the lack of a powerful and strong political party that could lead the revolution to victory. He decided "learn from Russia", adopted the "three great policies" of associating with Russia, associating with the Communist Party and

Site of the Huangpu Military School of Land Army of KMT.

assisting peasants and workers, and gave a new explanation to the Three Principles of the People, which viewed opposing imperialist aggression and "controlling monopoly capital and seeking development of the national capital" as the important contents. In January 1924, after plenty of preparation, the First National Congress of the Kuomintang of China was held in Guangzhou in southern China. At the conference Sun Yat-sen followed the mode of the Russian Communist Party to found the Kuomintang, finished the alteration on the Kuomintang of China, stressed "founding a country on the base of the Party" and "administering a country on the base of the Party", and absorbed the Communist Party members of China into the Kuomintang to start the first cooperation between the Kuomintang and Communist Party of China. After the First National Congress of the Kuomintang, Sun Yat-sen adopted the organizational system of the Soviet Union Red Army School, and founded the Chinese Kuomintang Military Academy in May 1924. As the site of the Academy was on Huangpu Island in a suburb of Guangzhou, it was also called the "Huangpu Military Academy".

From 1924 to 1927 under the cooperation and joint efforts of the Kuomintang and the Communist Party, the national revolutionary movement in China showed new development. Workers movements and farmer movements reached their climax, Guangdong revolutionary base was united, the National Government was founded in Guangzhou, and the National Revolutionary Army conducted a northern expedition. On March 12, 1925, the forerunner of the Chinese democratic revolution Sun Yat-sen died of illness in Beijing. The power of the Kuomintang had a vacuum due to the death of Sun Yat-sen, and all sects struggled for the leadership, and the views of opposing cooperation between the Kuomintang and Communist Party appeared to advocate "cleaning the party" (cleaning Communist Party members out of the Kuomintang). In April and July 1927, with the successive triumphant songs of the northern expedition by the national revolutionary army, Chiang Kai-shek and Wang Jingwei who held the military power and party power of the Kuomintang respectively began to clean the party, and the first cooperation between the Kuomintang and the Communist Party failed.

On April 18, 1927, the Nanjing National Government of the Kuomintang was founded. In April 1928 Nanjing National Government declared to keep up the northern expedition. In the first ten days of June, the National Government armies marched into Beijing, and the Beijing Government controlled by Beiyang Warlords for 16 years was tumbled. On June 15, Nanjing National Government issued a proclamation that China was united. On December 29, the local government of northeastern China declared to "submit to the National Government and change its banner." At that point the power established by the Kuomintang in Nanjing united China.

After Japan fabricated the September 18th Incident in 1931 and the Nanjing National Government adopted the policy of not resisting, large pieces of Chinese territory were occupied by the enemy, and the anti-Japanese democratic movements of Chinese people gradually ran high. Especially after Japan invaded

Soldiers of the Eighth Route Army fighting the Japanese invaders on the Great Wall in 1937. (Photo by SHA FEI)

northern China in 1935, the Chinese nation fell into a new crisis. On December 12, 1936 the patriotic generals of the Kuomintang, Zhang Xueliang and Yang Hucheng, initiated "armed remonstrance" and forced Chiang Kai-shek to resist the Japanese aggressors, which was the famous "Xi'an Incident". After the common efforts of the Communist Party of China and other parties, the incident was solved peacefully, which established the base for cooperation between the Kuomintang and Communist Party to resist the Japanese aggressors. On July 7, 1937 the Japanese aggressors launched an all-around invasion of China and the National Government declared war against Japan and accepted the proposal of cooperation between the Kuomintang and Communist Party suggested by the Communist Party of China, and then the second cooperation between the Kuomintang and Communist Party started. The battle field in China was a major battle field in the anti-fascist World War II, held down two thirds of the forces of Japanese fascists and strongly supported the anti-fascist war in Europe and on the Pacific Ocean. As the anti-Japanese war by Chinese people played an important role in the world anti-fascist war, when the United Nations was founded later China was selected as one of the five permanent members of the UN Security Council.

On August 15, 1945, the anti-Japanese war by Chinese people achieved final victory. Then the Communist Party of China and the Kuomintang conducted a vehement political and military struggle for establishing a democratic or an autocratic country.

Founding of the PRC
Led by the CPC

On May 4, 1919, a group of young students in Beijing started a demonstration in protest against the treasonable actions of the Beiyang government. Subsequently, a series of patriotic demonstrations broke out in many cities across the nation, leading to strikes of workers, shopkeepers and students. Thus was founded the epoch-making May 4 Movement in modern China. On that historic day, China's working class entered the political arena, and at the same time the Communist Party was founded as their representative. The May 4 Movement was led by the leaders of this Party, and their names were Li Dazhao, Chen Duxiu, Mao Zedong and Zhou Enlai.

Chen Duxiu and Li Dazhao were the original founders of the Communist Party of China, laying its earliest foundations in Shanghai and Beijing. On July 23, 1921, the first national congress of the Communist Party was held in Shanghai (although later, the Communist Party decided to make July 1 its official anniversary), at which 12 delegates representing approximately fifty party members participated. During the congress, they discussed the party program of the Communist Party and decided that its official title should be "The Communist Party of China". The historic founding of the Communist Party meant that at long last China's working class had its own political party, and the calamity-ridden China as a whole a new political hope. All at once the revolution in China had taken on an entirely new and significantly more favorable aspect.

After its birth, the CPC took on the task of building China into a real democratic republic, fighting against imperialism and feudalism together with the Kuomintang by promoting cooperation and forming a democratic united front. From 1924 to 1927, thanks to the efforts made by the Communist Party in firmly leading the worker-peasant movement, the national revolution under the cooperation of the Kuomintang and the CPC developed at great pace. However, after the 1927 purge of communists in the Kuomintang, the Communist Party-led revolution faced difficult and uncertain times. To restore the situation in their favor, the Communists, under the leadership of Mao Zedong, successfully established a method by which revolutionary bases were established in the rural areas, thus leading to agrarian revolution which itself became a platform by which control could be seized in the cities. For ten long years, from 1927 to 1937, the CPC, with its rural power-bases, found itself locked in confrontation with urban-dominating Kuomintang. However, in October 1934, the worker-peasant armed forces led by the CPC began the extraordinary and unprecedented large-scale strategic shift, the year-long, 25,000-li (12,500 km) Long March. It was during the March, in January 1935, that the leadership of Mao Zedong was established during an important meeting held in Zunyi of Guizhou Province.

In 1937, after the outbreak of the war of resistance against Japan, the united front between the CPC and the Kuomintang was reestablished in order

Site of the First National Congress of the CPC in Shanghai.

to fight more effectively against the common enemy, a truce that lasted until Japan's ultimate defeat in 1945. In the early days of the conflict, by analyzing the fundamental characteristics and the law of development of the Sino-Japanese war, the Mao Zedong-led CPC set out to demonstrate that only by launching a People's War using guerrilla tactics could China emerge victorious. The CPC correctly implemented the policy of an Anti-Japanese National United Front, developing the progressive forces, winning over the middle classes, and isolating the reactionary forces, thus protecting the fundamental interests of the Chinese nation and the Chinese people. Moreover, the CPC built up a series of anti-Japanese bases, and were able to establish fields of battle behind enemy lines —these actually became the principal theaters of conflict during the middle and later period of the war against Japan. This strategy pinned down Japanese forces and wiped out large numbers of Japanese invaders. Meanwhile, as the war progressed, Mao Zedong and his Communist Party comrades had also been improving the Theory of the New Democratic Revolution, the fundamental theory that would lead to the revolution in China. The theory stated that the revolution at this stage would be the New Democratic Revolution; upon the revolution's successful outcome China would become a new democratic country, but not a Western country or a socialist country.

In July 1945, shortly before victory in the war was finally achieved, the CPC held its 7th National Congress in Yan'an of Shaanxi Province. The CPC was by this time already a national political party that had over 900,000 party members, 1.2 million armed forces, and many revolutionary bases. The 7th National Congress of the CPC was already prepared for the ultimate and inevitable success of the Chinese revolution, but pointed out that this success was dependent on the abolition of the fascist dictatorial regime of the Kuomintang, practicing democracy, consolidating and expanding the anti-Japanese forces, finishing off the few remaining Japanese invaders, and, most importantly, rebuilding China as an independent, free, democratic, united, prosperous and powerful country.

After winning the War against Japan, and in spite of the common wish of the Chinese people to build an independent, democratic, united, prosperous and powerful People's Republic of China, the Kuomintang, under the leadership of Chiang Kai-shek, instead embraced a policy of civil war and dictatorship, and attempted to destroy the CPC-led people's army and its liberated areas. In its battle to safeguard the future of both the Chinese people and the Chinese nation, the CPC unfurled the banner of peace and democracy and threw itself into the struggle against the Kuomintang. In the month of June 1946, the Kuomintang's attack on the liberated areas brought about a full-scale civil war. The CPC, calling on all the progressive forces in the country, struck back, however, and managed to seize the military initiative. At last the strategically decisive battle was fought, the Kuomintang was defeated, and its leaders retreated to Taiwan.

The First General Assembly of the Chinese People's Political Consultative Conference

On September 21, 1949, the 1st Chinese People's Political Consultative Congress was held in Beijing, with delegates from the CPC and other non-CPC parties invited to participate. Mao Zedong chaired the meeting and announced, "The Chinese people, who account for one fourth of the world's population, have raised themselves up on their feet. The days when the Chinese people were considered uncivilized are now over." On October 1 of the same year, Mao Zedong declared on Tian'anmen Rostrum the founding of a the People's Republic of China on October 1, 1949 and the birth of the Central Government of the People's Republic of China. Henceforward, a brand new People's Republic of China proclaimed itself before all the people of the world.

基本路线一百年不动摇

Endeavors of the PRC and Reform and Opening-Up

Since the People's Republic of China was established in 1949, the Chinese people have enjoyed some success mixed in with setbacks and mistakes in the course of creating a modern nation. After arduous trials and tribulations, the CPC led the Chinese people to eventually create a road to modernization that was suited to national conditions, namely Socialism with Chinese Characteristics.

The year 1978 marked a turning point in the history of the PRC with the introduction of reform and opening up. Since that time, the Chinese people and the Communist Party of China have both undergone huge changes, and the relationship between China and the world has entered a new period of development.

Starting from Scratch

The establishment of the PRC heralded a new era in Chinese history. Chinese people celebrated the birth of the the PRC with pride and enthusiasm. But the new state was established on the basis of the old Chinese economy and culture and in a society of extreme backwardness. Chinese people commonly use the expression "poor and blank" to describe this low starting point.

If we look at the developmental level between the 1930s and 1940s, industry accounted for only about ten percent of the national economy, while agriculture and the handicraft industry accounted for more than 90 percent. At its inception, the PRC was a backward agricultural country.

In 1949, China had the largest population in the world; hence, on a per capita basis, its industrial and agricultural output ranked very low in the world.

Chairman Mao Zedong declared the founding of the People's Republic of China on October 1, 1949.

Industrial machinery production was almost zero. Large machinery such as aircraft, automobiles and tractors, could not be manufactured. Culture and education were backward. The illiteracy rate reached 80 percent. Average life expectancy was only 35 due to the low level of medical care and knowledge. The PRC also had to face the devastation left behind by the old regime.

At the beginning, the People's Government and the CPC as the ruling party put major efforts into consolidating political power and kick-starting economic development. By October 1951, the people's governments at provincial, city, county and township levels had been set up throughout the country. They began to progressively introduce regional ethnic autonomy for ethnic minority groups, ending long-term national divisions and turmoil. Economically, they confiscated the monopoly capital of old China and launched a State-owned industrial system (accounting for about 66 percent of the country's industrial capital) in order to establish a socialist State-run economy. At the time of the founding of the PRC, among the serious difficulties it faced were rampant speculative capital, chaotic

Peasants were given land to till during the Land Reform.

economic organization and runaway inflation. To cope, the State took various measures to combat speculation, enhance market management, stabilize the price system, and reunify national fiscal revenue and expenditure, so as to ensure continuous improvements to the financial and economic situation.

A nationwide land reform movement was launched. Old China's land system was practically feudal with landlords and rich peasants, who accounted for less than 10 percent of the rural population, holding 70–80 percent of the land. The landlords rented out their land and exploited farmers through land possession, acting as loan sharks. Land reform put an end to feudal land ownership, liberating productive forces so that more than 300 million landless farmers could gain access to farmland without exploitation, greatly arousing their productive enthusiasm.

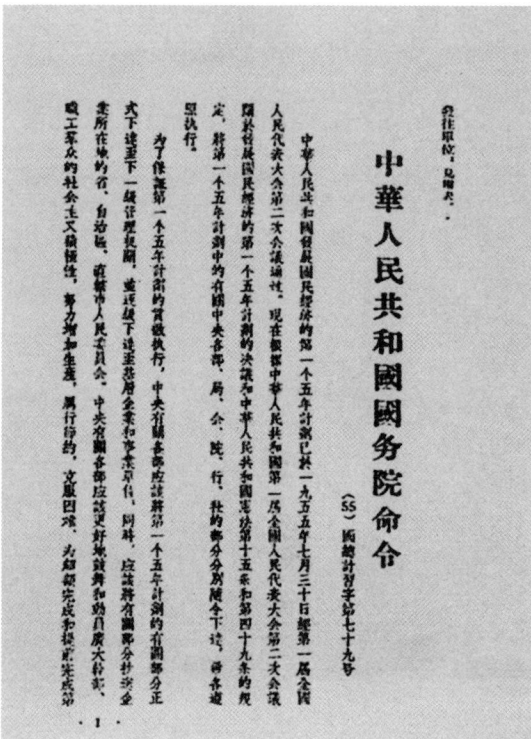

State Council decree signed by Premier Zhou Enlai on December 19, 1955 on the implementation of the First Five-year Plan.

A determined effort was made to get rid of the pernicious influences left over from the old society, including the social vices of prostitution, drug trafficking and addiction, and gambling. China had suffered a lot from opium addiction. During over 100 years following the First Opium War, opium smoking intensified and remained at epidemic proportions until the founding of the PRC. The number of drug abusers reached 20 million; nearly a quarter of local people in some places were opium addicts. By the end of 1952, opium smoking had basically been eliminated. In old China, visiting prostitutes was even more common and many rural girls were tragically sold into prostitution. The people's governments took effective measures to close brothels, banned prostitution and rehabilitated prostitutes.

After three years of hard work, the national economy had been restored and was beginning to show signs of initial development. In 1952, the value of industrial and agricultural output reached 81 billion Yuan, a growth of 77.6 percent since 1949, with an average annual growth rate of about 20 percent. The output of major industrial and agricultural products surpassed the highest levels before liberation. People's living standards generally improved. Compared with the average wage level in 1949, workers' wages had increased 70 percent by 1952, and farmers' income had grown 30 percent.

Based on this overall recovery in the national economy, the Chinese people launched a large-scale economic construction in 1953. According to Mao Zedong and the CPC, after the establishment of the PRC, there would be a very long transitional period towards building a new democratic society, strengthening national industrial development and ensuring a dominant State-owned economy. Socialism would be adopted in stages, as the government implemented nationalization of the private capitalist economy and began the process of agricultural collectivization. After three years of construction since the founding of the PRC, the CPC revised their original idea of how long it would take to achieve socialism. In September 1952, Mao Zedong proposed that the transition to socialism would be completed within 10 to 15 years. The main task of the

On September 15–17, 1956, the CPC's Eighth National Congress was held in the CPPCC Conference Hall.

transition was to basically complete national industrialization and the socialist transformation of agriculture, the handicraft industry and capitalist industry and commerce.

To achieve national industrialization had been the dream of many Chinese in the previous century. The Central Government put forward its first Five-Year Plan (1953–1957) to develop the national economy. It planned a program of large-scale industrial construction, and earmarked 156 major industrial projects including the construction of steel, aircraft, machine tools, automobile and petrochemical sectors. By the end of 1957, various targets had been significantly surpassed. The value of industrial and agricultural output amounted to 124.1 billion Yuan calculated in constant prices, a rise of 56.9 percent from 1952. The output of the main products of heavy industry grew significantly and the extremely backward situation of old China's heavy industry base was significantly transformed.

From 1953, socialist transformation occurred in all areas of agriculture, the handicraft industry, and capitalist industry and commerce. The overriding mission was to transform private ownership into something that belonged to the entire people; to transform labor-based private ownership of farmers and craftsmen into working mass collective ownership. By 1956, the socialist transformation of private ownership of the means of production was basically completed. In the national economy, the two forms of public ownership – ownership by the people and collective ownership – achieved a dominant position, and the socialist economic system in China was thus established.

In 1954, the first session of the National People's Congress was held in Beijing with 1,226 representatives drawn from the entire nation. Before that, representatives of the people at all levels of township, county, city, province (or municipal city directly under the Central Government) had been elected by the people and a People's Congress at all levels had been convened. The NPC formulated the Constitution of the PRC, discussed and adopted the report on the work of the government and elected new national leaders. Mao Zedong was elected Chairman of the PRC, Liu Shaoqi, Chairman of the NPC Standing Committee; and Zhou Enlai Premier of the State Council. The Constitution stipulated that the PRC was a people's democratic state led by the working class and based on an alliance of workers and peasants; that all power in the PRC belonged to the people; that the people exercised power through the National People's Congress and the People's Congresses at local levels; that the highest organ of State power was the National People's Congress, in fact that it was the only State organ exercising legislative power; and that the State Council, the Central People's Government, was the highest implementation organ of State power. On this basis, the PRC's political system was established.

In 1956, the PRC entered a new era of overall socialist construction. In September, the CPC held its Eighth Congress in Beijing. This was the first such gathering in 11 years. The meeting decided that the principal contradiction facing the people was between the requirements to establish an advanced industrial country and the reality of backward agricultural development, the contradiction

between the people's requirements for rapid economic and cultural development and the reality of an existing system unable to meet these needs. The main task of the CPC and the people was to focus their efforts on resolving such contradictions and thus transform China from a backward agricultural country into an advanced industrial one as soon as possible.

Setbacks and Mistakes in Exploration

It was an arduous and tortuous task to achieve rapid modernization in a country like China with its vast land, large population, backward economy and culture and uneven regional development. This was an unprecedented situation. In the 1950s, the CPC was still in the exploratory stage of establishing a socialist system yet they were well aware of the fundamental problem of how to build it.

With the revolutionary task completed, however, the State could enter into a period of overall construction. But there were many distractions posed by international and domestic affairs, in particular the Cold War and the need to consolidate the new regime. The CPC had to adhere to the theory of class struggle to guide its nation-building project and the pursuit of pure socialism. In 1957, the Anti-Rightist struggle came to the fore, but with hindsight, it was a bad mistake to allow national construction to be dominated by the theory of class struggle.

To enhance the CPC's construction, to overcome bureaucracy, subjectivism and sectarianism, in March 1957, the CPC decided to carry out a rectification campaign within the party to sweep away wrong ideas in order to better build a new nation. During the rectification campaign, the CPC attached particular importance to inviting non-Communist Party persons to become involved. Some leaders of the democratic parties and non-party democratic personages provided criticisms to the CPC. But there were also some people who took the opportunity to attack the party leadership and the socialist system. Mao Zedong believed a small number of right-wing elements wanted to overthrow the CPC leadership and overthrow the socialist system, and so the party had to urgently counterattack. Therefore, he launched the Anti-Rightist struggle. This campaign,

however, seriously damaged the people's enthusiasm for nation-building and, damaged socialist democracy, so that social and political life became at times chaotic.

The 1958, the "Great Leap Forward" movement was designed to shake off poverty and backwardness and promote the advance to communism. But it was a painful lesson in failure.

With the establishment of the socialist system and the first Five-Year Plan completed, large-scale construction was in full swing. The CPC thought it possible to speed up economic construction to overcome China's backwardness in a short time and achieve national prosperity in one great leap. To that end, it formulated a general line of socialism and launched the so-called Great Leap Forward along with the creation of people's communes. The contents of the general line were as follows: go all out, aim high and achieve greater, faster, better and more economic results in building a socialist country. This general line focused on the urgent demand of the CPC and the universal desire of the masses to overcome the country's economic and cultural backwardness, but also it was overly impetuous and over-anxious in its thinking. It placed excessive emphasis on the pace of economic construction, it exaggerated the people's will and the role of subjective efforts, and it tended to overlook or just ignore objective law.

In November 1957, Mao Zedong led the CPC delegation to Moscow to attend a meeting of world communist parties. During this meeting, the Soviet Union proposed that socialist countries catch up with and surpass the United States within 15 years. In regard to China, Mao Zedong proposed to catch up with or surpass the United Kingdom in steel output within 15 years. That winter, the Great Leap Forward movement began. In industry, it constantly raised steel output targets; in 1958, for example, steel output was set to double that of the previous year to reach 10.7 million tons. To achieve this goal, the whole country was forced to engage in iron and steel production. In agriculture, crop yield production targets were constantly raised; again, in 1958, the second Five-

Year Plan envisaged a gain in grain output from 250 billion kg to 350 billion kg. To achieve this objective, people's communes were set up in rural areas and small-scale agricultural production cooperatives were abolished. The rural people's commune was both a government and economic organization, the most prominent feature being "large in size and collective in nature" and certainly large in population, which in theory made it easier to undertake the mammoth tasks set out for it. Nationwide, there were more than 50 large communes each containing over 20,000 families. Collective in nature meant public ownership and the cancellation of individual household production, household sideline production and market trading; instead, there was a unified accounting system and communal distribution.

The blind pursuit of speed regardless of objective fact, and the fundamental disregard for the laws of economic construction, showed that the CPC had underestimated the arduous and long-term nature of building socialism in China.

Small steel-making furnace built in 1958 in Shizuishan, Ningxia Hui Autonomous Region.

The essence of the movement of people's communes was to establish a so-called universal equality, an average, fair and equitable society on the basis of developed productivity. It was an unrealistic fantasy beyond the capabilities of the nation. The result of the Great Leap Forward and the people's communes was not the development and progression of Chinese society, but rather retrogression. The Chinese economy declined sharply for three consecutive years and the people faced serious difficulties. Collectivization in China lasted more than 20 years until 1978, when the reform and opening-up policy was introduced.

From 1959 to 1962, the CPC adopted many policies and measures to correct the errors made earlier and to adjust the direction of the national economy. By 1965, through the efforts of both party and the masses, China's domestic economic situation had considerably improved. By the end of that year, calculated in real terms, the value of national industrial and agricultural output had increased 59.9 percent over 1957, with agricultural GDP growing 9.9 percent, and industrial output 98 percent. The consumption level of urban and rural residents increased 7.7 percent in 1965 compared to 1957. However, the mistaken "Leftist" thinking in CPC guiding ideology hadn't been fully corrected, and the mistakes of expanding the class struggle continued to develop, resulting in the emergence of a guiding ideology that saw "taking class struggle as the key link".

In 1966, when the national economy was showing good developmental momentum after years of adjustment, another major downturn occurred with the outbreak of the "cultural revolution" (1966–1976). These years would result in great suffering.

After more than 10 years of exploration and practice since the founding of the PRC, national construction under the leadership of the CPC had enjoyed considerable success, but also there were some hard lessons of failure. Based on a summary of these experiences and lessons, some senior Party leaders came up with a new understanding of China's development model and how to build socialism in the country, so that new working ideas begin to form. But this clashed with the ideas of Mao Zedong. He thought these different ideas revealed a class struggle between the proletariat and the bourgeoisie, and that certain elements in the inner sanctums of the CPC were promoting revisionism and taking the road back to capitalism. Thus, he felt China was in serious danger of a capitalist restoration. In order to ensure the CPC leadership remained truly Marxist, Mao determined to launch a public, comprehensive, bottom-up nationwide political revolution involving mass participation.

Mao Zedong always sought to ensure that China hewed to its own road of socialist construction based on his longstanding political ideals. But, because his political ideals and practices were somewhat divorced from the reality of the actual situation then prevailing in China, the desired results in strengthening the nation could not be achieved. Some people within the Party, acting out of ulterior motives, attempted to use the "cultural revolution" to further their own political ambitions. This was totally against Mao Zedong's desires and it resulted in great losses to Chinese society.

Reform Injecting Vigor and Vitality into Socio-Economic Development

After a chaotic decade of the "cultural revolution" (1966–1976), China's economy was brought to the brink of collapse in 1976.

Chairman Mao Zedong passed away on September 9, 1976. He was the principal founder of the Chinese Communist Party, the People's Liberation Army and the People's Republic of China. The CPC's second generation of central collective leadership with Deng Xiaoping as its core ended the precarious situation left behind by the "cultural revolution" and blazed a path of Socialism with Chinese characteristics.

坚持党的基本路线一百年不动摇

Portrait of Deng Xiaoping by Shennan Avenue in Shenzhen.

Finger prints of 18 members of Xiaogang Village in Fengyang of Anhui Province on an application. They did so to pioneer the rural contract responsibility system, ushering the rural reform in China.

The end of the "cultural revolution" provided China with a chance to return to the road of sound growth. At that time, a discussion on the problem of the criterion of truth was launched. Its central issue was what exactly is the criterion for judging what was right and what was wrong, the directives of the late Chairman Mao Zedong or actual practice? At last, all the members of the CPC unanimously agreed that Practice could only be the sole criterion for testing truth. Through this discussion, people's minds were emancipated from traditional socialism with rules and regulations and people's thinking became much less shackled to the cult of the individual. The Third Plenary Session of the Eleventh Central Committee of the Communist Party of China, convened at the end of 1978, rectified some mistakes in the guiding ideology of the CPC in the past and denied completely the erroneous theory and practice that took class struggle as the basis for all analysis and decision-making. At the same time, the session decided to shift the focus of the work of the Party and the State to economic development and implemented the historic decision to introduce a policy of

reform and opening up. It started a new period in China's modernization. After this, the State began to work to set things right, redress all unjust and false or wrong cases in all respects, and solve appropriately problems throughout the country which had been left over by history. In June 1981, "Resolution on Certain Questions in the History of Our Party since the Founding of the People's Republic of China" was adopted after discussion and approval at the Sixth Plenary Session of the Eleventh Central Committee of the CPC. The resolution drew definitive conclusions on major events in history, particularly the "cultural revolution", since the founding of the PRC, and evaluated Mao Zedong's place in history based on factual analysis.

While it set wrong things right and summed up historical experience, the CPC began to push forward the cause of reform and opening up. Since 1978, China has carried out a comprehensive reform from the countryside to the city and from the economic sector to all other sectors. Furthermore, China has opened up to the outside world in the coastal areas, along the rivers and the country's borders, as well as in east, central and west China. The unprecedented large-scale reform and opening-up fully motivated the initiative and creativity of hundreds of millions of people, and created a hugely successful historical transformation from a highly concentrated planned economy to a viable socialist market economy and from a closed and semi-closed state to a state open to the outside world.

China began to carry out the restructuring of the rural economic system at the end of the 1970s. Since 1982, the responsibility system of fixing farm output quotas on a household basis and work contracted to households rapidly spread across the countryside of China. The work contracted to households (later renamed the rural household contract responsibility system with remuneration linked to output) enjoyed great popularity among farmers. This form of agricultural production and operation established a direct link between farmers' labor and their benefit. This simple and easy system overcame the drawbacks of ideological distribution systems in the past and it has become the basic management system for agriculture in China since the initiation of the policy of reform and opening up. As a result, the household contract responsibility system not only aroused enthusiasm for production to the fullest extent, but also enabled China to make continuous gains in grain production. From 1979 to 1984, the average annual growth rate of the gross agricultural output value was 8.9 percent, while per capita grain production rose to 395.5kg in 1984 from 319kg in 1978, the output of major agricultural by-products quickly increased and people's living standard was improved considerably. The success achieved by the rural economic system reform solidified people's confidence in reform, laid a strong foundation and provided a good example for comprehensive reform of all other sectors.

China's urban economic reform started up at approximately the same time as the rural economic reform. Due to irrational structure arising from the planned economy that China had adopted for a long time, problems arising in the urban

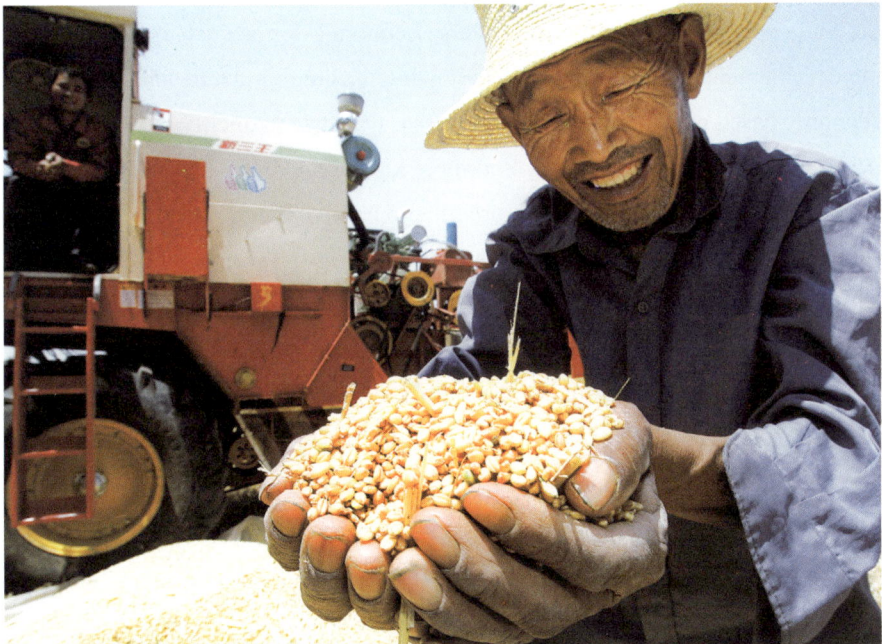

Farmers benefit.a lot from the rural reform.

economic reform were more complicated than those in the countryside. China adopted a system of pilot sites where reform could be hot-housed and assessed. This increased the decision-making power of enterprises. With the scope of pilot sites extending, the state embarked on some reforms in the managerial responsibility system and in the ownership structure of enterprises. These reforms gradually broke down the single ownership economy and realized diversified forms of economic organization. With the deepening of reform and opening up, and learning extensively from the beneficial achievements of human civilization, China kept exploring economic theory and modes of economic development which were suited to China's reality and actual developmental conditions in the 1980s and 1990s. In 1981, the State rectified incorrect notions that were traditionally not in accordance with the facts and confirmed that a market economy could exist in a socialist society. In 1982, it also put forth the declaration that the "planned economy was primary and regulation through the market was secondary." That is, while persisting in taking public ownership as the mainstay, the State was striving to develop diverse economic forms such as encouraging the development of cooperatives and allowing the appropriate development of an economy based on individual profit. In 1984, the State explicitly put forward the declaration that private economy and three kinds of foreign-invested enterprises (Sino-foreign joint venture, Sino-foreign cooperative enterprise, solely foreign-funded enterprises) were all necessary and beneficial complements to the socialist public economy. In 1992, it supported the establishment of a socialist market economic system which made market forces play an essential role in the allocation of resources under the state's macroeconomic control. In 1997, it emphasized the country would achieve a transformation in its economic system and in the means of economic growth as quick a time as possible. This effectively meant changing the planned economy to a socialist market economy and from a focus on extensive economic growth to intensive economic growth. Thus, China entered into an important period of development for deepening economic restructuring and speeding up the socialist modernization drive. Entering the

21st century, in terms of economic development, China has begun to strengthen macroeconomic regulation and control. By readjusting its economic structure and transforming the modes of economic growth, China has stepped up its efforts to promote reform and opening-up and self-renovation. Over the past 30 years, with the aim of establishing progressively a full set of economic theories and modes of economy, China had undertaken an omni-directional reform to state-owned enterprises and other sectors including finance, taxation, investment, pricing, foreign trade, commerce, labor, education, healthcare and transportation. At present, China's socialist market economy has taken shape initially and entered a new stage of constant improvement. The introduction of market competition mechanisms will inject new vitality into China's economic development.

When it carried out economic structural reform, not for a moment did China relax the reform of its political structures. It endeavored to establish and improve the political system corresponding to the socialist market economy system. By drawing on experiences and lessons from the "cultural revolution", the Chinese Communists, with Deng Xiaoping as their chief representative, started with the system of party and state leadership in their efforts to carry through reform of political structures. Deng Xiaoping deemed the systems' drawbacks to be bureaucracy, over-concentration of power, patriarchal methods, life tenure in leading posts, privileges of various kinds, and remaining thought of feudalism. He resolved to root these out, claiming that some serious problems which appeared in the past would arise again if the defects in our present systems were not eliminated.

Opening to the Outside World

China was once a closed or at least a semi-closed country. Despite the Silk Road, which served as a channel for cultural exchange, China, on the whole, didn't realize the necessity of opening up, especially in terms of the concept of national development and the benefits of communication with the outside world. Thus, again and again, China unfortunately let its opportunities of developing relationships with other countries slip away. Since 1978, however, the Chinese Government has specified opening up as a basic state policy and has unswervingly integrated China's development into the overall development of the world.

This process of opening up began with the establishment of economic special zones. In 1980, the first such zones were built in Shenzhen, Zhuhai and Shantou in Guangdong Province and Xiamen in Fujian Province in south and southeast China, with the term "economic special zone" broadly defined as an area receptive to foreign investment and advanced technology with the specific purpose of developing the national economy. After the instigation of economic special zones, a strong momentum for change and opening up was set in motion. A multi-directional and multi-tiered pattern was created covering a wide area. In 1984, a total of 14 coastal port cities were officially opened, including Dalian, Qinhuangdao, Tianjin, Yantai, Qingdao, Lianyungang, Nantong, Shanghai, Ningbo, Wenzhou, Fuzhou, Guangzhou, Zhanjiang and Beihai. In 1985, coastal economic open zones were set up in the Yangtze River Delta, Pearl River Delta, Xiamen-Zhangzhou-Quanzhou delta area in the south part of Fujian Province, Liaodong Peninsula and Jiaodong Peninsula. The intention was to develop the economy of inland China by accelerating the development in coastal areas. In 1988, Hainan Province was founded. It became the largest economic special zone

Lujiazui in the Shanghai Pudong Area today.

in China. By then, a vast opened-up area had been formed, including Hainan Province, five economic special zones, fourteen coastal open cities, three coastal open zones and two opened peninsulas located all the way from the south to the north of the country. In the following decade, China accelerated the pace of opening up. 1990 saw the official opening of Pudong New District in Shanghai. Within only a brief period of hard work, an export-oriented, multi-functional and modern district emerged spectacularly on the horizon, stimulating the economic development of Shanghai and other regions in the Yangtze River Delta, and even having an effect the entire length of the Yangtze River.

In the spring of 1992, Deng Xiaoping, the general architect of China's reform, went to Wuchang in central China, Shenzhen and Zhuhai in south China and Shanghai in the east, and delivered the now famous speech as a result of his inspections, during which he outlined his vision of sticking to the

path of socialism with uniquely Chinese characteristics. A key point focused on accelerating the pace of reform and opening up by grasping the best opportunities and concentrating efforts on economic development. Henceforth, the third generation leaders of CPC, headed by Jiang Zemin, led the next stage of China's reform and opening up. In 1992, some border cities in northern China were opened, including Heihe, Suifenhe, Huichun and Manzhouli. In the same year began the construction of tax-free zones in some of the coastal open cities. This is a preferential policy that accords with international conventions but works with a greater degree of flexibility than the economic special zones. Meanwhile, nearly 60 cities, counties and towns were granted approval to be opened-up and a further 10 major center cities along the Yangtze River were all given the go-ahead to solicit foreign investment and trade. As of the late 1990s, a multi-directional and multi-tiered pattern of opening up had been created covering the broadest possible area.

On November 10, 2001, after 15 years of negotiation, China's accession to the World Trade Organization was agreed unanimously through deliberation of the fourth WTO Ministerial Conference held in Doha, the capital of Qatar. This played an extremely important role in the process of China's opening-up to the outside world. Being a WTO member helps China to maximize its potential in the global market place, turning its regional opening up policy towards a multi-directional one, extending the traditional market economy to embrace the modern service industry, and increasing transparency and regulating the market access conditions.

Attracting foreign direct investment (FDI) is a basic element of the fundamental state policy of opening up. It has played an important role in promoting China's economic development and shaping the modern economy. Up to the first half of 2012, foreign investment had resulted in over 745,000 enterprises in China, covering virtually all sectors including agriculture, manufacturing and service industries. In 2012, China has, in total, attracted more

Contribution of Foreign-Funded Businesses to China's Import-Export Trade (2007–2012)						
	2007	**2008**	**2009**	**2010**	**2011**	**2012**
Import-export trade volume (US$ 100 million)	21,738	25,616	22,072	29,728	36,421	38,668
Foreign-funded businesses	12,549	14,106	12,174	16,003	18,601	18,939
Proportion (%)	57.7	55.1	55.2	53.8	51.1	49.0
Source: China National Bureau of Statistics.						

than US$ 1.3 trillion of foreign direct investment, ranking it the number one among all developing countries over the past 20 years. In 2011, industrial added value made by foreign-invested enterprises reached 22 trillion Yuan, accounting for 26.1 percent of the total; and tax revenue paid by foreign-invested enterprises stood at 1963.8 billion Yuan, taking up nearly 20.5 percent of the total. By the end of 2011, these enterprises had directly employed more than 45 million people, or 14 percent of the total workforce in all Chinese cities and towns.

Attracting foreign investment both actively and rationally has resulted in many gains. They include: effectively making up the domestic construction fund shortage; technological advancements; transference of management mode and experiences; the introduction of modern concepts of circulating and marketing; and the implementation of international competition mechanisms, international regulations and concomitant international standards. In short, the pace of change was greatly speeded up in the formation of China's new open economy, while its investment actively and effectively also helped the Chinese population to

broaden their international perspectives and free themselves from antiquated ideas and concepts.

Beijing successfully hosted the 29th Summer Olympic Games in August, 2008. It was the first time China hosted an Olympic Games, and International Olympic Committee (IOC) President Jacques Rogge said it is a real incomparable Olympic Games. The Beijing Olympic Games' theme slogan is "One World, One Dream", which expresses the beautiful dream shared by the Chinese people and the people of other parts of the world in owning a beautiful home, sharing the achievements, and working hard together to create a better future. On April 30, 2010, the 41st Session of the World Expo opened in Shanghai. It officially began on May 1 and closed on October 31. The theme of the Shanghai World Expo is "Better City, Better Life". This is China's another international event after the Beijing Olympic Games. Both events show a new stage of relationship between China and the world at large.

Creating a New Miracle in Economic and Social Development

Since 1978 China's economy has developed quickly, the society has advanced comprehensively and the construction of modernization has achieved great accomplishments due to continuously deepened reform and expanded opening-up.

World Ranking of China's Major Industrial and Agricultural Production in 1978 and 2012					
Projects	Unit	1978		2012	
		Production	Ranking	Production	Ranking
Cereals	10,000 tons	26546	2	53,935	1 ★
Cotton	10,000 tons	217	3	684	1 ★
Rapeseeds	10,000 tons	187	2	1,401	2 ★
Pork	10,000 tons	856	3	8,387	1 ★
Steels	10,000 tons	3178	5	72,388	1
Coal	10,000 tons	6	3	36.5	1
Crude oil	10,000 tons	10405	8	20,748	4
Power generation	100 million kWh	2566	7	49,876	1
Cloth	100 million meters	110	1	849	1
Cement	10,000 tons	6524	4	220,984	1
Chemical fertilizer	10,000 tons	869	3	6832	1 ★
TV sets	10,000 sets	52	8	12,824	1
Source: China National Bureau of Statistics. ★ means 2011 ranking.					

China's GDP has increased from US$ 140 billion in the early period of the reform and opening-up to US $9.43 trillion in 2013, with the average annual rate of increase above 9.6 percent. In this aspect China is listed as second in the world, rising from the fifteenth. The GDP per capita increased from less than US$ 200 in 1978 to US$ 6,750 in 2013. The production of some important products has leaped number one in the world.

China's foreign trade volume increased from US$ 20.6 billion in the early period of opening up to US$ 4.16 trillion in 2013, listed as number 2 rising from

Comparison Between China and World Top 10 in GDP in 2006 and 2012 Unit: US$ 100 million						
Ranking	2006			2012		
	Countries and Regions	GDP	Proportin of world GDP(%)	Countries and Regions	GDP	Proportin of world GDP(%)
1	USA	132,446	27.5	USA	156,848	21.9
2	Japan	46,593	9.1	China	82,270	11.5
3	Germany	28,970	6.0	Japan	59,640	8.3
4	China	26,301	5.5	Germany	34,006	4.7
5	UK	23,737	4.9	France	26,087	3.6
6	France	22,316	4.6	UK	24,405	3.4
7	Italy	18,526	3.8	Brazil	23,960	3.3
8	Canada	12,691	2.6	Russia	20,220	2.8
9	Spain	11,280	2.5	Italy	20,141	2.8
10	Brazil	8,820	2.2	India	18,248	2.5
Source: International Monetary Fund WEO database.						

No. 29 in the world. Since 2002 the growth of foreign trade has been above 20 percent for five successive years. From 2002 to 2004 the total trade volume rose every year; in 2002 it was listed as No. 5 in the world, in 2003 it rose to No. 4, in 2004 it exceeded Japan and listed as No. 3 in the world, and in 2006, due to quick growth, it approached Germany which was listed as No.2. By the end of 2013, the national foreign exchange reserves reached US$ 3.82 trillion, exceeding Japan and leaping to number one in the world.

People's living standard has been enhanced continuously, from solving the issues related to enough food and clothing to becoming comparatively well-off and marched on to a fairly comfortable life on the whole. Since 1978 the per-capita disposable income of urban residents has multiplied by more than 70 times; the per-capita net income for rural residents has multiplied by nearly 60 times; the number of people living in poverty has decreased from 250 million to 23 million in 2006. At the end of 2011, China had increased poverty alleviation allowances from 1,274 Yuan per person per year to 2,300 Yuan. According to the new stipulation, people eligible for the State subsidies increased to about 120 million in number. As of 2013, the number of people living under poverty line reduced to 82.49 million. This means some 40 million people have got rid of poverty in two years.

Since 1978, the Engel coefficient of urban families decreased sharply to 35 percent in 2013, a 20-plus percentage points fall. The family Engel coefficient of rural residents was 37.7 percent, a decline of about 30 percentage points. At present, China has 1.23 billion mobile phone users and 0.6 billion Internet users, both ranking first in the world; automobile consumption stays after the United States, ranking second in the world.

The undertakings of science, technology and education have developed quickly. From 2001 to 2005, the expenditure on research and development and experiments across China was 820.3 billion Yuan, a proportion of 1.16 percent of the GDP of the same period, higher than the average level of 0.7 percent in

developing countries. In 2011 expenditure in these fields reached 861 billion Yuan, or 1.83 percent of the GDP. In 2013, the figure rose to 1,190.6 billion Yuan, a proportion of over 2 percent of the GDP. However, this is still low when compared to the figure in developed countries (5 percent). Though low, the increase in this regard is impressive.

At present the number of professional technical staff and persons engaged in scientific research in China is listed as number one in the world. At present, China leads the world in number of technical workers and researchers.

By 2009, the overall enrollment rate of compulsory education exceeded 99.7 percent, and the gross enrollment ratio for secondary school education and higher education respectively was 85 percent and 30 percent.

Medical treatment and health care shared by Chinese residents exceeds the

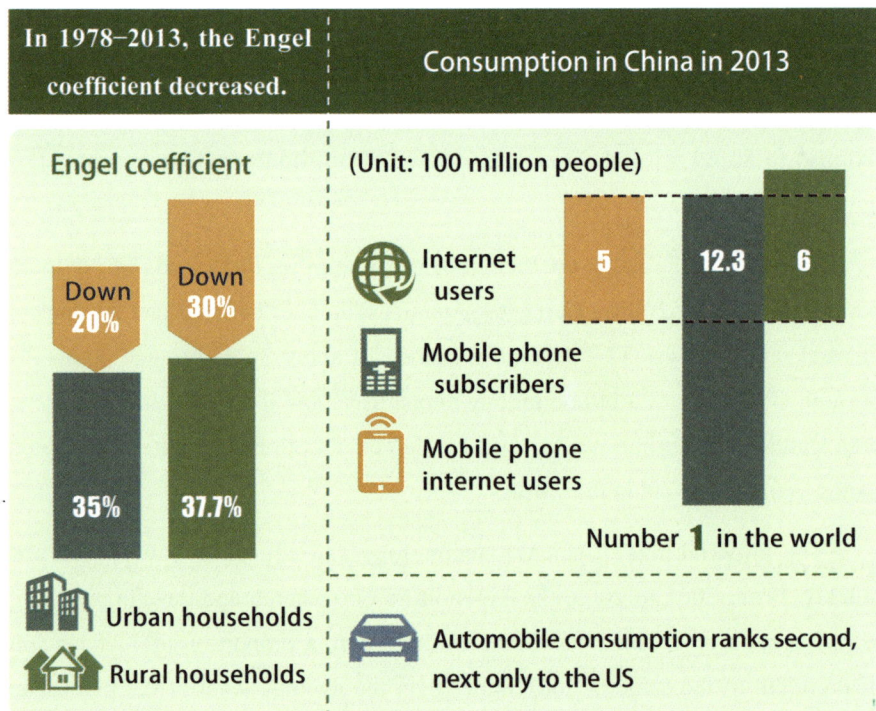

In 1978–2013, the Engel coefficient decreased.	Consumption in China in 2013

Engel coefficient

Down **20%**

Down **30%**

35%

37.7%

🏢 Urban households

🏠 Rural households

(Unit: 100 million people)

🌐 Internet users   5   12.3   6

📱 Mobile phone subscribers

📱 Mobile phone internet users

Number **1** in the world

🚗 Automobile consumption ranks second, next only to the US

world average. At present there are 970,000 medical institutions, complete with 7.18 million doctors of various types and 6.18 million hospital and clinic beds, all listed as number one in the world. The pilot range for a new rural cooperative medical service system was expanded to 2,489 counties (cities, prefectures), with the participation rate reaching 99 percent. The State subsidizes 12.293 million urban residents with financial difficulties to take part in medical insurance. By 2010, the expected life-span per capita is above 74.8 years, higher than the world average level 69.6 years; the infant mortality rate dropped from 200 per thousand before the birth of the People's Republic of China in 1949 to 13.9 per thousand in 2010; and the mortality rate of women in child-birth dropped from 1,500 out of 100,000 in 1949 to 30 out of 100,000. All these indexes are listed at the top among developing countries.

Healthcare Makes Great Progress

Over **970,000** medical and health institutions

7.18 million doctors

6.18 million hospital beds

2489 counties (cities, districts) implement the new rural cooperative medical system

New rural cooperative medical participation rate was **99.0%**

Some **12,293** million poor citizens receive government allowances in participating in medical insurance

Some **41,325** million poor rural people receive government allowances in participating in medical insurance

Educational Development in China in 2013 Unit: 10,000 people			
Various kinds of education	Enrolment	In-school students	Graduates
Graduates	61.1	179.4	51.4
Ordinary higher education	699.8	2,468.1	638.7
Secondary vocational education	698.3	1,960.2	678.1
Ordinary high schools	822.7	2,435.9	799.0
Middle schools	1,496.1	4,440.1	1,561.5
Primary schools	1,695.4	9,360.5	1,581.1
Special education	6.6	36.8	5.1
Source: China National Bureau of Statistics.			

The social security level in China has also been enhanced continuously. In towns 20.613 million residents have received the minimum living guarantee from the government. In rural areas 53.821 million rural residents have received the minimum living guarantee from the government.

China's economic and social development has enhanced China's international competitiveness year on year. The *World Competitiveness Year Book of 2006* compiled by the International Institute for Management Development, Lausanne, Switzerland has since 1994 been evaluating China's international competitiveness ever since 1994, putting China at number 34 then. In 2006, China's ranking rose from number 31 to number 19. In 2007, of the 55 countries and regions in the world, China ranked number 15 in terms of international competitiveness. In 2013, China's ranking moved to number 21, compared to number number 23 in 2012.

Building a Democratic Country Under the Rule of Law

In the past 100-odd years, Chinese people had made unremitting efforts for democracy, freedom and equality. Due to different national situations, the Chinese people chose the path of building a socialist democratic legal system with Chinese characteristics under the leadership of the Communist Party of China.

Since the adoption of the reform and opening-up policy toward the end of 1970s, China has entered a new era of developing socialist democracy and building a socialist country under the rule of law. The national democratic systems such as the system of people's congress, the system of multi-party cooperation and political consultation under the leadership of the Communist

Democracy and the rule of law publicity activities.

Party of China, the system of regional national autonomy and the system of grass-roots people autonomy have been developed and improved, the basic rights of citizens are respected and safeguarded, the Party's democratic governance capability has been further enhanced, the government's democratic administrative capability has been strengthened, and the construction of the judicial democratic system has been promoted continuously. The reform of the political system has been advanced unceasingly, and the reform on the state's leadership system, legislation system, administrative system, decision-making system, judicial system, personnel system and supervision and restriction system have had

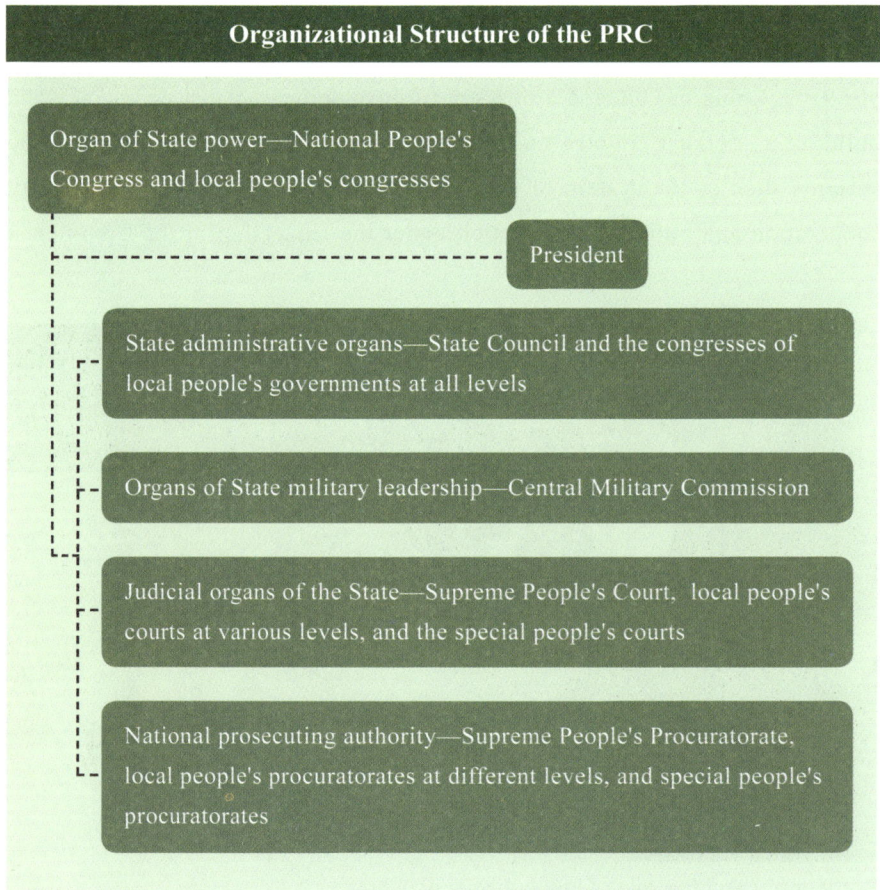

Organizational Structure of the PRC

Organ of State power—National People's Congress and local people's congresses

President

State administrative organs—State Council and the congresses of local people's governments at all levels

Organs of State military leadership—Central Military Commission

Judicial organs of the State—Supreme People's Court, local people's courts at various levels, and the special people's courts

National prosecuting authority—Supreme People's Procuratorate, local people's procuratorates at different levels, and special people's procuratorates

obvious effect. With the guiding aim of carrying out the rule of law and building a socialist country under the rule of law, the construction of institutions, standards and procedures for the socialist democracy has been strengthened continuously, the Constitution-centered socialist law system with Chinese characteristics has been formed basically, and there are laws to follow in the major aspects of political, economic and social life in the country.

According to its own national situation, China adopts the unicameral system instead of the bicameral system adopted by Western countries. In China people exercise the national power through the National People's Congress and local people's congresses at all levels. All citizens of China who have reached the age of 18 have the right to vote and stand for election, regardless of nationality, race, sex, occupation, family background, religious belief, education, property status or length of residence, except persons deprived of political rights according to law. There are more than 2.8 million deputies in all the people's congresses at all levels across China. The deputies have the right to put forth proposals, examine and discuss all proposals and reports, and vote on all proposals according to law, and may not be called to legal account for their speeches or votes at all meetings

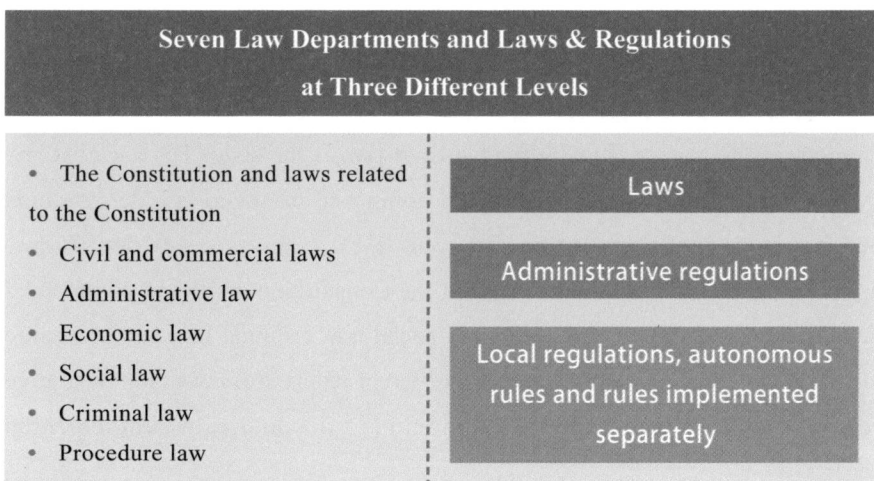

Seven Law Departments and Laws & Regulations at Three Different Levels	
• The Constitution and laws related to the Constitution • Civil and commercial laws • Administrative law • Economic law • Social law • Criminal law • Procedure law	Laws Administrative regulations Local regulations, autonomous rules and rules implemented separately

Contemporary Chinese law system.

of the people's congress. In China all administrative, judicial and procuratorial organs of the state are created by the people's congresses to which they are responsible and under whose supervision they operate. The major issues of the state are decided by the people's congresses. Administrative organs are in charge of implementing the laws, resolutions and decisions passed by people's congresses. Courts and procuratorates shall exercise respectively judicial and procuratorial power independently and are not subject to interference by administrative organs, public organizations or individuals. The functions and powers exercised by people's congresses mainly include four items: legislation, supervision, appointment and removal of personnel and decision-making on major issues.

Since the adoption of reform and opening-up in 1978, the National People's Congress and its Standing Committee have stipulated more than 240 laws currently in effect, the State Council has stipulated more than 690 administrative regulations, local people's congresses at different levels and their standing committees have stipulated more than 8600 local regulations currently in effect, and the people's congresses of national autonomous regions have stipulated more than 600 autonomous rules and rules implemented separately. The socialist law system with Chinese characteristics has been formed basically, in which the Constitution holds the core and commanding position. The Constitution prescribes the political system, economic system and citizens' rights and freedom of the state and is the fundamental law of the state. The socialist law system with Chinese characteristics is composed of seven law departments and laws and regulations at three different levels. The seven law departments are the Constitution and laws related to the Constitution, civil and commercial laws, administrative law, economic law, social law, criminal law, and procedure law. The laws and regulations at three different levels are: laws, administrative regulations, local regulations, autonomous rules and rules implemented separately.

The Fifth Session of the Tenth of Zhejiang Provincial Committee of the CPPCC, was concluded in the Provincial Great Hall on January 15, 2012.

The system of political parties is decided by the nature and conditions of a state. China's system of political parties is different from both the two-party or multi-party system adopted by the Western countries and the one-party system adopted by some countries. It is a system of multi-party cooperation and political consultation under the leadership of the Communist Party of China. At present there are nine political parties in China. Besides the Communist Party of China, they include the Revolutionary Committee of the Chinese Kuomintang, China Democratic League, the China Democratic National Construction Association, the China Association for Promoting Democracy, Chinese Peasants and Workers Democratic Party, China Zhi Gong Dang, Jiu San Society and Taiwan Democratic Self-Government League. As most of these political parties were founded during the Anti-Japanese War (1937–1945) by Chinese people and the Liberation War (1946–1949) for striving for national liberation and democratic freedom, they are also called "democratic parties". The political parties system of China is

distinctively characterized by: multi-party cooperation under the leadership of the Communist Party of China, and the Communist Party of China in power with multiple parties participating in the administration of state affairs. All the democratic parties are intimate friend parties and parties participating in the administration of state affairs in unity and cooperation with the Communist Party of China, instead of opposition parties. All the democratic parties participate in the state political process, the consultation on the major policies and guidelines and leaders of the state, the management of state affairs, and the stipulation and implementation of state guidelines, policies, laws and regulations. The Chinese People's Political Consultative Conference is a broadly representative organization of the untied front, an important organ of multi-party cooperation and political consultation under the leadership of the Communist Party of China and an important form which carries forward democracy in the political life of China.

China is a unitary multi-national state today, and there are 56 identified ethnic groups affirmed by the Central Government. Among them the Han ethnic group has the largest population and the other 55 ethnic groups have less population and are customarily called ethnic minorities. According to the Sixth National Census in 2010, the total population of the 55 ethnic minorities is 113.79 million, occupying 8.49 percent of the total population of China. The multi-national states in the world have different modes of dealing with national issues. In accordance with its historical development, cultural characteristics, national relations and distribution of ethnic groups, China adopts regional national autonomy. Regional national autonomy means that under the unitary state leadership, regional autonomy is adopted and autonomous organs are established to exercise autonomous power in the places the ethnic minorities inhabit. The national autonomous areas are divided into three levels of autonomous regions, autonomous prefectures and autonomous counties. At present 155 national autonomous areas are established across China, including five autonomous regions, 30 autonomous prefectures and 120 autonomous counties. 44 of the

55 ethnic minorities set up autonomous areas and the population of the ethnic minorities with regional autonomy is 71 percent of the total population of ethnic minorities. Meanwhile the state has set up 1,173 national townships in places ethnic minorities inhabit as supplement to the national autonomous areas.

Among the 1.36 billion population of China more than 670 million people live in rural areas. How to enlarge and develop the grass-roots democracy in rural areas and enable peasants to really hold the position as masters of the country and fully exercise their democratic rights is a significant question in the construction of democratic politics in China. After years of exploration and practice, the Communist Party of China has led hundreds of millions of peasants on the path to grass-roots democratic political construction in rural areas that accord with the national situation of China, implementing villagers' self-government. The

Sketch Map of the Ethnic Autonomous Regions in China

Heilongjiang Province

Jilin Province

Liaoning Province

Xinjiang Uygur Autonomous Region

Inner Mongolia Autonomous Region

Gansu Province

Beijing

Tianjin

Hebei Province

Shanxi Province

Shandong Province

Qinghai Province

Shaanxi Province

Henan Province

Jiangsu Province

Anhui Province

Shanghai

Tibet Autonomous Region

Sichuan Province

Chongqing

Hubei Province

Zhejiang Province

Hunan Province

Jiangxi Province

Guizhou Province

Fujian Province

Yunnan Province

Guangxi Zhuang Autonomous Region

Guangdong Province

Taiwan Province

Hong Kong Special Administrative Region

Macao Special Administrative Region

Hainan Province

South China Sea Islands

Ethnic minority autonomous regions

Other provinces and autonomous regions

Distribution of Autonomous Regions in China

On September 2, 2009, people with Zhulin Village in Ximei Town, Suining City, Sichuan Province, met to elect the Villagers Supervision Committee.

villagers' self-government organization is villagers committees whose members are elected directly by villagers. In the course of the election, the candidates for membership in a villagers committee are nominated and voted for by villagers and the voting result is made public on the spot. Villagers are ebullient to vote and according to incomplete statistics the average ratio of voting participation of rural residents across China exceeds 80 percent. At present most provinces, autonomous regions and municipalities directly under the Central Government have completed five to six sessions of election of villagers committees.

In the governance practice for more than half a century, the Communist Party of China formed a series of important thoughts on democratic governance, initially established the system of democratic governance and explored new ways and methods of democratic governance. In China the leadership of the Communist Party of China is mainly materialized in such aspects as politics, ideology and organization. By means of stipulating major guidelines and policies, it puts forth suggestions on legislation, recommends important cadres, and conducts ideology propaganda, plays the role of Party organizations and members, sticks to the governance according to law and carries out the Party's leadership of the state and society. In practice, the Communist Party of China has continuously reformed and improved the leadership system and working mechanism, made efforts to explore the practical form of democratic governance, and standardized the relations between the Party committee and the National People's Congress, Governments, the Chinese People's Political Consultative Conference, and people's organizations according to the principle that the Party in power assumes overall responsibility and coordinates all parties involved. To drive people's democracy by developing inter-Party democracy is an important content of the democratic governance by the Communist Party of China. After unremitting efforts over a long period, the Communist Party of China has gradually found a set of systems, mechanisms and methods to oversee and restrict powers and effectively undertake the work of combating corruption and upholding integrity, which accord with the national situation of China, and initially established and improved a system of punishment and corruption prevention paying equal attention to education, system and oversight.

In accordance with the requirement of democratic governance, the Chinese governments at all levels strengthen powerfully the construction of the capability of democratic administration. The Chinese government attaches importance to the exercise of power strictly in accordance with the statutory limits of authority and procedures, and in the course of administrative law-enforcement, the rights and interests of parties concerned and stakeholders should be safeguarded according to law and various illegal actions in administrative law-enforcement such as pursuing private interests through power should be firmly corrected. While accepting the oversight from the People's Councils, the Chinese People's Political Consultative Conference, judicial organs, public opinion and common people, the Chinese government has also established and improved a series of administrative oversight systems. According to the requirement of democratic

governance, the Chinese government sped up the transformation of governmental functions, powerfully promoted the innovation in the management system and mechanism, made efforts to construct a government with integrity, high efficiency and practicality, and made the government's administration full of efficiency and vitality.

China has continuously established and improved the judiciary system and working mechanism, strengthened the judiciary democratic construction and made efforts to safeguard citizens' and legal persons' legal rights and interests by judiciary activities so as to realize fairness and justice in the society. At the same time as establishing administrative organs under the People's Congresses, China has also set up independent judicial and procuratorial organs and carries out the judiciary system with separation between judicial and procuratorial organs. The judiciary organs view facts as basis and laws as criteria, and handle affairs strictly according to law, punish crimes and safeguard citizens' legal rights and interests. In the aspect of system and procedures, the justice in China persists in the principles that all people are equal before laws, and charges and punishment are stipulated by laws, and maintain and realize the judiciary justice and democracy and safeguard people's democratic rights by carrying out the trial classification system, withdrawal system, open trial system, people juror system, people supervisor system, lawyers system, legal aid system and people's mediation system.

In recent years along with the development of the state's modernization, the democratic system in China has been improved continuously, the forms of democracy become more colorful, the channels for democracy have been expanded gradually, and democratic election, decision-making, management and oversight have been carried out more widely, and people's rights to know the facts, participate, express and supervise have been further safeguarded.

—The democracy in legislation in China has been promoted forward continuously and almost every draft of a law adopted such forms as expert discussion, group evaluation, and collection of public opinion. In 2008 when the *Food Safety Law (Draft)* was promulgated, the public made 11,327 proposals.

—The *Law on Lawyers* promulgated in 1996 confirmed the basic framework of the lawyer system in China.

—In March 2004 the Second Session of the 10th National People's Congress examined and passed the amendment of the Constitution in which it is formally stipulated that "the state respects and protects human rights."

—The transparency of the government's work has been continuously enhanced by promoting electronic government administration with governmental portals as windows, building and improving the system of governmental spokespeople and the mechanism of news reports on incidents occurring suddenly.

—The social hearing and public demonstration have gradually become the methods usually adopted by governments at all levels at the time of decision-making.

—On July 1, 2004, the *Administrative Licensing Law of the People's Republic of China* was implemented formally, which stipulated a series of principles and systems of administrative licensing.

—On October 1, 2007, the *Property Law of the People's Republic of China* was formally put into effect. Public opinions were solicited before its promulgation.

—In May 2011, 15 people went to the NPC Office to air their view on the *Amendment to the Individual Income Tax Law (Draft)*.

Largest Developing Country in the World

China is the most populous developing country in the world. Large population, relative lack of resources, and weakness in environmental bearing is the basic national situation of China at present, which is hard to change in a short time. The developing issues facing China are mainly manifested in the contradiction between underdeveloped economy and people's increasingly growing material and cultural demands and in the contradiction between economic and social development and the comparatively large pressure from population, resources and environment.

China's construction of modernization is a very arduous duty, and there is a long way to go before realizing the development targets which will need several, more than ten and even scores of generations' long and unremitting efforts. At present the Chinese people are striving to build a well-off society in all aspects and are creating continuously a better and happier new life.

Huge Burden of Population

The most significant situation of China is large population and underdevelopment. The pressure from population that China is facing is unimaginable for other countries. The food consumed by Chinese people in a day can accommodate the people in New Zealand for a year, the people in Japan for 13 days and the people in the United States for 4 days. The population issue is a key factor in China's economic and social development and it is also a significant issue that China will face for long time.

By the end of 2013, China had a population of 1.36072 billion, about 22 percent of the total population of the world and more than quadruple of that in the United States, ten times that of Japan and scores of times of that in Canada and Australia. In China any issue disregarding how small it is will become a very

A shot of the waiting room of the Shenyang North Railway Station during the summer rush period.

big issue when multiplied by 1.3 billion; and any financial and material resources disregarding how considerable they are will become a very low per-capita when divided by 1.3 billion. If counted per capita, China is listed behind in the world in many aspects. The area of territory of China is listed as number 3 in the world but the per-capita tillable field is only 0.103 ha, about one tenth of that in the United States and one thirtieth of that in Canada; and the per-capita fresh water resource is only one fourth of the average level in the world. The GDP of China at present is listed as the second in the world, but the per-capita GDP is very low, ranking No. 89 in the world in 2013.

After 30 years of reforming and opening-up, the wealth of China is increased and the people's living standard has been enhanced. However, China is still listed in the range of underdeveloped countries in the world. At present, more than 20 million poor people in the urban areas are enjoying the minimum living allowances. By the end of 2013, there were still some 82.49 million people in the rural areas who have not solved the issues related to having enough food and clothing, and 53.82 million people in the rural areas eke out a living by enjoying State subsidies. According to the second national census on the handicapped population in 2006, nearly 82.96 million people are disabled.

China began to follow the family planning policy in the 1970s. Thanks to China's population policy, the growth of the total population in the world was delayed. China has entered the range of low birth-rate countries, but, due to the inertial effect of increasing population, China's population still increases at the rate of 6 million per year in recent years.

The huge population impacts on various aspects of economic and social development in China. While offering abundant labor resources for the economic and social development, it also puts heavy pressure on economic development, social progress, utilization of resources and environmental protection.

China has entered into an aging society. In 2013 there were 131.61 million people above the age of 65 (which is more than the total population of Japan),

Manchuli City in Inner Mongolia expands in size, just like cities in other parts of the country.

or 9.7 percent of the population of the country. It is predicted that by 2020 there will be 164 million people above the age of 65, or 16.1 percent of the population of the country, and there will be 22 million people above the age of 80. The aging in China is presented by such characteristics as high speed, large scale and "becoming old before wealthy."

Regarding the gender structure of the population, in 2013 the male population was 51.2 percent, 697.28 million; and the female population was 48.8 percent, 663.44 million. The sex proportion of total population is 105.1 and the sex proportion of birth population is still very high, reaching 118, much higher than the normal level of sex proportion of birth population recognized in the world (103–107).

The Third Plenary Session of the 18th CPC Central Committee held in November 2013 adopted the *Decision of the CPC Central Committee on Some Major Issues Concerning Comprehensively Deepening the Reform*. It points out:

"While persisting in the basic national policy of family planning, we will initiate a policy that allows married couples to have two children if one of the parents is a single child, and gradually adjust and improve the birth policy to promote balanced population growth in the long run." At present, the country is actively promoting a policy, which allows couples both being only child to have two children of their own. The purpose is to help improve the population structure. Zhejiang, Beijing, Jiangsu, Guangxi and other places take the lead in doing so.

The overall level of scientific and cultural qualities of the Chinese population is not high: first, the gross illiteracy rate of the population is much higher than the level of developed countries which is below 2 percent; second, the gross enrollment ratio for colleges and universities is much lower than developed countries; and third, the average number of years receiving education is lower than that of developed countries and even than the world average. According to the Sixth National Census conducted in 2010, people aged 15 and above receive an average of 9.05 years of school education, much less than in

Doing morning exercises in the park.

developed countries. At the same time, there are obvious differences between urban and rural population in terms of years of education received.

Among the 1.36 billion population of China, there are more than 1 billion people of the ages between 15 and 64, at least 300 million more than the total population of developed countries. It is predicted that by 2016 the population between the ages of 15 and 64 will reach its peak, 1.01 billion, and will be still around 1 billion by 2020.

The population of laboring age continues the trend of growth. At present in urban areas in China there are nearly 10 million new laborers every year and in rural areas there are more than 200 million surplus laborers. The growth of employment is mainly in cities. Every year tens of millions of people migrated from rural to urban areas for employment, and in urban areas there were more than 9 million increased employment opportunities every year, which made it hard to satisfy the demands of new laborers and unemployed persons. The current growth rate of the population in China has dropped down obviously and the total women birth ratio has decreased below the replacing level, but due to the inertial

Job promotion activities held for migrant workers in Beijing.

effect of population growth in the past, the total population and the population of laboring age are both in the trend of rising, and the employment situation is tense on the whole with more supply of laborers than demand. By 2030 in this situation the total population of laboring age every year in China will not be lower than the current level.

The urbanization level in China has been enhanced continuously. Due to the accelerated promotion of population urbanization and upgrade in industrial structure, the population urbanization ratio grows at the speed of more than 1 percent every year. By 2006 the urban population in China was 577.06 million, about 43.9 percent of the total population of the country. In 2010, urban population got closer to rural population. In 2011, urban population surpassed 50 percent of the national population for the first time in history. In 2013, the resident population in urban areas reached 731.11 million, or 53.73 percent of the total population.

Population of All Age Groups and Pproportion (Unit: 10,000 people,%)							
Year	Year-end population	Population of various age groups					
		0–14 years old		15–64 years old		65 years old and older	
		Population	Proportion	Population	Proportion	Population	Proportion
2007	132,129	25,660	19.42	95,833	72.53	10,636	8.05
2008	132,802	25,166	18.95	96,680	72.80	10,956	8.25
2009	133,450	24,659	18.48	97,484	73.05	11,307	8.47
2010	134,091	22,259	16.60	99,938	74.53	11,894	8.87
2011	134,735	22,164	16.45	100,283	74.43	12,288	9.12
2012	135,404	22,287	16.46	100,403	74.15	12,714	9.39

In the course of quick urbanization, as the change in the use of agricultural lands became an important source for driving economic growth and increasing financial revenue, there was an impulse for large-scale land requisition and the speed of land urbanization was accelerated. But meanwhile as the peasants who lost land due to requisition entered the urban society from rural society, broke off the traditional mutual-assistance network in villages, entered the urban society with strange human relations, they did not complete the course of becoming townspeople soon due to change of domiciliary register. The land urbanization was vastly quicker than the citizenization of peasants, which tends to cause social contradiction and conflicts.

China remained underdeveloped for a long time and the contradiction exists for a long time between the people's growing demands for welfare and the satisfaction of such demands. This lasts until in recent years; however, the social security in China faces a comparatively severe situation, with much work to be done in social insurances, social welfare and social relief. The traditional mode of families themselves providing care for the aged which has lasted for thousands of years in China is facing an unprecedented challenge. The current system of basic old-age insurance in China can only cover about 60 percent of all the employees in the whole society and most peasants cannot receive it. Even for the urban employees, about 40 percent of them have no old-age insurance, including a great number of migrant rural workers and informal employees. The medical security system is not sound. The urban medical security system has a small coverage and the strength of the rural cooperative medical service system is not enough. The security of basic rights and interests of nearly 245 million migrant people requires strengthening. At present the Chinese government is adopting a series of measures to change the situation gradually.

Disparity and Imbalance in Development

In today's China, whereas people's income level and standard of living are continually improving, there is still a growing disparity between the financial circumstances of different social members. The development of a range of social undertakings is moving comparatively slowly, and various issues relating to the day-to-day interests of the people, such as education, health care and housing, have not been adequately taken care of.

The excessively large disparity of income is a serious issue in the social development of China. According to relevant statistics, the income disparity between at the richest people, who represent 10 percent of the total population,

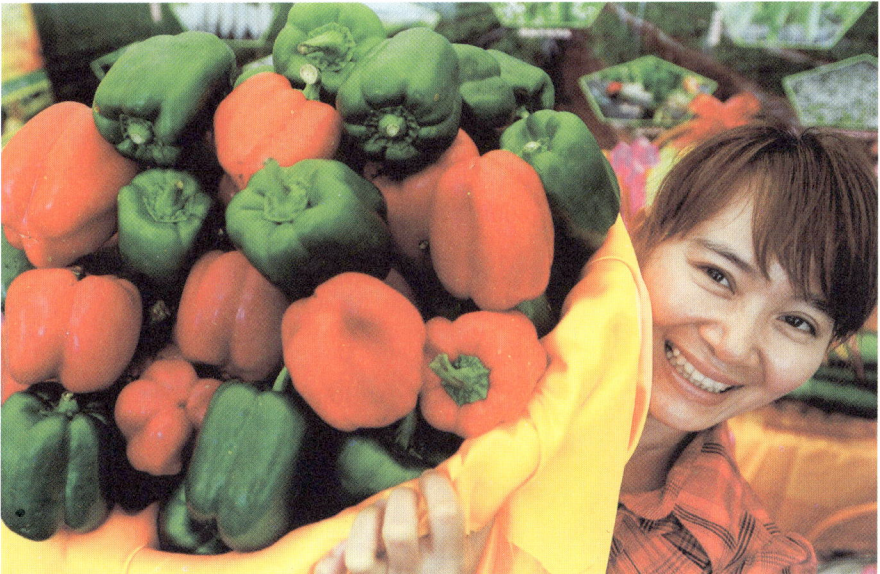

Farmers in Kaifeng, Henan Province happy to have a new bumper harvest.

281

and the poverty-stricken people, who make up 10 percent of the total population, is more than 20 times. According to the World Bank, China's Gini coefficient is about 0.47, as against 0.4 recognized as the warning line internationally. The Chinese government is taking a series of measures to narrow the income gap.

The issue of income disparity in China is manifested collectively in the following aspects: first, the income disparity between urban and rural areas. In 2013 the net per-capita income for urban residents in China was 26,955 Yuan while the net per-capita income for rural inhabitants was 8,896 Yuan, resulting in a ratio of urban to rural net per-capita income of 3.03:1. Secondly, there is the income disparity between different regions. In 2012 Zhejiang Province had the highest net per-capita income for urban residents (excepting municipalities directly under the Central Government) of 34,550 Yuan, and Xinjiang the lowest, 17,157 Yuan; furthermore, Zhejiang Province also had the highest net per-capita income for rural residents, 14,552 Yuan, while Gansu Province had the lowest, 4,495 Yuan. Lastly, there is the income disparity between different sectors. In 2012 the service sector, with the highest income, had an average payment of 89,743 Yuan, while the sectors with the lowest income (agriculture, forestry, animal husbandry and fishery) had an average payment of 22,687 Yuan, a ratio of 3.96:1.

The imbalance in social development is caused by the imbalance in economic development, itself mainly manifested in the imbalance of economic development between urban and rural areas (between industry and agriculture). Agriculture in China is mainly in rural areas while industry is mainly in cities and the development imbalance between urban and rural areas can be seen in the imbalance between industry and agriculture. The issue of agriculture, rural areas and peasants is the most problematic in the economic and social development of modern China. When closely analyzed, the situation with regard to agriculture, rural areas and peasants is the result of a dualistic economic structure with the long-term separation between urban and rural areas in China, manifested in the contradiction between a superabundant rural population and the limited and continuously decreasing agricultural production materials such as suitable farming land. At present, agricultural workers account for 46 percent of the total population in China; the number of people involved in the primary industry (agriculture, forestry, animal husbandry and fishery) is 260 million, or 33.6 percent of the total number of employees - however, their production yield accounts for 10.1 percent of the GDP.

The imbalance in economic development is also manifested in the imbalance between different regions. In 2012 the per-capita GDP for west China was 31,357 Yuan, that for east China 57,722 Yuan, the ratio between west and east being 1: 1.84.

In 2010, China issued a the National Program for Medium- and Long-Term Education Reform and Development (2010–2020), which calls for efforts for China to seek further development in education and cultivation of talents,

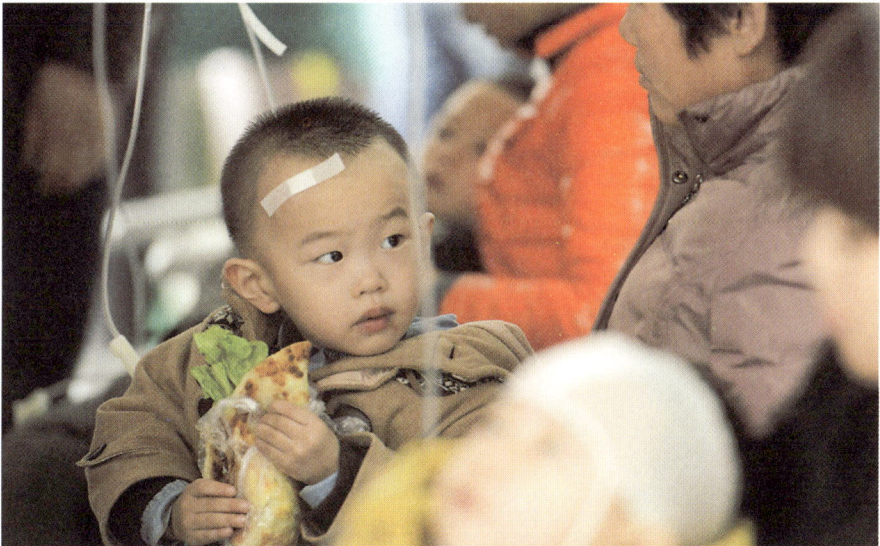

Children receiving treatment in the Taiyuan Health Institution for Women and Children.

A primary school for children of migrant workers in Beijing.

achieving modernization in education by the year 2020. According to the Program, more funding will be allocated for educational development purpose. The sum was 2,116.5 billion Yuan in 2012, or 4.1 percent of the 2012 GDP. Although China has narrowed the gap with developed countries in this regard, some problems remain: Case in point is the imbalance in educational resources between urban and rural areas, between east and west China, and even between different schools. Children from poverty-stricken families and children of migrant workers still have poor access to better education.

The issues surrounding medical treatment and health care are most prominently manifested in the unreasonable allocation of health care resources. Across the country, 80 percent of the health care resources are concentrated in cities; whereas high-quality medical treatment and health care resources are excessively concentrated in big city hospitals, there is a concomitant shortage of community health care service resources, and the service system of "giving priority to prevention" and reasonable access to a doctor have not come into being. In rural areas there is a shortage of medical treatment and health care resources. In addition, China's health investment is insufficient, accounting for 5.15 percent of the GDP in 2011, a figure which is higher than India (4.2 percent), close to Russia (5.6 percent), and far less than other BRICS countries including Brazil (8.8 percent) and South Africa (9.2 percent).

China's per capita GDP has exceeded US$ 6,000, which means China approaches the average level of medium-income countries in the world. This is fact that China has gone from the transformation period to a new historical period featuring high income. It is historical fact, having reached the level of US$ 6,000 per capita GDP, some countries declined and some others continued to move forward. Given this, China needs to find a new way of development.

The Decision of the CPC Central Committee on Some Major Issues Concerning Comprehensively Deepening the Reform adopted at the Third Plenary Session of the 18th CPC Central Committee held in November 2013 stipulates in explicit terms: "We will regulate income distribution procedures and improve the regulatory systems and mechanisms and policy system for income distribution, establish an individual income and property information system, protect legitimate incomes, regulate excessively high incomes, redefine and clear away hidden incomes, outlaw illegal incomes, increase the incomes of low-income groups, and increase the proportion of the middle-income group in society as a whole. We will strive to narrow the income gap between urban and rural areas, different regions and different sectors, thus gradually forming an olive-shaped distribution structure in the country." Generally speaking, when the proportion of middle-income group reaches 40–50 percent, it indicates that a society has formed an "olive" structure, with the majority of people enjoying middle income and the lower and high income earners forming the minority. At present, the proportion of medium income group in China makes up about 25 percent of the population. The Chinese society will have to wait to form an "olive" structure. This period is full of opportunities and challenges.

Conflict Between Economic Development and Resources Environment

China is vast in size. However, 52 percent of its land area belong to arid or semi-arid areas. The Qinghai-Tibet Plateau, highly cold and scarce in oxygen, covers an area of 2.4 million square km; the Loess Plateau, which suffers serious soil erosion, covers an area of 640,000 square km. In addition, Rocky desertification covers an area of 900,000 square km. China today boasts 122 million hectares of cultivated land, averaging less than 0.1 hectare per capita, a figure which is half of the world average level. Moreover, 70 percent of the cultivated land in China fall into the category of medium- or low-yield ones. Land exerts a heavy pressure on China with 1.36 billion mouths to feed.

The economy in China is growing very fast, but the extensive economic growth with high investment, high levels of energy consumption, high materials

China's Energy Consumption in 2012

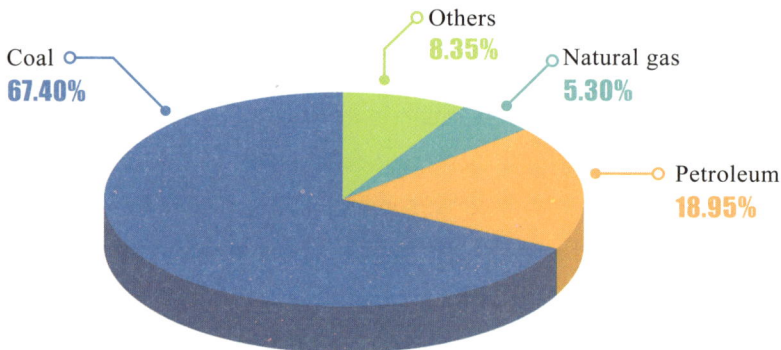

Coal
67.40%

Others
8.35%

Natural gas
5.30%

Petroleum
18.95%

consumption, high pollution and large requisition of land has not fundamentally changed. In particular, China is currently at a time of accelerated development in both industrialization and urbanization, and due to a comparatively high consumption of energy and various resources and a heavy emission of pollutants, the conflict between economic development and the conservation of natural resources is becoming ever more prominent.

In particular, the added value of tertiary industry as a proportion of GDP is 46.1 percent, higher than the secondary industry (43.9 percent). This compares sharply with the added value of the tertiary industry in developed countries (70 percent).

At present, China has overtaken the United States and Russia to become the world's number one energy producer and consumer. In 2013, China's primary energy production was 3.4 billion tons of standard coal while its energy consumption reached 3.75 billion tons of standard coal. Moreover, China is

China sees fast development of new coal chemical industry.

irrational in consumption pattern largely because it is the most populous country suffering from shortage of energy.

China also has relatively low energy resources. At present the per-capita petroleum resource is 17.1 percent of the world average, the per-capita natural gas resource even less, at 13.2 percent. Coal represents a major part of China's natural resources, but per-capita is only 42.5 percent of the world average.

In China there is a wide but imbalanced distribution of energy resources. Coal is mainly found in north and northwestern China, hydraulic resources are principally distributed in the southwestern regions, and petroleum and natural gas are mostly concentrated in the eastern, central and western regions as well as under territorial waters. The major regions with regard to energy consumption are concentrated in the southeastern coastal areas which have the more developed economy. The large-scale and far-distant transportation of coal from north to south, of petroleum from north to south, of natural gas from west to east and of electricity from west to east represents the distinctive and basic structure of the flow of China's energy transportation.

The demand for resources in China has grown fast. In the 1990s petroleum consumption increased at an average annual growth of 7.2 percent; that of natural gas increased at an average annual growth of 9.3 percent; that of steel increased at an annual average growth of 9.3 percent; and that of copper increased at an annual average growth of 11.2 percent. Recent yeasrs saw China make efforts to take controlling fast energy consumption growth as a major goal, with the result that energy consumed in 2012 and 2013 grew by only 3.9 percent and 3.7 percent respectively.

Regarding energy technology, China has made great progress, but compared to the demands for development and the advances that have been made at international level, there is still a significant gap. The development of new technology in such fields as recyclable energy, clean energy and alternative energy is comparatively fast and the application of such technology as energy-saving, consumption-reduction and pollution treatment is not nearly so wide as it might be. In 2010, China's energy consumption per-unit GDP stayed 2.2 fold when compared to the world level, and was higher than developed countries including the United States, Japan and Europe.

An extensive economy results in low efficiency and output. The labor productivity in China is obviously lower than that of western developed countries. Recent years saw fast growth of labor productivity, with the 2010 labor productivity doubling that in 1990, which, however, was still half of that of OECD, and even less than Latin American countries. According to the report by the Chinese Academy of Sciences, China's labor productivity is only equivalent to 1/12 of the United States and 1/11 of Japan.

The serious pollution we are currently witnessing is the result of an extensive development of the Chinese economy. Although China has adopted a variety of measures so that emissions of major pollutants has decreased year by year, but the emissions remain to be a serious problem plaguing China today. In 2012, the national wastewater COD emissions were 24.237 million tons, and the sulfur dioxide emissions in exhaust gas were 21.176 million tons.

Scientific Outlook on Development

In recent years the Communist Party of China and the Chinese government have developed a strategy of commanding the overall situation of economic and social development by adopting a scientific outlook on development after summarizing the successes and failures of economic and social development since the beginning of reform and opening up, by drawing upon the experiences and lessons learned during the foundation of modernization in all parts of the world, and by analyzing the conditions, situation and general trends that China faces in both the new century and the new stage in its development.

As to the scientific outlook on development, development is the first essential, putting people first is the core ideal, being comprehensive, balanced and sustainable is the basic requirement, and overall consideration is the fundamental method.

—As to development, we must firmly commit ourselves to the central task of economic development, concentrate on construction and development, seek for development whole-heartedly, and keep releasing and developing the forces of production.

—Putting people first means prioritizing the interests of the people as a whole, focusing on promoting the all-around development of the people, realizing their will, satisfying their demands, and safeguarding their interests.

—As to comprehensive, balanced and sustainable development, we must promote economic, political, cultural and social development, harmonize economic growth with the needs of the population, the best use of resources and the greatest benefit to the environment, and encourage the whole of society to follow the kind of enlightened approach to development that results in expanded production, a better standard of living and sound ecological and environmental conditions.

—As to overall consideration, we must correctly understand and handle the major relationships that occur in the construction of modernization in China and consider the overall situation and planning process as a complete entity.

According to the requirements of maintaining a scientific outlook on development, in recent years China has changed its outlook on development, both by innovation and quality enhancement, and has made great efforts to realize a positive and accelerated development of economy and society, achieving positive results. China will redouble its effort to tackle environmental problems and build up a beautiful country.

Persist in strengthening and improving macro-regulation, accelerating adjustments in economic structure and independent innovation. Targeting such major issues in development as the excessively fast growth of investment in economic operations, putting excessive currency credits on the market, and having too high a favorable balance in foreign trade, the Central Government adopted a series of measures on macro-regulation. By adopting such measures as strengthened land control, stricter management on currency credits, the

Wind power generators in Urumqi, capital of the Xinjiang Uygur Autonomous Region.

regulation of economic operations by finance and taxes, and regulation and supervision over the real estate market, the government avoided violent ups and downs in the economy. The government furthermore instigated policies to optimize the industrial structure, stipulated and carried out policies and measures aimed at adjusting the structure of eleven principal industries including steel and iron, coal and cement, and eliminated a previously sluggish production capacity. It made great efforts to develop the service sector, enhance industrial levels and standards, and promote the national economy and levels of public information. It accelerated the development of hi-tech industry, rejuvenated equip manufacture, actively developed recyclable energy, and moved in the direction of renewable energy. It implemented state key scientific and technological projects, and made efforts to overcome outdated core and key technologies concerning the national economy, people's livelihood and national security. It strengthened both basic research and the more advanced avenues of research in frontline technology and social welfare.

Persist in the energy strategy of giving priority to saving, basing on the current domestic situation, multiple development and protecting the environment; construct a stable, economical and clean energy supply system; and make efforts to construct a resource-efficient society. In pursuit of these goals the government has carried out the strictest land management system. The energy supply in China mainly depends on domestic sources and for a number of years the self-support ratio has been maintained at over 90 percent.

Pay more attention to saving energy, reducing consumption, protecting the environment and reducing intensive land use. The government has significantly improved its policies regarding energy-saving, consumption-reduction, and the concomitant reduction in the emission of pollutants, and has widely established a system of target responsibility on energy-saving and emission reduction. It has actively promoted the work of energy saving in key industries, enterprises and projects, and developed experimental units of recyclable economy. It has improved and firmly maintained standards on energy consumption and environmental protection, eliminated sluggish production capabilities with a firm hand, and accelerated progress in energy-saving and environmental protection technologies.

Strengthen the policies regarding pollution treatment and environmental protection. From 2006 to 2010, small thermal power generation units of 76.825 million kW will be decommissioned and 120 million tons of inefficient iron-making production capacity and 72 million tons of poor-performance steel-making production capacity will be eliminated. Meanwhile, some 370 million tons of cement production capacity has been wiped out. Efforts have also been made to clean seriously polluting factories involved in paper-making, chemical production, textiles, printing and dyeing, etc.

In mid-April 2012, Huangjiawan landfill Gas power station, the first landfill gas power station of Yichang City, Hubei Province, was completed by the acceptance, preparing to supply power to the grid.

China views energy saving as a significant strategy, is making a wholehearted attempt to develop a recyclable economy, and is endeavoring to realize a system of development based on the minimum consumption of resources. A few years before 2006, energy consumption per unit kept rising; but after 2006, it fell and the fall was 3.6 percent in 2012 and 3.7 percent in 2013. China is currently persisting in its policy of the multiple developing strategy on energy, the systematic development of coal resources, the active development of electric power, and is paying no less attention to petroleum and natural gas. In recent years the State has put a great deal of effort into developing new forms of energy and investigating renewable sources of energy such as wind, biological, solar, geothermal and wave-powered, and the consumption of high-quality clean energy has exhibited a corresponding although gradual rise. China has announced that by 2020 the proportion of renewable energy in the overall energy structure will be increased from the current seven percent to approximately 16 percent.

At the same time as promoting economic development, China has adopted a series of measures aimed at strengthening environmental protection. The State has persisted in giving priority to preventative and integrative treatment, emphasized the prevention of pollution and the protection of the environment at source, and fully applied the methods of laws, economy, technology and necessary administration in the interests of environmental protection. It has also persisted in a policy of comprehensive promotion with breakthroughs in key points, and established programs to solve the most prominent environmental issues, i.e. those which represent a danger to people's health and which negatively influence the future of sustainable development. No less than these, it has furthermore persisted in giving priority to protection and orderly development, viewed the control over unreasonable resource exploitation as a key issue, and strengthened ecological protection in the area of natural resources. Finally, it has persisted in saving resources, actively advocated the path of environment-friendly consumption, continuously cultivated and accelerated an environment-friendly social atmosphere, and persisted in combining the prevention and treatment of pollution with the work of ecological protection, at all times sparing no effort to improve the quality of the ecological environment.

The work of environmental protection in China is making extremely positive progress. The aggravation of environmental pollution and ecological destruction is slowing down, the pollution treatment in some river drainage areas is beginning to show positive results, the air quality in some cities and regions has been enhanced, the emission of pollutants in the industrial sector has shown a small but encouraging decrease, and the awareness of environmental issues across the whole of society has been steadily broadened. In urban areas the air quality has improved. In 2011, of 330 cities monitored, 88.8 percent or 293 cities had a level of air quality reaching or exceeding the State-stipulated Class II, an increase of 28.6 percent compared to 2002. The growth in gross emission levels of major pollutants correspondingly slowed down. In 2012 the growth of emission of chemical oxygen and sulfur dioxide decreased by 3.05 percent and 4.52 percent respectively from that in the previous year. The ecologically motivated planting of new forest areas underwent steady development over the same period, coinciding with a decrease in the level of desertification. Across the country forests cover an area of 208 million hectares, with the forest coverage rate reaching 21.63 percent. However, the wetland coverage drops to 53.6026 million hectares.

The State has persisted in the implementation of an overall strategy of regional development, made wide-ranging plans, and taken all known factors into consideration. It has made a reasonable program, brought advantages into play, carried out appropriate policies, and accelerated a balanced development across the various regions. The Development of the Western Region has been steadily promoted, the benefits of returning farmland to forests and animal breeding grounds to pastures have been solidified and developed, and key ecological projects such as protection of natural forests and prevention and treatment of desert areas have been carried out. The work of rejuvenating the

old industrial base in northeast China has been successfully carried out, the adjustment of industrial structure solidified, the construction of commercial grain bases strengthened, and the renovation of old towns accelerated. Those policies aimed at speeding up the development of China's middle regions have started to be implemented, just as the grain yielding capacity and the production of energy, raw materials and the traffic transportation system have been boosted. The eastern region has made significant progress in leading the way in development; the industrial structure has kept on optimizing, and independent innovative capacity and international competitiveness have been very much strengthened.

Building a Harmonious Society

In a big country with a large population and imbalanced development such as China, the implementation of modernization should be conducted according to the overall requirements of democracy and the rule of law, according to fairness and justice, integrity and fraternity, vitality, stability and order and harmony between man and nature. Importance should also be attached to those issues relating to the actual day-to-day interests of the people as a whole, efforts should be made to develop social undertakings, accelerate social fairness and justice, construct a harmonious culture, improve social management, strengthen social creative vitality, and follow the path of common wealth. It follows as essential that a balanced development between social construction and economic, political and cultural construction should be actively promoted.

When the Legal Publicity Day on December 4 approached, volunteers with the College of Life science, Liaocheng University, Shandong Province, went to the university town construction site, where they carried out law promotion activities.

Aiming at the realization of social development in China, despite some existing conflicts and problems influencing social harmony, China has developed a significant strategy of building a harmonious socialist society. The main objectives and tasks for building such a society by 2020 are as follows: the socialist democracy and legal system must be further improved, the fundamental principle of administrating the country according to law must be generally implemented, people's rights and interests should enjoy concrete respect and be guaranteed, the widening gap between urban and rural development and between different regions must be steadily reversed, a reasonable and orderly income distribution pattern must take general shape, household wealth should increase across the board, thus enabling all people to lead more affluent lives, employment rates must be relatively high and a social security system covering both the urban and rural population be established; the basic existing public service system should be further improved and the government attain relatively significant improvements in administrative and service levels; the ideological and

A shot of the dining room of the Dapo Town Central Primary School in Rong'an County, Guangxi Zhuang Autonomous Region.

moral standards, scientific and cultural qualities, and health and welfare status of the whole nation must be markedly improved, and further progress made in fostering a sound moral atmosphere and encouraging harmonious interpersonal relationships; the overall creativity of society must reach a new level, and an innovation-based national characteristic be established; the public administration system must be further improved and social order given a stronger platform; resources must be used more efficiently and the environment visibly improved; and finally the objective of turning a society with more than a billion population into one that has a moderate but achievable prosperity and standard of living within a harmonious social framework is the responsibility of everyone to try and achieve.

In recent years both central and local governments at all levels in China have adopted various powerful measures and made significant progress towards building a harmonious society.

On November 28, 2013, the Bubgquabg County Tianjin Hospital, invested by Tianjin in the form of aid after the devastating Wenchuang Earth Quake in 2008, was built.

Regarding developments in education, the Chinese government has persisted in prioritizing education policy, accelerating its development at various levels, and has had the general desire of popularizing and solidifying compulsory schooling, accelerating the development of vocational learning, and sparing no effort to enhance the quality of higher education. Recent years saw the Central Government increase financial input in education, health care and cultural undertakings. In 2007 the tuition and miscellaneous expenses of the compulsory education stage were exempted in rural areas across the country so that the economic burden of the families of 28.21 million secondary and primary school students in 25,900 cities were lightened, with each student exempted from 190–350 Yuan per year.

Regarding developments in the sphere of health care, a significant amount of attention has been paid to the construction of a basic health care system covering urban and rural residents. A new rural cooperative medical service

The Taiyuan City Employment Service Cente in Shanxi Province adopts the "one-card" social security card for urban employees.

system is being actively promoted. Toward the end of 2013, some 2,489 counties (cities and districts) introduced the new rural cooperative medical service system, with the participation rate reaching 99 percent. Meanwhile, the development of a new urban health care service system based on communities was being accelerated. The State has already started experimental units offering basic medical care for urban residents with the overall emphasis on treating major diseases, and is offering financial aid to poor people in respect of medical treatment. In 2012, the central financial arrangements 204.82 billion Yuan for medical and health expenditure. In 2013, the government funded 12.293 million urban residents in their participating in medical insurance, and 41.325 million rural residents in doing the same. China has made much headway in reforming its basic medical insurance system, with the government subsidy reaching 320 Yuan per capita. Pilot reform has expanded to cover 1,000 counties, covering some 500 million rural people.

Regarding employment and social security, the State has further improved and implemented its policies on employment and re-employment, exploited employment possibilities through a wide variety of channels, and actively supported independently created businesses and encouraged opportunities for self-employment. After years of endeavor, the proper correlation between unemployment insurance and a basic living guarantee for laid-off employees of state-owned enterprises has been fundamentally worked out. The system of labor contracts has been comprehensively overhauled and rigorously promoted to safeguard workers' legal rights and interests. In 2012 the central financial department put aside 575.373 billion Yuan for necessary expenditure on social security. The system of basic pensions for retirees from enterprises has kept on improving, and the establishment of a social security system geared to the demands of migrant rural workers has been accelerated. The urban and rural social assistance system has been improved; the basic framework of a social assistance system established, and procedures to take into account a minimum living guarantee for urban residents, urban and rural medical assistance, and

assistance for urban vagrants and beggars put into place.

Regarding the important issue of a balanced development between urban and rural areas, from 2006 the agricultural tax and agricultural specialty tax were both shelved, thus ending over 2,600 years of peasants having to pay taxes for planting crops. The government also subsidized peasants who planted grain, as a direct consequence of which agriculture expanded for three successive years. Investment into infrastructural development in rural areas has been increased, and the construction of irrigation works, roads, power grids, telecommunications, safe drinking water, and production of marsh gas. The government has increased the farmers' incomes through a variety of means, made efforts to increase the income from planting, cultivation and forestry, has actively developed the secondary and tertiary industries in rural areas, and endeavored to promote the modern, industrialized operation of agriculture.

Regarding the reconstruction of the judiciary system, the government has tried to safeguard the independence and fairness of judicial and procuratorial power according to law by implementing systems that take full account of protecting people's democratic and legal rights and interests and maintain the balance of social fairness and justice. The Supreme People's Court has taken back the power to approve the death penalty and the handling procedure for capital cases has been further improved. Transparency in trial and procuratorial affairs has been targeted and the mechanism of procuratorial jurisdiction over litigation activities much improved, especially in respect of that concerning malfeasance by judiciary staff. A uniform judiciary authentication system has been set up.

During the 17th National Congress of the Communist Party of China, held in October 2007, the goal of building a moderately prosperous society in all aspects by 2020 was again definitely advocated. By 2020, when the goal of building such a society has been realized, China, an ancient civilization with a long history, now an important developing socialist country, will become a country where industrialization is basically realized, integrative national power is distinctively strengthened, and the overall scale of its domestic market is number one in the world. It will be a country whose people have a universally high standard of living, both with regard to wealth and environment, where people share a greater degree of democratic rights and maintain higher levels of civilized quality and spiritual pursuit, whose systems in all aspects have become more greatly improved, where society is more active, safe and united, and which has become further opened up, has more affinity with the people, and makes an even greater contribution to human culture.

The 18th National Congress of the CPC held in November 2012 put forward the goal of building a well-off society in 2020. According to its Report, China will attain the goal of completing the building of a moderately prosperous society in all respects by 2020. The Report also stresses that China will surely complete the building of a moderately prosperous society in all respects when the CPC celebrates its centenary and turn China into a modern socialist country that is prosperous, strong, democratic, culturally advanced and harmonious when the PRC marks its centennial. China will achieve national rejuvenation by persisting in taking the road to socialism and have a more beautiful tomorrow.

Beautiful China Dream

Chinese civilization once made significant contributions to the development of human society. In modern times, the Chinese nation experienced a great deal of hardship with huge sacrifices rare in world history. To realize the great national rejuvenation has become the ambitious goal of the Chinese people from generation to generation. Leading the whole nation to achieve the goal is the great historical mission placed on the shoulders of the Chinese Communist Party.

The Chinese people have chosen the road of socialism with Chinese characteristics. According to the 18th CPC National Congress, great efforts will be made to meet the goal of building a moderately prosperous society when the Party celebrates its 100th birthday, and the goal of turning the country into a modern socialist one prosperous, strong, democratic, culturally advanced and harmonious when the PRC marks its centennial (2049). These goals represent China's objectives in the future and embody the "China Dream" featuring national prosperity and rejuvenation and people's wellbeing.

The China Dream is one for peace, development, and win-win cooperation. It is closely related to the beautiful dreams of the people in different countries. The China Dream will integrate China's revival into the progress of the world and thus become a bridge to connect the country and the rest of the world.

Two Century Goals

When the Communist Party of China, an advanced working-class party, was established in 1921, the disaster-ridden country saw signs of hope. It has since taken on a new look. In 1949 the People's Republic of China was founded. The socialist system was set up, fundamentally changing the political landscape of East Asia and the world. In the late 1970s, China began to introduce the reform and opening up policy. Due to establishment of a socialist market economy, the Chinese social economy has been able to maintain fast growth over a fairly long period, helping radically reshape the economic landscape of East Asia and the world. All these are monumental historical events occurring in the 20th Century.

On August 29, 1987, Deng Xiaoping met with Italian Speaker of the House of Representatives Yorty (first left), who was also a leader of the Italian Communist Party.

Under the leadership of the CPC, the country has made unremitting efforts in exploring ways to modernization and national renewal. In the 1950s and the 1960s, China set the strategic goal of achieving the modernization of agriculture, industry, national defense, and science and technology, to be achieved by the end of the 20th Century. Despite many subsequent twists and turns, the goal never changed. In August 1987 when Deng Xiaoping met with the guests from Italy, he said: "China is developing its economy in three steps. Two steps will be taken in this century, to reach the point where our people have adequate food and clothing and lead a fairly comfortable life. The third step, which will take us 30 to 50 years into the next century, is to reach the level of the moderately developed countries. There are our strategic objectives and our high ambitions." Later, both the Party and the society reached consensus on the three-step strategic objectives, further enriched from the 14th to the 18th CPC National Congress.

At the 15th CPC National Congress convened at the eve of the 21st Century, the new "three-step" development strategy was presented: efforts to double the 2000 GDP by 2010 and ensure the people could lead a more comfortable life and a fairly sophisticated socialist market economy having taken shape; in 2021 or the 100th anniversary of the CPC, the national economy will have achieved further development, with improved systems and institutions in place; in the mid-21st century (2049), the goal will basically be achieved in terms of modernization and building a prosperous, strong, democratic and culturally advanced country. The targets were updated at the 16th CPC National Congress in November 2002: GDP of 2000 to be quadrupled in the first 20 years of the 21st Century, the goal of building a moderately prosperous society in an all-round manner to be realized; by the middle of the 21st Century, the goal of modernization will have been achieved in the main by a prosperous, democratic and culturally advanced socialist country. The 17th CPC National Congress held in October 2007 decided to work hard to quadruple the per capita GDP of 2000 in the first 20 years of the 21st Century while accomplishing the task of building a moderately prosperous society in all aspects.

As a matter of fact, the first step of the new three-step development strategy was realized by 2010, raising China to the second largest economy in the world. In November 2012, the 18th CPC National Congress pledged great efforts to fulfill the task of building a moderately prosperous society in all aspects by the Party's 100th anniversary and work hard to accomplish the task of turning China into a modern socialist country prosperous, strong, democratic, culturally advanced and harmonious by the time of the PRC's centennial. In this way, the China Dream of national revival will be embodied in the overall planning and pursuit of the "two century goals".

To achieve the great rejuvenation of the Chinese nation doesn't mean to restore China's glory in history, but to regain its due status in the world under new historical conditions. In a word, it is to achieve the modernization of China. Deng Xiaoping borrowed the phrase "a moderately prosperous society" from the traditional Chinese classic – *The Book of Songs* to describe "modernization with Chinese characteristics". "A moderately prosperous society" refers to a kind of ideal society in ancient China when people lived a peaceful, happy, and harmonious life. Actually what is called "a moderately prosperous society" means a "great society", including everything from economy to politics, culture, etc.

According to the fifth plenary session of the 15th CPC National Congress convened in October 2000, China had finished the first two steps of the modernization drive and generally completed the building of a well-off society. However, it was a substandard one, paying more attention to material consumption and featuring unbalanced development between regions. The 16th Party Congress proposed to build a well-off society at a higher level to benefit the entire population so that the economy would be more developed, democracy even sounder, science and education more advanced, culture more prosperous, society more harmonious, and people living a happier life. At the 17th Party Congress, the goal of doubling the GDP of 2000 by 2020 set previously was amended to quadrupling per capita GDP in the same period. It means that the

Chinese economy must grow faster through optimizing its economic structure and improving economic returns while saving energy and reducing emissions so as to promote harmony between humans and nature. According to the 18th Party Congress, hard work was needed to ensure the building of a moderately prosperous society in all aspects by 2020 while, at the same time, greater efforts should be made to help the economy develop in a more balanced, more coordinated and more sustainable manner so as to double both the GDP and the per capita disposable income of urban and rural residents between 2010 and 2020. It is obvious that China has been working hard to raise the standards for a "moderately prosperous society" continuously, make "two century goals" clearer and push them forward.

The Communist Party of China will celebrate its 100th birthday in less than 10 years; and the PRC will mark its centennial in less than 40 years. Relevant monitoring results show that the degree of realization of building a moderately prosperous society reached 80.1 percent in 2010, 20.5 percentage points higher than that in 2000. Economic growth made the greatest contribution. From the per-capita perspective, World Bank data indicates that the Chinese figure was US$ 4,260 in 2010, for the first time exceeding US$ 3,976, the bank's dividing line between lower and upper-middle income. Such a fast growth amazes the world. People have no reason to doubt whether China can attain the "two century goals" and make its great dream of national rejuvenation come true.

China Dream Has Rich Connotations

Since the new leadership group of the CPC took office in November 2012, the "China Dream" has quickly become a key word for understanding the national development trend. On many occasions at home and abroad, President Xi Jinping has spoken about its specific connotations, development goals, overall planning, and the way of realization. It's fair to say that the "China Dream" is much richer than "moderately prosperous society" in connotation. It not only embodies the aspiration of the Chinese people from generation to generation, but also reflects the interests of the whole Chinese nation. Now, the "China Dream" has become a word well known domestically while causing widespread concern internationally.

According to *Power and Potential of the China Dream* recently published by WWP, the largest advertising and public relations group in the UK, the "China Dream" is likely to surpass the "American dream" in the future. It is becoming a spiritual power and shared vision encouraging the Chinese people to move forward. People attach to it abundant and profound connotations through theoretical discussion and concrete practice.

When visiting the exhibition "Road to Revival" in November 2011, President Xi Jinping said: "Now, we are all discussing the China Dream. I think that achieving the great rejuvenation of the Chinese nation is the greatest Chinese dream in modern times. Because the dream carries a long-cherished wish of generations of Chinese people. It reflects the interests of the Chinese people as a whole, and it's a common expectation of the Chinese nation." In April 2013 when Xi made the keynote speech at the Boao Forum for Asia, he said again: "the main goals we set for China are as follows: By 2020, China's GDP and per capita incomes for urban and rural residents will double the 2010 figures, and the

Visitors to the Road to Rejuvenation exhibition enjoying space suit used by space astronaut Yang Liwei.

building of a moderately prosperous society in all respects will be completed. By the mid-21st century, China will be turned into a modern socialist country that is prosperous, strong, democratic, culturally advanced and harmonious; and the China Dream, namely, the great renewal of the Chinese nation, will be realized." "On the other hand, we are aware that China remains the world's largest developing country, and it faces many difficulties and challenges on its road to progress. We need to make relentless efforts in the years ahead to deliver a better life to all our people. We are unwaveringly committed to reform and opening up, and we will concentrate on the major task of shifting the growth model, focus on running our own affairs well and make continued efforts to boost the socialist modernization drive."

"People's longing for a better life is the objective we strive for." On November 15, 2012 when the new Standing Committee of the Political Bureau of the CPC Central Committee met the media, Xi Jinping delivered a nearly

20-minute speech focused mainly on the people, in particular their livelihood. In the speech, there is a passage that is so impressive: "Our people love life. They expect better education, steadier jobs, higher income, and more reliable social security. They expect better medical and health services, more comfortable housing conditions, and more beautiful environment. They expect their children can grow more healthily, get a better job and live a better life." On March 17, 2013, at the closing ceremony of the First Plenum of the 12th National People's Congress, the newly elected President Xi delivered his inaugural speech. Over a period of under 25 minutes, he mentioned the "China Dream" nine times and "the people" 44 times. The "ten betters" in his speech are the main concerns of the ordinary Chinese people, including education, employment, distribution of income, medical service, etc. They are absolutely the key words related to the people's livelihood. Through the "ten betters", President Xi expressed his great concern for the issues related to people's livelihood in a positive manner while painting a rosy picture for people's life in the future. Actually, the "ten betters"

The First Session of the 12th NPC closed in Beijing on March 17, 2013.

Music fans gathering at the Rending Lake Park in Beijing.

also represent the beautiful future of social construction based on the "China Dream".

Thanks to more than 60 years of hard work, China has made great achievements. Social productivity, comprehensive national strength and people's living standard have all risen by a large margin. However, China remains the biggest developing country in the world. Not only its economic and social development but also its reform and opening up program have entered into a critical period. This is a rare historic opportunity for the country and at the same time, it also brings about numerous risks and challenges. In this period, the Chinese people have a strong desire for a prosperous and strong country, national renewal, and a happy life, which constitute the powerful driving force behind the China Dream.

The most unique feature of the China Dream is to take the country, nation, and individual as an integral whole with a common destiny while closely linking

State interests, national interests and those of the individual. The China Dream is a combination of "individual's dream" and the "dream of the nation". The realization of individual's dream cannot do without the support of the latter. Different industries and places across the country all presented their China Dreams on the basis of their own realities. For instance, to make their own China Dreams come true, the young generation is endeavoring to upgrade "Made in China" to "Created by China" so as to improve the international influence of Chinese brands.

The China Dream is a dream for happiness that not only belongs to the whole nation, but also to every Chinese. Meanwhile, it is also a dream to make contributions to the world. With such a great dream, China stands at a new historical starting point.

"Five-in-One" Blueprint for Development

On November 8, 2012, Hu Jintao, General Secretary of the CPC Central Committee, on behalf of the 17th CPC Central Committee, delivered a keynote report titled the *Firmly March on the Path of Socialism with Chinese Characteristics and Strive to Complete the Building of a Moderately Prosperous Society in All Respects* during the opening ceremony of the 18th CPC National Congress. In the report, he pointed out: In building socialism with Chinese characteristics, we base ourselves on the basic reality that China is in the primary stage of socialism. Our overall approach is to promote economic, political,

On November 14, 2012, the 18th CPC National Congress closed in the Great Hall of the People in Beijing.

Shengzhou-10 landed at Siziwangqi in Inner Mongolia on June 26, 2013.

cultural, social, and ecological progress, and our general task is to achieve socialist modernization and the great renewal of the Chinese nation. The so-called five-in-one approach means to promote the harmonious development of economic, political, cultural, social and ecological civilization construction in order to provide strong support for the building of a moderately prosperous society in all respects and realization of the "China Dream".

The five-in-one layout is an organic whole. Economic construction plays a fundamental role; political construction serves as the guarantee; cultural construction is the soul; social construction is the condition; and ecological civilization construction is the foundation. Only persisting in the comprehensive and harmonious development in the five aspects can we create a sustainable development pattern characterized by developed economy, democratic politics, prosperous culture, social fairness and healthy ecosystem. Undoubtedly, the implementation of the development plan is the expectation of the CPC and all Chinese people.

Economic Construction. In the past over three decades, the Chinese economy maintained fast growth more than three times higher than the three percent AAGR of the world economy. Despite the outbreak of the international financial crisis in 2009, the Chinese economy still kept growing rapidly. In promoting the great rejuvenation of the Chinese nation, enhancing the living standard of the people has always been the core goal. By 2012, the per capita disposable income of urban and rural residents had risen to more than 24,500 Yuan and over 7,900 Yuan from less than 100 Yuan and less than 50 Yuan respectively in 1949; the proportion of food consumption as a percentage of total expenditure stayed at 36.2 percent and 39.3 percent respectively, down 21 percentage points and 28 percentage points respectively from 1978 when the reform and opening up program was launched. Obviously, fundamental changes have taken place in the life of Chinese people. At the 18th CPC National Congress in November 2012 and the subsequent Central Economic Working

In October 18, 2013, the Party branch of Zizhuang Village of Yongrong Town, Yongchua District of Chongqing City met to elect its new member committee.

Conference in the same year, "ensuring the people's livelihood and improving the people's living standards" were high on the agenda. We will work harder to improve the people's life further and spare no efforts in helping all Chinese benefit from the reform and opening up policy and socialist modernization drive.

Political Construction. To achieve the people's democracy is an objective both the CPC and the Chinese people have long struggled to achieve. To effectively guarantee the people's right to govern the country, China has chosen the system of people's congresses as the fundamental political system, always upheld and always sought to improve the multi-party cooperation and political consultation system. To solve the issues related to ethnic minorities, it has introduced the system of regional national autonomy. It also makes positive efforts in promoting the democratic autonomy at the grassroots level, greatly enhancing people's awareness of participation, right, and independence. At present, the system of villagers' assembly or villagers' representatives' assembly is adopted in the rural areas to formulate the rules of villager's autonomy or village regulations and non-governmental agreements. A series of management systems are in place including those for democratic management of financial affairs, financial auditing, and village management. Moreover, effective electoral methods have also been created to ensure peasants fully enjoy their democratic rights, including direct election based on nominees recommended by the public, and election based on the nominees recommended by both CPC and non-CPC members. In cities, efforts are being made to improve self-governance among urban residents and build new-type, well-managed, and well-served communities with beautiful environment and featuring civilization and harmony across the country.

Cultural Construction. Culture is the lifeblood of a nation, and it gives the people a sense of belonging. In recent years, there is growing recognition that culture plays an important role in promoting social development and cultural soft power is of great value. To complete the building of a moderately prosperous

society in all respects and achieve the great renewal of the Chinese nation, hard work must be done to create a new surge in promoting socialist culture and bring about its great development and enrichment, increase China's cultural soft power, and enable culture to guide social trends, educate the people, serve society, and boost development. The government's investment in the public cultural sector keeps growing. According to relevant statistics, during the period of the 11th Five-Year Program (2006–2010), the State spent a total of 122.041 billion Yuan in promoting the cultural cause, about 2.46 times of that in the 10th Five-Year Plan (2001–2005). In the 12th Five-Year Program (2011–2015), cultural construction has been upgraded to improve the nation's soft power. Recent years have witnessed fast development of the cultural industry, which is making a bigger contribution to economic growth. China's protection of its intangible cultural heritage started late. However, it has now become internationally advanced in this regard. In applying for and protecting the world cultural heritage, China has done a very good job in the world.

In April 2014, opera lovers in Nantongling Industrial Society attended the Shaoxing opera genres concert.

China also works hard for cultural exchanges with foreign countries and in enhancing the international influence of Chinese culture. Up to now, the country has established a good relationship for cultural exchange with more than 160 countries and regions. The extensive emergence of the Confucius Institute and interest in the Chinese language also means that the international influence of Chinese culture is on the rise.

Social Construction. In China, a populous country with fairly fast social-economic development, social administration is really a very difficult and arduous job. Through long-term exploration and practice, the country has gained a fairly complete organizational network for social management. It has formulated a series of basic laws and regulations in this regard, promoted grid management, information platform and other new achievements in line with the times, and effectively maintained social stability and harmony.

China has put improving the people's livelihood high on its agenda,

A public bicycles rental station in Huhan, Hubei Province.

energetically pressed ahead with the development of education, and actively explored to establish a social security system suitable for its socialist market economy. From 2002 to 2012, the country created over 100 million new jobs in cities and towns. Moreover, it has continued to deepen health system reform, with more than 1.2 billion people covered by basic medical insurance. The 18th Party Congress in 2012 decided to work harder and ensure that all the people enjoy their rights to education, employment, medical and old-age care, and housing so that people can lead a better life. After the 18th Party Congress, a number of policies for the improvement of the people's livelihood were unveiled one after another. Cases in point include the college examination scheme for the children of the migrant population and the income-doubling program. By February 2013, 25 provinces had increased their minimum wage standards by about 20.2 percent on average. The long-awaited income distribution system reform program, which had garnered particular attention, was finally released, while the government-subsidizing housing projects for low-income urban residents have developed apace. All these aspects ensure the people can enjoy a happy and contented life.

Ecological Civilization Construction. Ecological civilization results from human's rethinking of traditional civilization, in particular the industrial civilization. It represents a major progress of human civilization and the development concept, road and model of civilization. It tallies with the traditional Chinese culture especially when the latter touches upon the relationship between humans and nature and between people, as well as the harmonious coexistence of humans and society. China endeavors to develop its economy and, at the same time, it also attaches great importance to environmental management and ecological construction. According to the 18th Party Congress in November 2012, promoting ecological progress is a long-term task of vital importance to the people's wellbeing and the nation's future; China will give high priority to making ecological progress and work hard to build a beautiful country and achieve lasting and sustainable development of the nation. All these things have struck a chord with people in all walks of life. The progress of concepts has greatly speeded up the pace of practice. China is saying goodbye to "black development" while embarking on the road to green development. From the 17th to the 18th Party Congress, from the Bali Weather Summit to those held in Copenhagen and Durban, China took the lead in making a promise of green development and has effectively fulfilled it. The responsible spirit of the Chinese nation for its descendants and the world will be recognized and appreciated by more and more countries.

Deepening Reform Comprehensively

Since entering the 21st Century, China has maintained its good momentum for development, overcome various risks, difficulties and challenges, and made a slew of new historic achievements. Its comprehensive national strength, international competitiveness, and international influence have all improved significantly. But at the same time, as extensive and profound changes are taking place domestically and internationally, China's development faces a series of prominent dilemmas and challenges, and there are quite some problems and difficulties on its path of development: Unbalanced, uncoordinated and unsustainable development remains a big problem. It is weak in scientific and technological innovation. The industrial structure is unbalanced and the growth mode remains extensive. The development gap between urban and rural areas and between regions is still large, and so are income disparities. Social problems are on the rise markedly. There are many problems affecting the people's immediate interests in education, employment, social security, health care, housing, ecological environment, food and drug safety, workplace safety, public security, law enforcement, administration of justice, etc. Some people still lead hard lives. Going through formalities and bureaucratism as well as hedonism and extravagance are serious problems. Some sectors are prone to corruption and other types of misconduct and the fight against corruption remains a serious challenge for us. To solve these problems, the key lies in deepening reform.

In November 2013, the Third Plenary Session of the 18th Party Congress passed the *Decision of the CPC Central Committee on the Major Issues Concerning Comprehensively Deepening Reforms*. The Decision presented the ideas on and the program of deepening reforms through an all-round approach. In a long run, it will exert far-reaching influence on every Chinese, Chinese society, the Chinese nation and even the world. According to some media, the historical task and orientation of the meeting is very clear, namely, continuing to deepen the reform and opening up program.

In 1992, Deng Xiaoping pointed out in his southern tour talks: "If we did not adhere to socialism, implement the policies of reform and opening to the outside world, develop the economy and raise the living standards of the people, we would find ourselves in a blind alley." Just based on the historical lessons we have learned and the needs of current times, the CPC Central Committee has been repeatedly stressing that there are no bounds to practice and development, to emancipating the people's minds, or to the reform and opening-up effort. We will reach an impasse if we stall and go into reverse on our path, and reform and opening up only transpires in the progressive sense, there is no end to it. The Decision passed at the plenum embodies the ideological consensus and wisdom of the whole Party and society on comprehensively deepening reforms. The major issues and measures it contains include:

First of all, letting the market play the decisive role in allocating resources and letting the government play its functions better. This is a major theoretical proposition in the Decision, because economic restructuring is still the focus of deepening reform comprehensively, and the appropriate handling of the relationship between the government and the market is still the core issue of the reform of the economic system. Such a positioning is conducive to transforming the economic development pattern and government functions, as well as reining in corruption and other forms of misconduct.

Second, adhering to and improving the basic economic system.

Third, deepening the reform of the fiscal and taxation systems. Fiscal and taxation system reform is one of the key points in deepening reform comprehensively. The reform mainly includes improvement of the budgeting and taxation system, and establishment of a system in which authority of office matches responsibility for expenditure.

Fourth, improving mechanisms and institutions for the integrated development of urban and rural areas. To complete the building of a moderately prosperous society in all respects and accelerate socialist modernization, we must eliminate the unbalanced development between urban and rural areas.

Fifth, promoting wide, multi-tiered and institutionalized consultative democracy.

Sixth, reforming the judiciary and its operation mechanism. Miscarriage of justice has been a major concern of the people in recent years. Judiciary reform is one of the key points in deepening reform comprehensively.

Seventh, improving leading and working mechanisms for anti-corruption efforts. Fighting corruption has always been a widely discussed topic inside and outside the Party. The Decision lays out plans for promoting innovation in the anti-corruption mechanisms and institutions, and strengthening institutional guarantees.

Eighth, accelerating the improvement of the leadership for the management of the Internet.

Ninth, establishing the Council of State Security.

10th, improving the country's natural resources management system and oversight system. It is aimed at solving some prominent problems plaguing China's efforts in ecological environmental protection.

11th, establishing the Leading Group for Deepening Reform Comprehensively under the CPC Central Committee. The leading group will be responsible for the reform's overall design, planning and coordination, advancing on the whole, supervision and implementation.

It is not hard to see that the Decision makes a series of new major breakthroughs in the theory and policy on China's reform and lays out plans for the systematic reform of significant and pressing issues currently facing China.

After the Third Plenum of the 18th CPC National Congress, China, from

On September 13, 2013, the China Telecom and the Alibaba signed an agreement for strategic business cooperation, under which both parties will cooperate in cloud computing, mobile Internet, data center and other fields.

the local to the central level, had a swift response and released an array of reform measures for economic and other sectors. Statistics show that by January 2014, more than 100 reform-related documents had been unveiled by the CPC Central Committee, State Council, Central Government and relevant departments of State organs and over 200 reform-related files issued by the Party committees and government at the provincial level. Moreover, many of them have been carried out in practice. Since the new leadership group took office, a total of 400 administrative approval items have been abolished and streamlined.

Recently, the State Council released the *Circular of the Reform Policies on the Capital Registration System for Companies* to lay out plans for carrying out capital registration system reform. The reform of industrial and commercial registration system and others will also be implemented step by step. According to the Circular, China will relax the thresholds of registered capital, adopt the subscribed capital registration system, and greatly lower the threshold of start-ups so as to stimulate the social enthusiasm and give full scope to the decisive role of the market. Facts have proved that the number of the main market players

in the pilot areas skyrocketed. For instance, in Shenzhen, newly registered market players surged 130 percent year on year, the growth of private businesses being the fastest.

China has ushered in another spring of reform and opening up. It has prepared well to solve various problems in development and address risks and challenges in various respects. The releasing and implementation of the *Decision of the CPC Central Committee on the Major Issues Concerning Comprehensively Deepening Reforms* not only gives full expression to the foresight of the new leadership group on the difficulties facing reform, but also declares its determination to solve problems. Just as President Xi Jinping said when he was interviewed by a Russian television station on February 7, 2014: "It is no easy job to deepen reform in China, a country with over 1.3 billion people. After more than 30 years' hard work, China's reform efforts have entered a critical stage. It's fair to say that all the easy work has been done and what we have to do next is to put the axe in the helve. We must be courageous and careful. Being courageous means no matter how hard the reform is, we'll continue to move forward, we'll be willing and ready to fulfill responsibilities, we'll crack the hard nuts, and we'll travel through rough waters. Being careful means that we must set the right goal and move towards it carefully and we absolutely cannot make subversive mistakes in this process."

China and the World in the Era of Economic Globalization

Before the adoption, in 1978, of the policy of opening-up, the Chinese economy was basically self sufficient and separated from the world economic system. After the adoption of reform and opening-up, China conformed to the developing trend of economic globalization, set itself upon the path of peaceful development, and not only made use of the changing international environment to develop itself but also used that development to help maintain world peace and aid the pace of common development.

The contemporary-era relationship between China and the rest of the world is undergoing a major historical change and the future and fate of China is closely and increasingly connected with the future and fate of the world.

China has become an important participant in, a builder and maintainer of, the contemporary international system and plays a significant role in international affairs. As a large, responsible, developing country, China has committed itself, along with the other nations of the world, to building a more harmonious global environment with long-lasting peace and common prosperity for all.

Joining the Process of Economic Globalization

The economic and trading relations between countries is becoming ever closer, a continuation of a basic trend that has been in progress for a number of years. From 1950 to the present time, for example, the world trade dependency rose from just 5 percent to over 50 percent. It can be said that, excepting a few countries, almost all the world's separate nations are involved in the global division of labor, and commercial systems and foreign trade have become an important engine for the economic growth of most of the countries of the world.

The Principal Speaker of Asian-Pacific Policy Center of the American Rand Corporation has passed the following comments on China and Japan's

Beijing Central Business District (CBD).

accession into the process of economic globalization: "Although arriving late," he said, "China has acceded to the system of globalization with a far greater ardor than Japan. The opening degree of China's economy is much higher than that of Japan. " (*China and Globalization*) The policy of reform and opening-up introduced in late 1978, coinciding with economic globalization, made relations between China and the rest of the world much closer and the trade dependency rose proportionately. In 1978 China's foreign trade dependency was only 10 percent, but in 1994 it reached 42 percent. In the next few years it dropped a little but in 2002 it reached 43 percent, further rising until, in 2006, it attained its highest historical level of 67 percent. In recent years, China worked hard to seek growth of domestic consumption. There is still a high foreign trade dependency which reaches 46 percent in 2013. As a consequence, China's participation in the process of economic globalization was becoming continually more important.

The level of China's opening-up has entered a new stage and the degree of internationalization is all the time increasing. American former trade representative Charlene Barshefsky said that China has in the last 10 years undergone unprecedented changes unseen in the world. In the ten years subsequent to its accession to the World Trade Organization in 2011, China abided by the WTO rules, carried out its undertakings as set down at the time of its entry, adjusted and reformed its economic system according to the correct timescale, amended and improved relevant laws and regulations, and became a fully integrated member of the world economic system. At present, China's general tariff level has dropped from 15.3 percent to 9.8 percent, lower than the world tariff level of other developing countries. China's non-agricultural products and agricultural products tariff levels stand at nine and fifteen percent respectively, against global counterparts of twenty-nine and sixty percent respectively. Among all the sectors in China, the greatest degree of opening up occurred in the service sector, and among the 160-odd service departments distinguished by WTO, China made undertakings in 100 departments, close to the average level of WTO's developed members.

China is both the participator in, and architect of, an international multilateral trade system, and it actively participates in global and regional economic cooperation courses and plays an important and constructive role. China takes an active part in the multilateral and regional economic cooperation organizations and activities such as the WTO, International Monetary Fund, World Bank, and Asian Development Bank, has held dialogues with Group 8 and Group 12, and has strengthened the macro-policy coordination with major economic bodies and dialogues in such fields as finance, foreign exchange, industry, trade and energy. China, as a developing country, has also participated in the international multilateral commercial system and the stipulation of international economic rules and here too has played a leading role.

China attaches great importance to the role played by the regional bilateral economic cooperation mechanism. China has made positive progress in the negotiations aimed at facilitating trade and investment under the regional

On April 11, 2014, the Boao Forum for Asia Annual Conference discussed role of the central banks, responsibilities, objectives and crisis management.

economic cooperation mechanism of Shanghai Cooperation Organization, Asian-Pacific Economic Cooperation Organization, Asian-European Conference, ASEAN and China, Japan and Republic of Korea (10+3), Greater Mekong Sub-Region Cooperation, and Asian-Pacific Trade Agreement. By means of such activities as ASEAN and China (10+1) Cooperation, Sino-Africa Cooperation Forum, Sino-Arab Cooperation Forum, China-Caribbean Economic and Trade Cooperation Forum and China-Pacific Island Countries Economic Development and Cooperation Forum, China has done much to strengthen the regional economic cooperation with relevant countries and regions. Thus far, China has established more than 160 bilateral trade cooperation mechanisms and more than 150 investment agreements with countries and regions concerned; meanwhile, China has established dialogue channels with the United States, Europe, Japan, UK and Russia.

China is committed to speeding up the foundation of free-trade regions, expanding fields of cooperation and enhancing cooperation levels. Thus far, China has set up 15 free trade zones and signed 10 free trade agreements with 28 countries and regions. In 2010, the trade volume of Chinese inland with the 10 free trade partners (including ASEAN, Pakistan, Chile, Singapore, New Zealand, Peru, Costa Rica, and Chinese Hong Kong, Macao and Taiwan) made up 26.3 percent of its total trade volume.

Bringing New Opportunities for Development to the World

"In history no one has maintained such a dazzling economic growth rate as China has in the past thirty years." Those words are taken from an article in the British magazine *The Economist* on September 29, 2007. Since 1978 China's economy has maintained an average annual growth rate of nearly 10 percent, much higher than that of Japan and the "Four Small Dragons" in Asia (Republic of Korea, Singapore, and Chinese Hong Kong and Taiwan) in the same period. In recent years, the world economy enters into a period of transformation and readjustment, but fails to form a new growth point. In order to improve the growth quality, China is making effort to readjust its economic structure. Although this leads to slower economic growth, it will solve long-term economic problems. Even though, in 2012 and 2013, China's growth rate stayed at 7.8 percent and 7.7 percent, respectively.

China's development provides a positive driving force in the growth of global trade. A growing China will make greater contribution to the world.

China's development serves to stimulate global trade. The contribution made by China's economy on the world economic development has risen from 2.3 percent in 1978 to 19.2 percent in 2007, overtaking the United States to be number one in the world. In 2013, the Chinese contribution rose further to reach nearly 30 percent, pushing forward the world economic development.

Since its accession to the WTO in 2001, China has imported goods with an annual average total value in excess of US$ 750 billion, which means China has created 14 million employment opportunities for relevant countries and regions.

China's Development Serves to Stimulate Global Trade

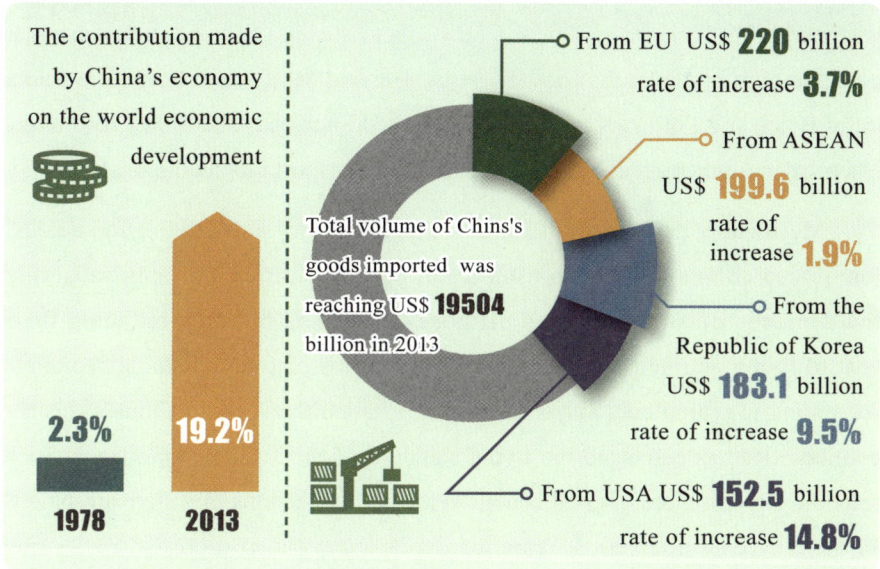

The contribution made by China's economy on the world economic development

2.3% 1978

19.2% 2013

Total volume of Chins's goods imported was reaching US$ 19504 billion in 2013

From EU US$ **220** billion
rate of increase **3.7%**

From ASEAN
US$ **199.6** billion
rate of increase **1.9%**

From the Republic of Korea
US$ **183.1** billion
rate of increase **9.5%**

From USA US$ **152.5** billion
rate of increase **14.8%**

In 2013, China continued to increase its imports, with the value of goods imported reaching US$ 1,950.4 billion, an increase of 7.3 percent from the previous year. Of this, the value of China's imports from EU and ASEAN was US$ 220 billion and US$ 199.6 billion, an increase of 3.7 percent and 1.9 percent respectively; and that from the Republic of Korea and the United States was US$ 183.1 billion, an increase of 8.5 percent, and US$ 152,5 billion, or 14.8 percent increase. In addition, China's imports in the form of services in 2013 were valued at US$ 329.1 percent, an increase of 17.5 percent over the previous year.

The rapid growth of China import scale, provides a broad market for other countries. According to a report released by the National Committee on US-China Trade of the United States, from 2000 to 2011, American exports to China increased by about US$ 88 billion. The Chamber of Commerce with 240 noted companies including Coca-Cola and Procter & Gamble, said that American exports to China is of great importance to US economic health, and create good

jobs for Americans. China is America's third largest export market, and will continue to provide growth opportunities for US enterprises. China has become a vast market for America products. Coca-Cola's sales in China keep increasing at a double-digit rate over the past few years. General Motors and Ford have sold a lot of Buick and Ford cars in China. The United States has also sold China many electrical equipment, machinery, computer and transportation equipment.

Meanwhile, the growth of China's export industry also offers good quality, low-priced commodities to consumers in many countries, not only satisfying the demands of large numbers of those consumers but also reducing their cost of living and helping the importing countries maintain a stable economy. According to (admittedly as yet incomplete) statistics, access to China's cheaper commodities has enhanced the living standard of the average Americans. Such imports, therefore, are of great benefit to the poorer sections of American society. In the ten years after 2001, American consumers saved more than US$ 600 billion by buying Chinese goods, and each family in EU saved 300 Euro dollars a year.

Chinese-made products, combining good quality with cheap price, help to maintain the inflation ratio in some countries at a comparatively low level, thus extending the upturning cycle of their economy. The United Nations Industrial Development Organization Director General Kandeh K. Yumkella pointed out that China's trade-driven economic growth is a boon for other developing countries in their economic development as consumers in these countries can afford buying Chinese products indispensable for their life. This is fact that what China does serves to help boost the purchasing power of other developing countries, a boon for the poor there.

A considerable part of China's foreign exchange reserves have been used to buy the national debts of Western countries such as the United States, a fiscal policy which has helped those countries escape some of the pressure of economic deficit.

338

China's participation in economic globalization has expanded the space for global optimization in industrial structure, accelerated economic relationships between the countries, and become an important factor in maintaining a healthy world economy. In the course of opening up and entering into the world market, China has offered opportunities and wealth sources to the world. It has been a driving force in effecting changes in the global systems of labor, pricing, and supply-and-demand, and has accelerated the optimization and upgrading of economic structure. What has rapidly become known as the "China factor" has played an extremely active role in the world economy.

China's development soon offered a wide market for international capital investment, and that investment has seen many positive returns. The huge market surrounding infrastructural construction, for example, has provided a large number of foreign companies with major business opportunities. From 2001 to

In November 2011, Sinopec and Yum Group signed the cooperation framework agreement, announced that Yum will open KFC restaurants and Pizza Hut at all filling stations and expressway service area under Sinopec.

2011, foreign companies in China remitted US$ 261.7 billion of their profits out of China, an annual average increase of 30 percent.

With the growth in power of Chinese enterprises, investment in foreign countries and regions has also been on the increase. China's foreign direct investment increased from US$ 2.7 billion in 2002 to US$ 74.65 billion in 2011, an average annual increase of 26.9 percent. By the end of 2011, China's foreign direct investment stock reached US$ 424.78 billion. China set up 18,000 business abroad, with assets valued at US$ 2000 billion. In 2012, Chinese investors invested US$ 77.22 billion in 4425 businesses in 141 countries and regions. In 2013, the sum rose to US$ 90.2 billion, or 16.8 percent more than in the previous year. In 2011, Chinese enterprises overseas paid taxes amounting to more than US$ 22 billion, or 88.7 percent more than 2010. Of the 888,000 workers they employ, 72.8 percent were locals.

In May 2011, sale of iPad 2 began in the Chinese mainland: A shot of the Xidan Apple Market in Beijing.

By the end of 2011, China's outbound tourist destinations totaled 140. In 2013, more than 98.19 million people in the Chinese inland visited abroad. They included 91.97 million who went out of China for private reasons, up 19.3 percent from the previous year. China has surpassed the United States and Germany to become the number one source of outbound tourists, with the number hitting more than 100 million, compared to 10.47 million in 2000. From 2000 to 2012, the number of Chinese outbound tourists increased 8 times. Chinese spending in this regard reached US$ 102 billion, with the Chinese contribution to world economy reaching 13 percent.

On October 22, 2013, Guiling in Guangxi Zhuang Autonomous Region saw the opening of the 7th forum on trends and prospects of the UN World Tourism Organization/Pacific Asia Travel Association. The World Tourism Organization Executive Director Matthew Favela said that in 2012, the number of outbound Chinese was 78 million, which made China the world's largest tourist source market. In the next 5 years to come, he predicted, the total number of Chinese outbound tourists is expected to surpass 400 million.

China has huge potential and excellent prospects for developing foreign economic and commercial cooperation. By 2020 the market size and total demand in China doubled that of 2000. Meanwhile, all the world's countries can identify and develop their own huge business potential in their mutual-beneficial cooperation with China, which will play an important and active role in driving forward world economic growth.

Regarding the development prospects for China's economy in the first half of this century, some worldwide economic research institutions have made their estimations and a broadly common outlook is as follows: China's economy will keep growing at an annual rate of above eight percent. By 2013 China's GDP reached US$ 9,430 billion, with the per-capita share reaching close to US$ 7,000. China ranked second in terms of goods imports and exports, and has become the world's number one exporter, and major foreign capital user and investor. By around 2020 China's GDP will increase further and China's national power will enter a new stage, making China to be somewhere between number 10 and number 15 in the world. It is estimated that from 2005 to 2020, based on purchasing power parity, China will have a contribution rate of 37 percent to the world's new growth GDP. China will offer the world more chances for further development.

A Responsible Developing Big Country

By the end of July 2011, China had established diplomatic relations with 172 countries, formed economic and commercial links with more than 230 countries and regions, participated in more than 130 inter-governmental international organizations, acceded to 27 international conventions on human rights and signed more than 300 international treaties. In international affairs China enjoys a broad range of privileges and takes its corresponding obligations seriously. It has become an important member of the international community.

China is a participator in, and a builder and maintainer of, today's international system.

On the evening of December 4, 2012, the first group of 135 Chinese peacekeeping officers and men reached the Bamako International Airport.

—Participate in UN affairs and safeguard UN authority. As one of the initiating states of the San Francisco Conference China has helped draw up its constitution. It is a member state of the United Nations, the first to sign the *UN Charter*, and made an outstanding contribution to the birth of the UN. After its resumption of the legal seat in 1971, China actively participated in the work of various fields, continuously deepened its cooperation with the UN, earnestly implemented its international obligations and firmly safeguarded the tenets and principles of the *UN Charter*. As a permanent member of the UN Security Council, China took a comprehensive part in the work of UN Security Council, strove to safeguard the authority and role of Security Council, worked hard to solve regional hot issues by means of peaceful methods such as discussion, dialogues and negotiation, and supported the UN Secretary-General in developing preventive diplomacy such as mediating and coordinating. China played a constructive role in helping the Security Council successfully deal with a series of issues such as the Iraq-Iran war, Cambodia and East Timor. China supported the UN in its adoption of necessary and reasonable reform in all aspects and various fields, and advocated that the UN should develop in the direction that is beneficial to maintaining the tenets and principles of its Charter, to unity of member states, and to the overall and long-term interests of those member states. China supported the UN's leading and coordinating role in the field of international anti-terrorism and nonproliferation, supported the UN in its deployment of peace-keeping forces, and actively promoted the solution of regional conflicts within the framework of UN policy. China widely participated in the international dialogues and cooperation held by the UN in various fields such as human rights, development, justice, environmental protection and cultural exchange.

—Participate in cooperation in global energy security and environmental protection. China has actively strengthened bilateral and multilateral cooperation in energy issues and attached great importance to working together with the international community in the field of world energy security. In such spheres as

On June 30, 2013, the 14th session of the ASEAN and 10+3 Ministerial Meeting was held in Brunei.

energy exploitation, utilization, technology, environmental protection, as well as new and renewable energy sources, China has, in recent years, actively developed dialogues and cooperation with a number of international organizations and countries. China has also planned its unified policy of domestic development and opening up, actively participated in the global exploitation and cooperation in regard of such resources as petroleum and natural gas, and maintained energy security in combination with political transparency. China has undertaken effective cooperation with more than 10 international inter-governmental organizations and non-governmental organizations including UNEP, has added its signature to more than 50 international treaties involving environmental protection, and has earnestly undertaken the work of implementation. China has signed bilateral agreements or memoranda of understanding on environmental protection cooperation with more than 40 countries including the United States, Japan, Canada and Russia, has established environmental cooperation mechanisms with the European Union and the League of Arab States, and has helped African countries develop along the path of environmental protection.

China has, with a fully committed and proactive spirit of cooperation, participated in regional environmental protection, has established a mechanism allowing environmental ministers of China, Japan and Republic of Korea to hold regular meetings, has initiated the Greater Mekong Sub-Regional Environmental Cooperation Mechanism, and has pushed for environmental cooperation under the mechanisms of ASEAN and China (10+1) and ASEAN and China, Japan and Republic of Korea (10+3).

—Commitment to the strengthening of international cooperation in arms control, disarmament and nonproliferation. China has always stood for the comprehensive prohibition and complete elimination of nuclear weapons. Since possessing a nuclear capability of its own, China has solemnly announced an unshakeable policy of no first strike use of nuclear weapons at any time and under any condition and it unconditionally undertakes neither to use nor threaten to use nuclear weapons against non-nuclear weapon states. China has always held an extremely restrained attitude regarding the development of nuclear weapons and the size of its nuclear arsenal is always maintained at the lowest possible level for adequate self-defense. China has never deployed nuclear weapons overseas. China was one of the first states to sign the *Comprehensive Nuclear Test Ban Treaty* and has maintained its position regarding that Treaty since the suspension of nuclear testing in July 1996. China firmly supports the implementation of the *Biological Weapons Convention* and *Chemical Weapons Convention* and thoroughly carries out its obligations as stipulated in those Conventions. China believes in the peaceful use of outer space, and encourages the international community to adopt practical methods to effectively prevent an extra-terrestrial arms race. China firmly opposes the proliferation of weapons of mass destruction and their means of delivery, and actively participates in the course of international prevention of proliferation. China has acceded to all the international treaties and relevant international organizations in the field of nonproliferation, actively undertaken exchanges and cooperation with other countries and mechanisms related to multinational export control, and has

On December 4, 2012, the Shanghai Cooperation Organization member states held their 11th meeting of the prime minister at the Kyrgyzstan capital of Bishkek.

promoted solutions to issues related to nonproliferation by means of peaceful methods such as dialogues and cooperation. China maintains a policy of ever tightening export control laws and regulations involving nuclear, biological, and chemical missiles, as well as conventional military hardware, and has also established an inter-agency contingency mechanism for nonproliferation export control, and has strengthened those powers by which it is enforced.

—Strive to maintain neighborhood and regional security and stability. By a series of practical actions, China has sought to establish good relations and mutual confidence with its neighbors, has accelerated bilateral cooperation and regional security cooperation, and has worked hard to improve the regional security dialogue and cooperation mechanism. Sticking to accepted guidelines for international relations, and in the spirit of equal consultation and mutual understanding and accommodation, China has properly solved its border issues with neighboring countries, dissolved disputes and accelerated stability. After sparing no effort to reach a mutually acceptable accord, China has now signed

border treaties with a dozen continental neighboring countries and has solved those border issues which came about for historical reasons. The resolution of border issues with India and Bhutan is already developing in a positive direction. China has signed a series of agreements with relevant neighboring countries to accelerate bilateral mutual confidence, has further signed the *Declaration on the Conduct of the Parties in the South China Sea* with ASEAN to maintain stability and develop cooperation in this area, and has made a significant breakthrough in the common development of the South China Sea region with The Philippines and Vietnam. China has more actively and practically developed its military relationship with the major powers, has strengthened its military communications with neighboring countries and extended its policy of military exchange with developing countries. By brokering reciprocal visits between high-level officials, it has solidified the basis for mutual and friendly cooperation; by undertaking strategic consultation and dialogues, it has promoted mutual communication and confidence; and by enlarging the scope and nature of these meetings, it has broadened mutual dependence, avoided confrontation and helped to realize common security and stability.

—Actively promote regional security dialogues and cooperation. China plays a constructive role in such regional and inter-regional mechanisms as China and ASEAN, ASEAN and China, Japan and the Republic of Korea, Shanghai Cooperation Organization (SCO), Asia-Europe Conference, ASEAN Regional Forum, and Asian Cooperation Dialogue. Under the framework of SCO, China and member states have comprehensively strengthened cooperation in defense security, established multi-level cooperation mechanisms in a wide field including meetings of heads of states, prime ministers, foreign ministers and national defense ministers, launched SCO Secretariat and Regional Anti-Terrorism departments, and advocated the setting up of a new global security structure with mutual confidence, benefits, equality and respect. China attaches much importance to the role of ASEAN Regional Forum, has put forward constructive proposals on its sound development, and has either sponsored or jointly held seminars on non-traditional security fields under the framework of the Forum. As a major country in the region, China has taken the lead in acceding to the *Treaty of Amity and Cooperation in Southeast Asia*, and has injected a new vitality into the peace and friendship between China and ASEAN countries. China actively participates in the regional cooperation in non-traditional security fields such as maritime search and rescue, combating piracy, and cracking down on drug production and trafficking.

—Participate in dealing with global and regional hot issues. China holds a strong position on solving international disputes and accelerating worldwide common security by political and diplomatic methods such as negotiation and dialogue. Regarding the nuclear issue on the Korean Peninsula, China has always advocated a dialogue-led peaceful solution, with the ultimate aim of denuclearizing the Korean Peninsula and maintaining the peace and stability of the Peninsula and Northeastern Asia. Since 2003 China has actively worked along diplomatic lines with the relevant parties, and succeeded in convening

On June 10, 2014, China's Foreign Minister Wang Yi met with Hwang Joon-kook, ROK Ministry of Foreign Affairs, Minister of the Korean Peninsula Pace Negotiations, and ROK delegation chief for six-party negotiation.

In March 2014, 218 Chinese peacekeeping officers and men were awarded UN peacekeeping medals. They have completed their peacekeeping mission in the Democratic Republic of the Congo and also assisted some 1,100-member medical aid teams in work.

and hosting first the Three-Party Talks between China, North Korea and the United States and then the Six-Party Talks between China, North Korea, the United States, Republic of Korea, Russia and Japan. China was instrumental in getting the participants of the fourth round of Six-Party Talks to issue a Joint Statement on confirming the target of denuclearization of the Korean Peninsula and achieved an important stage in the negotiations. Regarding the issues that surround the problems in the Middle East, China opposes any practice that might threaten regional peace and stability. Along with other countries it persuaded the UN Security Council to pass Resolution No.1701, and called on the concerned parties to return to the conference table in the light of the relevant UN decisions and the principle of "Land for Peace". China's position is to realize as soon as possible a comprehensive and just solution to the problems facing the Middle East, including that which exists between Palestine and Israel, and harmonize relations between the relevant countries with the ultimate objective of a lasting peace. Regarding the Iraq issue, China advocates seeking a political solution within the UN framework, and stands for maintaining the independent sovereignty and integrity of the territory of Iraq. China furthermore respects the Iraqi people's wish to become masters of their own country, and has done a great deal of work on how the future of Iraq will take shape when the country returns to peace. Regarding the issue of Iran's nuclear capability, China supports and safeguards the international nuclear nonproliferation system, advocates policies in support of peace and stability in Middle East region, opposes proliferation of nuclear weapons, and stands for a peaceful solution to the Iran nuclear issue by means of diplomatic negotiation.

—Continuously extend its participation in UN peacekeeping actions. From 1989 to 2013, China deployed over 22,000 military personnel on 24 UN peace-keeping initiatives; and nine Chinese officers and soldiers lost their lives in the cause of maintaining global peace. At present, nearly 2,000 Chinese officers and men are carrying out their missions in separate peacekeeping actions. Of the five permanent members of the UN Security Council, China sends more men to do the work than any others. China also pays more for the peace-keeping missions than other developing countries.

—Actively participate in the struggle against global terrorism. China adheres to the *UN Charter* and other accepted international law guidelines as the basis of its anti-terrorism policy. It brings the leadership and role of the UN and the Security Council into full play, prevents and combats terrorism in partnership with many other countries, roots out the sources of terrorism, strengthens cooperation in such respects as exchanges in anti-terrorism information, cuts off the monetary supply of terrorist organizations, apprehends and where appropriate extradites suspects of terrorist crimes, and has put a great deal of effective work into the international anti-terrorism struggle. China has acceded to ten international anti-terrorism conventions including the *International Convention on Stopping Terrorist Explosions*, has signed the *International Convention on*

Severing Financial Aid to Terrorism, and has thoroughly implemented a series of decisions on anti-terrorism issues passed by the UN Security Council. China advocates strengthening regional anti-terrorism cooperation, holds joint anti-terrorism exercises with relevant countries, and is continuously exploring new ways to combat terrorism, a policy which is having an impact on international terrorist forces.

—Adhere to a defensive national defense policy. China's national defense is subject to and serves national development and security strategies. It aims at safeguarding national security and unity and ensures the realization of the grand objective of modernization. Since the 1990s, on the back of its economic development, China has promoted the gradual growth and reconstruction of national defense and modernization of armies, which has suited the developing trend of new military reform in the world at large and yet still satisfied the demands of maintaining national security and protecting national interests. In 2013 Chinese defense budget was 720 billion Yuan, an increase of 10.7 percent higher than 2012, ranking second in the world, but still far behind the USA. In 2012 military spending as a proportion of GDP was 4.35 percent in the United States, 2.8 percent in South Korea, 1.99 percent in China, and 0.99 percent in

Military Spending as a Proportion of GDP of Some Countries in 2012

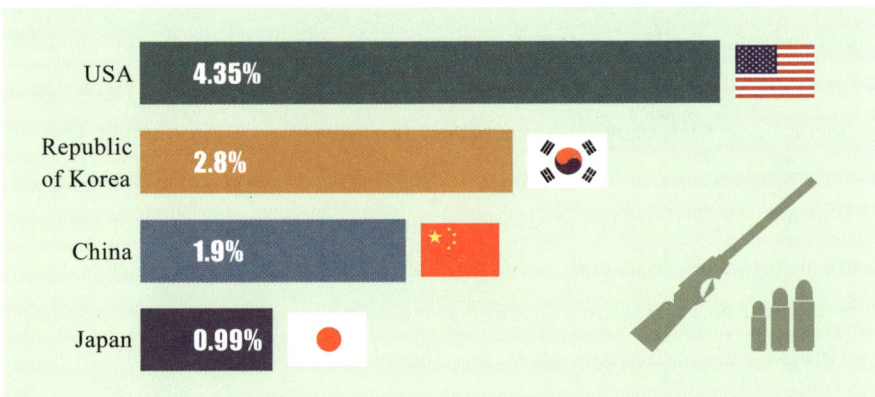

Country	Percentage
USA	4.35%
Republic of Korea	2.8%
China	1.9%
Japan	0.99%

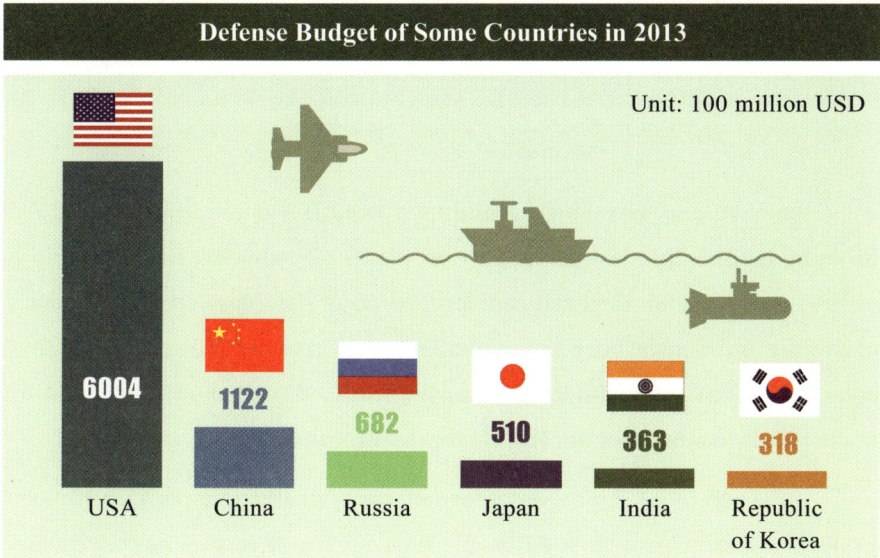

Defense Budget of Some Countries in 2013

Unit: 100 million USD

6004	1122	682	510	363	318
USA	China	Russia	Japan	India	Republic of Korea

Japan. IISS's 2014 report lists top 15 countries in terms of military spending in 2013: USA, US$ 600.4 billion; China, US$ 112.2 billion; Russia, US$ 68.2 billion; Japan, US$ 51 billion; India, US$ 36.3 billion; and Republic of Korea, US$ 31.8 billion. In terms of per-capita share, China's military spending is at a low level.

New Diplomatic Ideas and Image

We have only one Earth. Building a beautiful home to achieve global harmony is the lofty ideal pursued by people in all countries. But the world in reality is not peaceful. Regional conflicts and major flare-ups occur continuously, economic imbalance becomes wider, the gap between north and south is enlarged, traditional and non-traditional security threats interweave, and the peace and development of our world faces numerous difficulties and challenges.

At the end of 2012, this was solemnly underlined during the 18th National Congress of the Communist Party of China (CPC). "Peaceful development is

On June 5, 2014, the 6th Ministerial Meeting of the China-Arab Cooperation Forum was held in Beijing. After the meeting, Chinese Foreign Minister Wang Yi and Arabia National League Secretary General Alabi signed the Beijing Declaration of the Ministerial Meeting of the China-Arab Cooperation Forum, the Chinese Arabia National Cooperation Forum Plan for 2014–2016, and the China Arabia National Cooperation Forum Development Plan for 2014–2024.

the sure choice of socialism with Chinese characteristics. We should pursue development through opening up and cooperation to benefit all." According to the changes in the international situation and the development trend of China, and taking into account the long-term interests and strategic overall situation, the new central leadership with Xi Jinping as General Secretary has promoted innovation in diplomatic theories and practice, put forward a series of new diplomatic ideas and carried out a series of diplomatic actions, presenting a new image of the country as a major power with Chinese characteristics. China is creatively implementing the diplomatic strategy - taking its relations with surrounding regions as a priority, and that with major powers as crucial, that with developing countries as the base and multilateral diplomacy as an important operational mode.

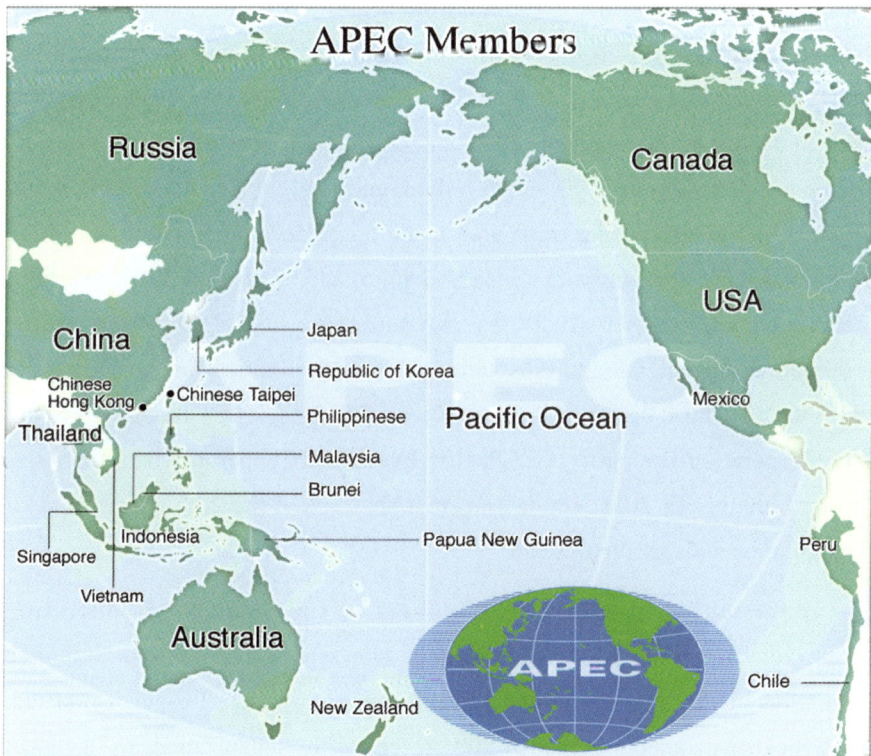

Putting forth the right approach to upholding justice and seeking interests with a view to enhancing friendship and cooperation with neighboring countries and developing countries. China has some 30 neighbors, either with a common border or facing each other across the sea. In the south are 11 small and medium-sized developing countries of Southeast Asia, including ten ASEAN countries and East Timor. All ten ASEAN countries are close neighbors of China, which is seeking to create a secure and prosperous neighborhood based on amity, sincerity, mutual benefit and inclusiveness. Currently, the relationship between China and ASEAN shows good development momentum featuring "equality, mutual trust and mutually beneficial cooperation". In the political sphere, over the past decade, both sides have successfully established the strategic partnership; in the security field, they are trying hard to enhance mutual trust through dialogue, peacefully solve disputes through negotiation and achieving the goals of regional security through cooperation, signing a number of cooperation documents; meanwhile, fast growth in trade, investment and cooperation has been witnessed in the economic field. The China- ASEAN Free Trade Area was officially launched on January 1, 2010, encompassing a population of 1.9 billion, a combined GDP of over US$ 6,000 billion, and total trade value of US$ 4,500 billion. It is the largest free trade area made up of developing countries in the world, and there are continuous efforts being made to upgrade it. In regard to international and regional affairs, the two parties are jointly promoting healthy development of regional and cross-regional cooperation mechanisms including ASEAN plus China, Japan, and South Korea (10+3), ASEAN Regional Forum, Asia Cooperation Dialogue, Asia-Pacific Economic Cooperation and the Asia-Europe Meeting. In 2011, China and ASEAN marked the 20th anniversary of their dialogue with great optimism.

The establishment and development of the Shanghai Cooperation Organization is another successful example witnessing China's efforts to build a harmonious neighborhood. China, Kazakhstan, Kyrgyzstan, Russia, Tajikistan, and Uzbekistan joined together in 2001 to create the organization in Shanghai.

Increase in China-ASEAN Import and Export Trade

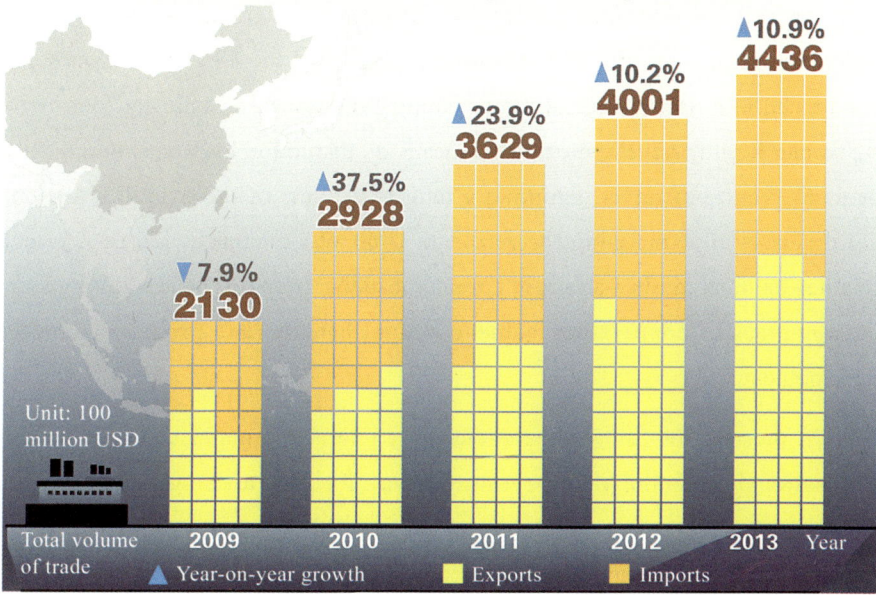

Total volume of trade	2009	2010	2011	2012	2013	Year
	▼7.9% 2130	▲37.5% 2928	▲23.9% 3629	▲10.2% 4001	▲10.9% 4436	

Unit: 100 million USD

▲ Year-on-year growth   ■ Exports   ■ Imports

It has unique advantages in geographical proximity, similar history and cultural empathy, and the members abide by the aims of peace and development, follow democratic principles, pursue an opening-up policy and actively carry out various forms of dialogues, exchanges and cooperation. Over the years, the SCO has unswervingly implemented the "Shanghai Spirit" advocating mutual trust, mutual benefit, equality and consultation, respect for cultural diversity and common development. It has become an important force in maintaining regional and world peace, stability and prosperity. In September 2013, the 13th SCO Summit was held in Bishkek, Kyrgyzstan. Chinese President Xi Jinping delivered a speech advocating further promotion of the "Shanghai Spirit".

Putting forth the vision of building a new model of major-country relationship between China and the United States while striving to advance relations with other major countries. The rapid development of China has profoundly changed the international and regional situation. It has helped to

break down the historic understanding that "a rising power will certainly conflict with the existing dominant power". To resolve international concerns about China's development, the 18th National Congress of the CPC put forward the need to build a new model of major-country relationship featuring long-term stable and healthy development. This means no disruption by some contingency or local event, but rather, adopting a long-term view of the overall situation. On the basis of abandoning the zero-sum Cold War mentality, the new model requires us to strengthen strategic communications, properly handle differences, enlarge areas of cooperation, achieve mutual benefits and promote common development.

At present, the Sino-US relationship is one of the major concerns by the international community, presenting the way for how a rising power and an existing dominant power can get along. In June 2013, when meeting President Obama, President Xi Jinping summarized the new model from three viewpoints: non-conflict and non-confrontation; mutual respect; and win-win cooperation. President Obama quite agreed with this approach. In November 2013, American President's National Security Advisor Susan Rice gave a speech entitled *America's Future in Asia*. She clearly put forward that America should seek a new model of major-country relations with China, try to improve the quality of bilateral relations through controlling competition, deepening cooperation and strengthening dialogue, and realize the best balance in competition and cooperation. On December 4, 2013, US Vice President Joseph Biden visited China, where he declared: "The Sino-US relationship is the most important bilateral relationship in the 21st century. America will actively join hands with China to build a new model of Sino-US relationship on the basis of mutual respect, mutual trust and equality." China and the United States also successfully held their fifth round of Strategic and Economic Dialogue, making good progress in implementing the agreement of the two presidents and advancing the building of the new model of major-country relationship.

On May 20–21, the Fourth Summit of the Conference on Interaction and Confidence Building Measures in Asia was held in Shanghai. President Xi Jinping delivered a keynote speech on the Summit, stressed that China would work with other sides to to advocate common, comprehensive, cooperative and sustainable security in Asia, establish a new regional security cooperation architecture, and jointly build a road for security of Asia that is shared by and win-win to all. The picture is the leaders of each country moving toward the venue after the group photo.

With active planning and facilitation, China's relations with other major countries have also made fresh progress and breakthroughs. Xi Jinping made Russia his first port of call on his first overseas visit as President, which strengthened bilateral cooperation in economy, trade, energy and strategic security and consolidated the basis of the China-Russia comprehensive strategic partnership. The two countries have maintained close coordination on major international and regional issues and in global economic governance, and achieved new progress in growing their comprehensive strategic partnership of coordination, setting an example for major countries to deepen trust and

cooperation in the new era. Meanwhile, China and the European Union have expanded their areas of cooperation, deepened their shared interests and continued to elevate strategic relations and cooperation to new heights. China has also made active efforts and achieved notable results in developing friendship and cooperation with other major developing countries and major regional countries.

Enhancing friendship and cooperation with neighboring countries and developing countries. Chinese leaders' successful visits to Africa and Latin America have fully reflected the great importance China attaches to developing countries. During his visit to Africa, Xi Jinping expounded on his Africa policy and stressed China's commitment to cooperation with sincerity, real results, affinity and good faith. In particular, he emphasized the win-win nature of China-Africa cooperation. China would fully honor its commitments, attach no political strings to aid, help African countries translate their strength in natural resources into progress in development and achieve diverse, independent and sustainable development. His remarks struck a chord among African leaders and people. The two sides achieved fruitful results in renewing friendship, enhancing mutual trust, advancing cooperation and identifying opportunities for common development. By visiting Trinidad and Tobago, Costa Rica and Mexico and holding bilateral talks with leaders of eight Caribbean countries, Xi Jinping has brought China's overall cooperation with Latin America and the Caribbean to a new high. A large number of major cooperation projects were agreed upon.

China attaches great importance to the promotion of world development through its own progress and the realization of common development of all countries. For years, it has actively promoted economic and trade relations with developing countries and constantly enlarged the mutually beneficial results. As a result, the broad cross-section of developing countries has gained more development opportunities and benefits from cooperation with China. Cooperation has been further strengthened through opening wider its domestic market, importing more products of other developing countries and providing other countries with production technologies. The Chinese Government supports competent domestic enterprises to carry out mutually beneficial cooperation in various forms overseas.

While focusing on completing its own arduous development tasks, China has supported the same cause in other developing countries with concrete moves and gradually increased economic aid to them. The scale of China's foreign assistance kept expanding from 2010 to 2012. Besides complete projects and goods and materials, which were the main forms of China's foreign assistance, technical cooperation and human resources development cooperation also saw remarkable increases. Asia and Africa were the major recipient areas of China's foreign assistance. To promote the realization of Millennium Development Goals, China directed most of its assisting funds to low-income developing

Students of the anti-poverty study program for developing countries financed by China.

countries. From 2010 to 2012, China appropriated in total 89.34 billion Yuan for foreign assistance. China provided assistance to 121 countries, including 30 in Asia, 51 in Africa, nine in Oceania, 19 in Latin America and the Caribbean and 12 in Europe. Besides, China also provided assistance to regional organizations such as the African Union. China provided foreign assistance mainly in the following forms: undertaking complete projects, providing goods and materials, conducting technical cooperation and human resources development cooperation, dispatching medical teams and volunteers, offering emergency humanitarian aid, and reducing or exempting the debts of the recipient countries.

Deeply engaging in and guiding the process of multilateral diplomacy. When meeting leaders of international organizations, Xi Jinping stressed China's commitment to the advocacy and practice of multilateralism and the great value it places on the important role of the United Nations and other international organizations. China will honor its due international obligations and work in close cooperation with relevant international organizations in maintaining world peace and security, promoting human development and progress and addressing global issues and challenges. Fresh progress has been made in China's relations with major international organizations. Attending the Fifth BRICS Leaders' Meeting in Durban, South Africa in March 2013, President Xi Jinping brought about progress in building organizational mechanisms. The Summit issued the *eThekwini Declaration* and *Action Plan*, decided to establish a development bank and a contingent reserve arrangement among BRICS countries, thus providing a strong impetus to the establishment of a new international political and economic order that is fairer and more equitable.

Inheritance and Development of Tradition

Thanks to the implementation of the opening-up policy and economic globalization, the contemporary society of China is now undergoing unprecedented changes. China is developing fast to become a modernized society. The history of human beings has never seen such a huge change that improves the living condition of more than one billion people so rapidly.

Today's China maintains its tradition. It is furthermore a country that keeps up with the times and is full of innovation. The development of China's society is at a transitional stage. China is taking a completely new attitude facing the future.

The structure of China's social economy is also undergoing changes.

Migrant workers looking for jobs in a Chongqing job fair.

Diversity features such changes. Further development of a socialist market economy diversifies the structure of the economy. It forms the pattern with the public sector remaining dominant and diverse sectors of the economy developing side by side. Meanwhile, the organization of economic activities, means of employment and distribution methods are also diversified. All these factors contribute to diversified relationships of different social interest. People at different social strata have different understanding about the development of the society as well as different requests related to their own interest.

Urbanization speeds up the changes in rural areas. The source of ancient Chinese civilization developed through agriculture. The small-scale peasant economy based on family production determined the value of the society and mode of development. Modernization and urbanization develop side by side. As a result of the quick development of modernization construction in China, the number of cities increases and the scale of the cities are enlarged. Thanks to the Chinese Government which actively promotes the urbanization, updates the

A total of registered voterswith Julong Village, Xianlong Town in Chongqing elected their new villagers committee.

October 31, 2013 was the traditional Halloween in the West. In Beijing, however, Jack-O-Lantern, zombies, vampires and other "monster" were deployed to start their Carnival night.

industrial structure and implements the strategy of "the development of cities brings along the development of rural area; the development of industry supports the development of agriculture", the peasants are no longer confined to rural areas. Some peasants long to live in the cities, because living in the cities enables them to have more opportunities and enjoy a more convenient life. Recent years have seen large numbers of surplus laborers moving into the cities. Villages are becoming smaller and smaller. The population in urban areas is increasing at an annual rate of more than one percentage point. The move of a large part of the population from rural areas into urban areas provides sufficient labor force to the cities and improves the economic condition in rural areas. The cities also offer a wider platform to the people from rural areas to put their abilities to good use. They can earn more and live a better life. Urbanization brings not only the shift in population ratio in urban and rural areas but also the change of concepts. The

In October 2007, *Harry Porter* 7 (Chinese version) began to hit the market in China.

peasants no longer regard land as their sole source of living. They overcome the old and closed concept of attaching sentimentally to their hometown and fearing changes, and become competitive and innovative.

The concept of value of the Chinese people is also changing. The traditional thoughts, such as the doctrine of the mean, are replaced by modern concepts of value. The development of the society greatly improves people's concept of value. People's understandings about concepts, such as time, efficiency, development, various key elements of production, justice, fairness, honesty and friendliness, etc, are greatly improved. The concepts of democracy, legal system, liberty, equality and fraternity are widely accepted by the whole society and are put into practice by people. The Chinese people used to advocate modesty and prudence. Nowadays, people publicize their individuality. The spirit of innovation runs high. The whole society is full of vigor. In recent years, the

Chinese people have more independence and choices in their thoughts, which are varied with obvious differences. All these make greater demands on the political and cultural construction of this country.

Development of culture is characterized by variety. Different forms of culture, no matter traditional or modern, from the east or the west, can be found everywhere in China. It becomes a common understanding that the artistic character of the artist should be stressed and the development principle of art itself should be respected. Art works are more likely to be produced for amusement. Different schools of art coexist. Art and life are mixed together. Literature is popularized. Ordinary people can write books. Web literature becomes fashionable. Pop music becomes an indispensable part of people's life. Songs are created on the websites. Rock and roll can be heard everywhere. Traditional Peking opera is protected and advocated. As people from all walks of life participate in TV cultural activities, TV shows become very successful,

The 3rd Beijing international top brand of life Expo site: more than 300 international high-end brands from more than 20 countries and regions make their luxury appearance.

White colars, Chinese and foreign, often come to play football here, located among high-rise office buildings in Beijng's CBD.

marking the coming of the age of popular cultural consumption. Holiday culture is also diversified. People are still fond of traditional festivals such as the Spring Festival and the Moon Festival. On the other hand, young people are also keen on Western holidays such as Valentine's Day and Christmas, etc. China ranks first in the number of netizens in the world. A lot of people write blogs and publish their own programs by using DV online.

Chinese opinion about marriage and family also undergoes changes. More women go out to work and earn stable incomes. The strengthened realization on equality between man and woman shook the dominant role of man in the family. The authority of man is downgraded. The traditional Chinese praised highly the marriage with only one spouse for the whole life. Now, this situation has changed. Recent years have seen an increase in the divorce rate in China. The uneven divorce rates show that there are more divorces in urban areas compared to rural areas. More than half of the divorces are asked for by women.

The majority of the people divorced are above the age of 30. Among them, most are females who have received higher education. Active social life, flow of population and strengthened self-awareness and awareness of freedom result in unstable relationships in families and sexual relationships outside of marriage. The traditional Chinese attached great importance to bringing up children. It was believed that people without children, especially a son, did not fulfill their filial duty. Nowadays, the view of bringing up children is changed. Some young people concentrate more on their career development and seeking of freedom, so they choose a DINK family. The change of view on bringing up children and the implementation of the birth control policy in China leads to a notable decrease in the rate of births and speeds up the aging of the society. The improvement of dwelling conditions and fast flow of population gradually minimizes the size of families. At present, the first "only child" generation is nearly at the age of getting married. The pyramid of the traditional Chinese family is developing in the opposite way. The mode of aged people living with their family, which has a several-thousand years' history, is facing unprecedented challenges. Nowadays, the average size of families in urban and rural areas has decreased to 3.1 persons from 4.8 persons in the 1970s. The number of single-person households and single-parent families is growing fast.

The development of social economy in China enhanced the people's standard of living. Chinese people's life style is changed. Their view of consumption is updated, level of consumption improved, structure of consumption optimized and method of consumption multiplied. The Chinese people are becoming more and more fashionable and are attaching importance to the current style and color of clothes. Compared to their fathers' generation, Chinese young people are facing too many changes in their life. The older generation experienced a long-time shortage of supply, so they formed the habit of working hard and living plainly. While on the other hand, it is more and more popular for the young generation to spend money on luxuries and fashionable products. Some world famous luxuries companies start to make inroads into the

market by opening their shops in China. Many Chinese young people are very fond of Western food. The cuisines from various countries can be found in big cities such as Beijing and Shanghai. Youngsters become fans of Western fast food such as KFC and McDonald's. They enjoy having birthday parties with their friends in these fast food restaurants. Some young people buy apartments by installments to build their own "world". Some do not live with their parents after they get married. They regard leisure as important as work and want to fully enjoy the happiness of life.

Foreign observers describe the changes in China as follows:

"The Chinese people are experiencing social changes. The changes are so dramatic and can never be overstated. However, it is just because that China welcomes such changes, there are no people in any other big countries in history that have ever experienced such rapid changes in their standard of living and working conditions. When the reform policy was firstly implemented, the workers in Shanghai, wearing the uniform in the same style, looked listless. Very few people could afford daily commodities such as a TV set or watch. In the rural areas, malnutrition could be found everywhere. Yet ordinary families in Shanghai nowadays easily own more than one TV set and malnutrition has been stamped out. By experiencing such changes, no doubt, the majority of the Chinese will support further globalization. " (William H. Overholt: *China and Globalization*)